Collision Course

Federal Education
Policy Meets State and
Local Realities

Paul Manna
College of William & Mary

CQ PRESS

A Division of SAGE
Washington, D.C.

CQ Press
2300 N Street, NW, Suite 800
Washington, DC 20037

Phone: 202-729-1900; toll-free, 1-866-4CQ-PRESS (1-866-427-7737)

Web: www.cqpress.com

Cover design: Auburn Associates, Inc.
Composition: C&M Digitals (P) Ltd.

♾ The paper used in this publication exceeds the requirements of the American National Standard for Information Sciences—Permanence of Paper for Printed Library Materials, ANSI Z39.48-1992.

Printed and bound in the United States of America

14   2 3 4 5

Library of Congress Cataloging-in-Publication Data

Manna, Paul.
    Collision course : federal education policy meets state and local realities / Paul Manna.
      p. cm.
    Includes bibliographical references and index.
    ISBN 978-1-60871-649-4 (alk. paper)
    1. Education and state—United States. 2. United States. No Child Left Behind Act of 2001. 3. Educational accountability—Government policy—United States. I. Title.
    LC89.M222 2011
    379.73—dc22

                                                        2010037290

Contents

Figures and Tables

Figures

Tables

Series Foreword

As the fledgling nation began spilling across the Appalachians into new states, the federal government set aside a small part of some of the territory to provide support for local schools in the form of land grants. The idea was simple: new settlements brought new opportunity and, to reach that potential, new settlers would need education. From the earliest days of the country, long before the robust federal grant system developed in the twentieth century, the federal government has been involved in providing national support for local education.

In the nation's history, however, few local programs have been more jealously guarded than education. Nothing more defines a community than its children and how the community chooses to educate them. Just what should children be taught? How much education should they receive? How can residents be sure that children are learning what they're taught? And, most important, because teaching is not only about substantive skills but also about values, how can parents be sure that local schools inculcate the values that will take a community where it wants to go?

The federal government has long recognized the primacy of this local role in education. Neither "education" nor "teach" appear in the Constitution. The closest the Founders came to suggesting a national role in education was the phrase "promote the general Welfare," but they also embraced the fundamental right of state governments in the Bill of Rights, which concludes that "The powers not delegated to the United States by the Constitution, nor prohibited by it to the States, are reserved to the States respectively, or to the people."

This sets up the collision course that Paul Manna so elegantly explores in his new book. State and local governments read the Constitution, and the precedent set throughout America's history, as giving them primary authority to shape education. The federal government has long viewed education as a keystone to a great society. And while the Constitution prohibits the federal government from pushing state and local governments around in the educational arena, federal support has been impossible for state and local governments to resist. There's an old proverb, "He who pays the piper calls the tune." For centuries, the federal government has paid for the music, and state and local governments haven't been able to resist dancing—but that doesn't mean they don't complain about the tune.

Manna's book explores these puzzles by looking carefully at George W. Bush's "No Child Left Behind" program. The passage of this law was the signature achievement of Bush's first year in office. A former governor, Bush came to the presidency with a keen appreciation for the importance of state and local control of schools. As president, he committed to coupling federal support with local performance. Yet conservatives worried about the expansion of federal programs, even as they applauded the oversight. Liberals fretted over whether the program would provide enough aid to allow local schools to meet the tough standards but found comfort in federal support. With this delicate compromise, Bush got the law passed. Surrounded by such divergent figures as the Senate's Democratic lion Edward Kennedy and conservative Republican representative John Boehner, Bush traveled to Ohio, a state that received one of the first land grants in the country's earliest days, to sign the bill.

As with all big policy initiatives, the passage of the bill only launched the real debate. No Child Left Behind frames the fundamental questions about education policy for the twenty-first century: Is a strong federal role inevitable in this traditionally local policy issue? What role should national performance standards play in local education policy? Can state and local governments resist federal cash? And, if they accept the money, how far can—and should—federal control go?

This book uses No Child Left Behind to bring a fresh and forward-leaning look to the dilemmas of education. These are not only questions about how Americans run their schools—they cut right to the heart of the balance of power among the federal, state, and local governments. Perhaps most important, they frame the fundamental questions about how government shapes the values that, in turn, shape life in the United States. Manna's book reads at all these levels, and it ought to be read by anyone who cares about how these debates will shape the future of governance and public life in this nation.

Donald F. Kettl
Dean, School of Public Policy
University of Maryland
August 2010

Foreword

It has become commonplace to note that we live in an increasingly interconnected world. Being a cliché, though, does not lessen the truth of that assertion.

A prime example of this interconnectedness occurs in elementary and secondary education. The world's major economically advanced countries, with federal systems of government placing schooling at the state, provincial, or local level, are all struggling to effectively use their national governments to improve education. To mobilize support, leaders in these countries use similar political rhetoric by arguing that international economic competitiveness demands rapid improvements in schools to ensure a better-educated citizenry.

Collision Course is about recent American experiences to find that proper role in education for the national government in Washington, D.C. The No Child Left Behind Act (NCLB) is the focus of analysis, given its attempt to raise academic achievement while operating in the nation's complex federal system of state and local governance of schooling.

In the half-century since federal policymakers created the National Defense Education Act, in response to the Soviet Union's *Sputnik* launch, no law has been as highly praised and as roundly condemned as NCLB. It is perhaps natural that over that same period of time, accountability for results—to determine what the public investment in education has produced—has risen to equally historic heights. Notably, also since the 1950s, international economic competitiveness has intensified, and so have pressures on the schools to produce better-educated citizens and workers.

While much has been written about NCLB, most often based on opinions or powerful anecdotes, what has been missing is a thorough examination of the law's roots and an objective description of the nation's experience since January 8, 2002, when the legislation was signed into law with great bipartisan fanfare.

One might ask, "Why is it important that we know all of this?" There is, after all, a new president and new congressional leadership who will surely write a new law. What general lessons could they, and their successors in the years or decades to come, learn by reflecting deeply on NCLB's implementation and its effects?

Unfortunately, in both policymaking and politics we have short memories and as a result all too often repeat our predecessors' mistakes. As philosopher George Santayana said, "Those who cannot remember the past are condemned to repeat it." If we wish to avoid that outcome, it is imperative for those who will shape the next generation of policy—at federal, state, and local levels—to understand the origins, the complexity, the successes, and the failures of what has come before.

In this important volume Paul Manna has done a great service by telling the story of NCLB while also considering the Obama administration's early reform agenda and looking ahead to the future. The analysis ranges from those initial days of euphoria to the nuts and bolts of how NCLB has played out. It also draws important conclusions that all who enter future stages of creating and implementing federal education policy should read. Manna concludes that the federal government is capable of producing the "enabling conditions" for better schools, but he also usefully shows the constraints on federal action.

All signs point to the world becoming even more interconnected, and to economic competitiveness intensifying still further. Therefore, pressures will continue to mount for the country to improve its schools as part of the national strategy to have a well-educated citizenry. We should learn from the experiences of NCLB in addressing that future challenge. This book provides us with the lessons that will help us to do just that.

Christopher T. Cross
Chairman, Cross and Joftus
Former Assistant U.S. Secretary of Education
and President, Maryland State Board of Education

Jack Jennings
President and CEO, Center on Education Policy
Former staff director and general counsel,
Committee on Education and Labor,
U.S. House of Representatives

Preface

My first job out of college was teaching social studies and coaching debate in the public high school that I had attended in Traverse City, Michigan. The work was demanding. The hours were long. My students came from a variety of backgrounds. Some of these young people eventually moved on to the best colleges and universities in the country. Others from my classes barely squeaked by or did not graduate. Like many new teachers, I poured all of my energy and time into the job, intending to make a difference in my students' lives. I loved the work, but like many new teachers I also didn't last long. After three years I realized that although working in the classroom and coaching debate provided me with tremendous satisfaction, there was a researcher in me dying to see the light of day. Seeking a better balance of teaching and scholarship, I was ready to shift gears in my professional life.

Nine years after I taught my first class in Traverse City, I spent the 2001–2002 academic year in Washington, D.C., as a graduate student working on my PhD in political science. Having finished my course work and designed my dissertation proposal, I headed for Washington that year to try to make sense of how the federal role in education had developed since the 1960s. It was an interesting and inspiring time to spend in the nation's capital. The city was still in transition as a new presidential administration and Congress faced challenges that tested the boundaries of their developing relationship. The bravery and heroism of the region's emergency responders was on dramatic display as they raced to the Pentagon on September 11. And finally, after a year of grinding on Capitol Hill, the No Child Left Behind Act (NCLB) came off the legislative assembly line and was signed into law with great fanfare. While my research ambitions in Washington were focused on long-term developments in the federal role, not simply current events, it was hard to avoid the hoopla and debates that NCLB sparked.

Since 2003, when I came to William & Mary, much of my teaching and research has continued to explore different dimensions of education policy. I have been especially interested in two things: (1) trying to better understand what NCLB can teach us about the federal role in education and, more broadly, about American federalism; and (2) considering NCLB's demands from the perspectives both of education policymakers with experience at state and national levels, many of whom I encountered in Washington during my dissertation research, and of teachers and local officials who work in schools each day, such as my colleagues from Traverse City. Reflecting on the experiences of the people who crafted NCLB and those who have implemented it, I am reminded of the legend in which six blind men each touched a different part of an elephant to determine what it was. In comparing notes, the men discovered they were in complete disagreement about the object before them. One could easily replicate a similar conversation by convening a gathering of education officials and teachers and then asking them to describe the federal government's role in American schools.

In exploring the wealth of studies that have examined NCLB's origins, impacts, and potential future, my students and I have learned much about how education policy unfolds in practice across levels of government. Still, despite all this reading and my own prior research, I was convinced that a book such as *Collision Course* was sorely needed. Specifically, three reasons motivated me to write it. First, no book on NCLB that I have encountered focuses specifically on the administrative and political challenges that the law has unleashed across federal, state, and local levels. In addressing those issues, *Collision Course* looks in detail at how people from the federal Education Department and state agencies to local communities and classrooms have attempted to implement NCLB's provisions. In examining the law from those vantage points, I hope readers will come to appreciate the complexities arising in the many corners of the nation's intergovernmental system.

Second, several books about NCLB, including some to which I've contributed, are edited volumes. Those works are great at offering multiple perspectives, but edited volumes tend to lack a coherent analytical or narrative thread that pulls together their sometimes fragmented chapters. By writing with one voice and using the specific lens of administration, I have attempted to provide a coherent analysis of the ties linking people across levels of government as they have implemented NCLB's many moving parts.

Finally, much writing about NCLB is either highly technical, densely presented in evaluation reports, or driven primarily by anecdotes, opinion, or a selective read of the evidence. In *Collision Course* I have attempted to craft an accessible work that draws on a diverse and balanced range of support. The evidence in the pages that follow includes my own analyses of public documents and quantitative data, findings from large-scale studies, reports from the nation's education journalists, and reflections from elected officials, agency administrators, and teachers.

The book's title foreshadows the metaphor that guides the overall discussion. As I explain in the ensuing chapters, policies hoping to promote accountability for results, such as NCLB, create collisions between the ambitions of leaders demanding higher performance and other individuals who manage the environments in which those ambitions unfold. In NCLB's case the law's accountability demands collided with the structures, policies, and educational practices in states and local communities. NCLB's strongest advocates suggested that the country needed those collisions to foster a sense of urgency to improve school performance and reduce inequities in achievement. Collisions from the advocates' perspective, then, were needed to transform American education and provide political cover to state and local reformers who had struggled to gain traction. In contrast, NCLB's critics have seen the collisions as inflicting harmful damage in states and local communities. That damage has undermined what some believe have been promising efforts aimed at helping disadvantaged students and the schools they attend. As the following pages will show, NCLB has produced many collisions of varying types that sometimes have prompted great change and at other times have seemingly produced few substantive effects.

Collision Course begins with a bit of history and context, continues down NCLB's implementation chain, and concludes by drawing broader lessons about the future. Chapter 1 orients readers to the federal role in education and the various factors that influence how education policy is implemented in the United States. In Chapter 2, I describe the theories of action that motivated NCLB's authors and the key parts of the law they designed to translate those theories into action. Chapter 3 begins examining the law's implementation, focusing on administrators at the federal and state levels. Implementation in schools and school districts is the focus of Chapter 4, while Chapter 5 investigates the law's effects on teachers and teaching. Chapter 6 attempts to summarize the large body of work that has assessed NCLB's impact on student achievement. Finally, Chapter 7 begins by considering early reform efforts of the Obama administration, before spending much time identifying some of the larger lessons that NCLB suggests about accountability and the future of the federal role in American schools.

I am optimistic that readers from diverse backgrounds and perspectives will find *Collision Course* an informative and lively read. I believe that students and scholars interested in American government, public policy, public administration and management, state and local politics, intergovernmental relations, policy implementation, and, of course, education policy will find it valuable. Similarly, individuals working in the policy world across levels of government, teachers and administrators in local schools, and researchers at think tanks or other institutes should find in *Collision Course* opportunities to reflect on their own practice. I am sure that all of the book's readers will discover points where they agree and other claims—perhaps many!—to challenge. My intention is not to offer the last word on NCLB or the broader federal role in the nation's schools. Debates in the United States will continue to persist about how to improve American classrooms while promoting the twin goals of equity and excellence. Given those ongoing disagreements, my goal is to provide a launching pad for informed, reasoned, and vitally important discussions as the country tries to figure out how to offer all its students an outstanding education.

ACKNOWLEDGEMENTS

Writing this book has reaffirmed my belief that I am incredibly fortunate to have a job where I get to spend so much time interacting with smart, generous, and hard-working people. Let me first thank the team at CQ Press, who embraced the project and helped me to improve it every step of the way. Series editor Don Kettl and editorial director Charisse Kiino have been supporters and valuable critics from the start. Many thanks as well go out to Joan Gossett, Christopher O'Brien, Erin Snow, and Janine Stanley-Dunham. The following CQ Press reviewers also provided important feedback that improved the book: Gene Brewer (University of Georgia), Sheron Fraser-Burgess (Ball State University), Jeffrey Henig (Teachers College, Columbia University), Peter Hinrichs (Public Policy Institute, Georgetown University), Patrick McGuinn (Drew University), Maike Philipsen (Virginia Commonwealth University), John Portz (Northeastern University), and Kenneth Wong (Brown University).

Since I began studying NCLB in 2001, I have encountered dozens of individuals who have been willing to share their insights and encouragement. That generosity has continued through to this current book. In particular, I owe many thanks to Christopher Cross, George Thompson, and my William & Mary colleague Chris Howard, who read and commented on the entire manuscript. Pamela Eddy, also at William & Mary, was generous enough to invite her graduate students in education policy—many of whom were full-time school employees—to read and provide reactions to an earlier draft. I am also grateful to Jack Jennings, who, along with Christopher Cross, coauthored the foreword. Jack and Chris were two of the first people I met when I began my research in Washington in 2001. Their encouragement during the past decade has been invaluable.

As a faculty member at William & Mary, where I began my academic career in 2003, I have been fortunate to work with truly outstanding students. Several have been instrumental in helping me to develop this book. I owe a collective thanks to those from my spring 2009 freshman seminar, which examined NCLB in detail. Their energy for the subject and willingness to engage me and one another in discussion, along with their comments on an early draft of the introduction, helped to convince me that I definitely needed to write this book. From that group Laura Ryan deserves extra special mention for literally scrutinizing every word, table, and figure in the manuscript. Her sharp mind and eagle eye improved all dimensions of the book, including its argument, prose, and presentation. Tim Harwood, who as a master's student in public policy was my assistant for two years, was equally valuable. His passion for education policy, work ethic, and keen attention to detail were vitally important for assisting me in gathering the evidence, organizing the data, and crafting the arguments that animate the book. Other current or former students who provided great assistance, feedback, or ideas include Brandie Burris, John Constance, Meghan Dunne, Joe Hayes, Stephanie McGuire, Sean O'Mealia, and Kimberly Walters.

Like all things in my life, this book and none of my other work would be possible without the support of my loving wife, Lisa, who teaches high school French in the local public schools here in Williamsburg. Thanks to her dedication and unmatched energy for her own students, I fear that I will always be the second-best teacher in our household. Finally, I dedicate this book to my two-year-old son, Theo. His presence in my daily life continues to inspire and amaze me. In the time that it took me to write *Collision Course,* he was hard at work learning to walk, talk, and feed himself. While I could not be more pleased with how this book turned out, I would bet that any objective observer would argue that Theo clearly had the more productive year. This one is for you, my son. You sure do make Papa proud.

Paul Manna
College of William & Mary
Williamsburg, Virginia

Abbreviations

AFT	American Federation of Teachers
ARRA	American Recovery and Reinvestment Act
AYP	Adequate yearly progress
DIBELS	Dynamic Indicators of Basic Early Literacy Skills
ELL	English-language learner
ESEA	Elementary and Secondary Education Act
ESL	English as a second language
GAO	Government Accountability Office for cited publications after July 7, 2004 and General Accounting Office for cited publications before that date
HOUSSE	High Objective Uniform State Standard of Evaluation
HQT	Highly qualified teacher
IASA	Improving America's Schools Act (ESEA reauthorization of 1994)
IDEA	Individuals with Disabilities Education Act
IEP	Individualized Education Program
K–12	Elementary and secondary education (kindergarten through 12th grade)
NAEP	National Assessment of Educational Progress
NCLB	No Child Left Behind Act (ESEA reauthorization of 2001)
NCTM	National Council of Teachers of Mathematics
NEA	National Education Association
NYPD	New York City Police Department
REAP	Rural Education Achievement Program
RTTT	Race to the Top fund
UMRA	Unfunded Mandates Reform Act

1

Contexts

EARLY IN THE MORNING ON JANUARY 20, 2009, tens of thousands of spectators began assembling on the National Mall to catch a glimpse of the west front of the U.S. Capitol. Some had traveled across the country to be in Washington, D.C. Others were residents of the nation's capital region who rose early that day, but not to face the usual punishing commute to work. That morning, all had gathered to witness history. At approximately noon John Roberts, chief justice of the United States, administered the oath of office to Barack Obama, who on that day became the nation's forty-fourth president and the first black person to hold the nation's highest political office.

Stepping to the lectern to deliver his inaugural address, President Obama peered out across the wide expanse of people, space, and monuments to the nation's history that lay before him. Perhaps fitting, facing the new president far in the distance was the memorial and larger-than-life statue of Abraham Lincoln, where Martin Luther King Jr. had delivered his famous "I Have a Dream" speech in 1963. Leading up to Obama's inauguration and during the ceremony itself, commentators remarked on the historical threads connecting the nation's sixteenth president and its hero of the civil rights movement to the man about to become America's new leader.

Despite such a powerful intersection of historical symbols and personalities, Obama's inaugural message did not dwell on the subject of race.[1] The president did note that the country had "tasted the bitter swill of civil war and segregation" and that his own father "might not have been served in a local restaurant" fewer than sixty years ago. But rather than celebrating the historical significance of his inauguration, Obama's more somber message called the nation's attention to several pressing crises. In the speech's opening paragraphs, the president reminded all listeners of the major challenges of the moment:

> Our nation is at war against a far-reaching network of violence and hatred. Our economy is badly weakened, a consequence of greed and irresponsibility on the part of some, but also our collective failure to make hard choices and

prepare the nation for a new age. Homes have been lost, jobs shed, businesses shuttered. Our health care is too costly, our schools fail too many—and each day brings further evidence that the ways we use energy strengthen our adversaries and threaten our planet.

It was notable that in the paragraph framing the nation's grand challenges, school performance appeared alongside concerns about ongoing wars in Iraq and Afghanistan, an economic crisis that Obama had labeled the worst since the Great Depression, and health care and energy policy, which both affect economic performance and the latter, energy, having crucial national security implications given the country's dependence on foreign oil.

FEDERAL LEADERSHIP AND EDUCATION

Historically, federal policymakers have possessed many tools to fight wars and promote economic growth. But education has been different. Although federal influence over schools has expanded, state and local governments are still the primary caretakers of elementary and secondary (K–12) education in the United States. Many citizens, in fact, would prefer that federal leaders remain focused on questions of war, peace, and prosperity and leave classroom matters to governments closer to home. Still, Obama's inaugural address appeared to signal a commitment to improving classrooms that was on par with his duties as commander in chief of the armed forces and lead steward of the nation's economy.

But what would the president do about "schools that fail too many"? On that question, in contrast with his discussion of the nation's other grand challenges, the president failed to elaborate. Whatever path Obama envisioned that morning, one thing was certain: His education agenda would not be written on a blank slate. Years of federal initiatives and state and local reform movements had created a context in which Obama's education plans would operate. That fact about education is also true of other policy areas. No new president governs with an entirely free hand. Policy legacies of prior presidents and congresses generate constraints and opportunities for new leaders. Breakthrough moments sometimes occur when presidents have a chance to remake the policy landscape, but most often changes are small and incremental.[2]

Roughly fifteen months before Obama's inaugural address, Secretary of Education Margaret Spellings delivered a less-celebrated, but still notable, message of her own. Speaking on September 17, 2007, in front of the department she had led since becoming President George W. Bush's second education secretary, Spellings dedicated the facility with a new name. Henceforth, it would be called the Lyndon Baines Johnson Department of Education Building, honoring the nation's thirty-sixth president. In her remarks, Spellings told audience members that "President Johnson worked tirelessly to provide an equal education to all children. Having his name on the Department of Education building is a daily reminder to all Americans that his goal is now our duty to pursue and achieve."[3]

Johnson's principal accomplishment in K–12 education was passage of the Elementary and Secondary Education Act (ESEA) of 1965. That act has been the federal government's main education law, focusing especially on the needs of disadvantaged students. The ESEA's mechanisms, programs, and even its popular name have evolved as subsequent presidents and congresses have adjusted the legislation during its various major revisions, known as reauthorizations. In 2001 the Congress reauthorized the ESEA as the No Child Left Behind Act (NCLB), and President George W. Bush signed that measure into law on January 8, 2002.

The ESEA's four-decade evolution into NCLB raises an important question, which this book explores. What happens when federal policymakers attempt to hold schools accountable for academic results? Increasing student achievement and decreasing achievement gaps between student groups were the principal goals that the authors of NCLB aimed to accomplish. As subsequent chapters will show, NCLB's implementation revealed many things about the ability of federal policy to ensure that all children learn challenging and interesting academic content. Given the many hands at federal, state, and local levels charged with making NCLB work, it was no wonder that the law's implementation produced uneven results. In fact, despite NCLB's provisions, as the law took hold, the entire notion of "educational accountability" assumed many different meanings in states and communities across the country.

Such adaptations across the American federal system revealed the power and limits of federal law to meet the challenge of promoting educational accountability. The choices and capabilities of agency leaders in the U.S. Department of Education and state governments, as well as officials and teachers in local districts and schools, all revealed how the administrative environments in which federal initiatives operate can assert much influence on the ability of federal policymakers to hold state and local governments accountable for results. Although this book examines NCLB's implementation from 2002 through 2009, while also considering future directions emerging during President Obama's first term in office, its overall insights about federalism and public administration are relevant to several other policy areas as well.

My primary argument is that the allocation of responsibility for K–12 education in America hinders federal efforts to hold schools accountable for academic performance. In developing that claim, the book contends that difficulties arise when the assumptions of government accountability systems are misaligned with the institutional environments in which they operate. In other words, for an accountability system to succeed, especially one involving actors across the nation's intergovernmental system, the logic and incentives linking relevant actors must be clear, consistent, and based on realistic understandings of how policy implementation works in practice. Designers of accountability systems are likely to produce frustrations when they overestimate the administrative capacities that governments possess or when they create incentives based on faulty assumptions about those capacities.[4]

Policies that promote accountability for results often create collisions between the ambitions of leaders demanding higher performance and other individuals who manage the environments in which those ambitions unfold. In NCLB's case the law's accountability demands collided with the structures, policies, and practices governing education in states and local communities. NCLB's strongest advocates suggested that the country needed such a collision to create a sense of urgency among state and local officials who, for too long in the advocates' minds, had tolerated lagging school performance and persistent inequities in achievement. Collisions from the advocates' perspective, then, were valuable for their potential to transform state and local policy and the political contexts in which education operates. *Value of collision*

In contrast NCLB's critics believed the collision was undesirable. They saw the law as inflicting damage, much like a construction site wrecking ball, on the state and local institutions that have primary responsibility for educating the nation's youth. That damage undermined what some of NCLB's critics have seen as potentially valuable state and local efforts aimed at helping disadvantaged students and the schools they attend. Some critics also suggested that NCLB represented a veiled attempt to advance certain political agendas, such as weakening teacher unions or tarnishing the reputations of otherwise effective public schools, rather than promoting high achievement.

The chapters that follow assess the collision between NCLB and the state and local institutions charged with carrying it out. Before considering those details, the next sections of this chapter establish three contexts that have shaped the nature of the collision. The first context involves the evolving ambitions of federal policymakers, who have demanded greater accountability for educational results. The second concerns how federal policymakers since 1965 have attempted to reform the ESEA to satisfy their changing ambitions. The third focuses on the all-important institutional and political contexts where policy implementation and student learning take place each day.

EVOLVING FEDERAL AMBITIONS

Americans have tremendous faith in education to help individual people and the overall nation to prosper. Those views date to the country's founding. National icons such as Benjamin Franklin and Thomas Jefferson, for example, believed that America's grand democratic experiment would flounder unless citizens developed the knowledge, skills, and sensibilities to govern the new nation. Across time the United States has relied on schools to improve and sustain its democracy while accomplishing several specific objectives. These have included assimilating new immigrants; defeating international rivals during the Cold War; helping the country's businesses compete with foreign companies; addressing racism and other forms of intolerance; alleviating poverty; reducing drug and alcohol abuse, teen pregnancies, and smoking; overcoming the legacies of slavery and legal segregation that prevented generations of blacks and other minorities from realizing their full potential; and finally, providing young people with opportunities to help them live better, more prosperous lives than their parents.[5]

As several items in the prior paragraph suggest, federal policymakers have frequently relied on schools to minimize persistent inequities. The view of education as a great equalizer, helping the most disadvantaged students overcome seemingly impossible barriers, has guided much federal education policy since the 1960s. Coming roughly a decade after the U.S. Supreme Court's seminal 1954 decision in *Brown v. Board of Education,* which declared that laws separating the races in education were inherently unequal, Lyndon Johnson pushed to pass the first ESEA as part of his larger War on Poverty.

Since the 1960s, developments in federal policy have reflected this equity theme. Subsequent revisions to the ESEA itself, for example, have incorporated programs to assist students learning English as a second language. The Education for All Handicapped Children Act of 1975, now called the Individuals with Disabilities Education Act (IDEA), dramatically increased opportunities for students with disabilities to attend public schools. Title IX of the Education Amendments of 1972 aimed to address persistent inequities that girls and young women faced in their academic and extracurricular activities. These federal initiatives have enjoyed varying levels of success and sometimes have stoked controversy. Overall, they have revealed a consistent federal drive to press states and local school districts to ensure equality of educational opportunity for all students.[6]

Concerns about educational excellence joined equity as a more consistent federal ambition in the 1980s. Perhaps the most influential voice in prompting this additional federal focus was the National Commission on Excellence in Education. Terrell "Ted" Bell, who served as President Ronald Reagan's first education secretary, created the commission in 1981. Bell charged its members with examining several issues, including the quality of teaching and learning in the nation's classrooms, the performance of schools and American students versus those of other nations, the factors influencing long-term trends in student achievement, and the major problems that undermined educational excellence. Bell created the commission because he was worried about popular perceptions that American schools were performing poorly, thereby jeopardizing the nation's future.

The commission's now famous report, *A Nation at Risk,* did nothing to allay Bell's fears.[7] The relatively brief document quickly became a media sensation and helped to enhance federal interest, especially presidential interest, in education.

One of its most frequently quoted passages made this bracing claim: "If an unfriendly foreign power had attempted to impose on America the mediocre educational performance that exists today, we might well have considered it an act of war. . . . We have, in effect, been committing an act of unthinking, unilateral educational disarmament."[8] To remedy that dire situation, the commission recommended several specific reforms to push American students to take more substantively demanding courses and to encourage all involved in education— elected officials, government bureaucrats, school personnel, and parents—to have high academic expectations for the nation's young people. Critics of *A Nation at Risk* claimed that the report overstated the country's predicament and understated the factors beyond the classroom, such as persistent poverty and policies fostering inequity, that kept some students from excelling.[9]

Despite the critics' claims and counterevidence, the report emboldened state reforms that were already under way and led federal leaders increasingly to embrace both equity and excellence in their policy deliberations. After *A Nation at Risk* appeared, observers became aware that several states had reforms in progress that anticipated the commission's recommendations. Governors used the report to build momentum for their own state-level efforts and to assert their priorities at the 1989 National Education Summit in Charlottesville, Virginia. That meeting was called by President George H. W. Bush and encouraged by industry leaders across the country in organizations such as the Business Roundtable. At the summit the governors persuaded the president to endorse the concept of creating national education goals that would guide the country into the future. The governors, including then Arkansas governor Bill Clinton, who played a leading role, hoped that the resulting goals that were developed shortly after the Charlottesville summit would bolster reforms based on academic standards, which governors were already advocating in their home states.[10]

Even with the flurry of state-level reform activity during the 1980s—one report called it the "education reform decade"[11]—substantive changes in federal policy came slowly. Federal officials rhetorically embraced the concerns about educational excellence articulated in *A Nation at Risk,* but sweeping action was missing. The stated support for excellence had joined the historical commitment to educational equity that federal leaders identified when the first ESEA became law in 1965. Yet it took more than a decade after *A Nation at Risk* appeared for the ESEA to demand that states hold all students, advantaged and disadvantaged alike, to challenging academic standards. Those adjustments came in 1994 with the Improving America's Schools Act (IASA), promoted by President Clinton and passed amid strong resistance from congressional Republicans. Further, it would take nearly another decade before the ESEA would incorporate specific consequences for schools that failed to make regular academic progress. Those shifts came in 2002 with NCLB and advocacy from President George W. Bush as well as congressional leaders from both parties.

[handwritten margin note: Story bou NCLB]

[handwritten note at bottom:] ESEA → IASA → NCLB → ESSA
LBJ   Clinton   Bush (W)   Obama

REFORMING THE ESEA [Federal Goals]

One reason why federal officials and national interest groups pushed for a stronger federal role with NCLB was because prior ESEA reauthorizations had fallen short of achieving their stated goals. Since its original enactment in 1965, the ESEA had embraced lofty and noble ambitions. While details have varied from reauthorization to reauthorization, in general, four main goals have stood out.[12] They have included: first, to direct federal dollars to impoverished local school districts to better serve disadvantaged students; second, to meet these students' specific academic needs while simultaneously helping them to catch up academically with their more advantaged peers; third, to accelerate the development of state standards, testing, and accountability systems; and fourth, to judge and then hold schools and school districts accountable for academic performance. The ESEA has embraced the first two objectives for its entire history. The more explicit concerns about standards, academic performance, and accountability, the last two goals, came later. They were first seriously incorporated into the ESEA under President Clinton during the 1994 reauthorization.

Despite good intentions to improve disadvantaged students' academic prospects, NCLB's supporters saw several weaknesses with past implementation of the ESEA. Previous efforts to incorporate explicit mechanisms to hold schools accountable for student performance were done without much thought and generally were unsuccessful. Some such efforts date to the law's initial passage in 1965. At that time Senator Robert Kennedy, a Democrat from New York, pressed Lyndon Johnson's White House team to include provisions in the original ESEA to force local school districts to report objective measures of their students' progress.[13]

Johnson and his advisers, including the president's commissioner of education, Francis Keppel, resisted Kennedy's pleas because they feared stoking political disagreements with local districts and teachers. The proposed ESEA represented a major step forward for federal involvement in the nation's schools. During the legislative process it came under political attack from different groups, especially the nation's business community, who feared its mandates would increase taxes and threaten state and local control of classrooms. Demanding such accountability would upset local officials, Johnson reasoned, and it would create administrative headaches for the relatively small federal Office of Education. That office, headed by Keppel and residing in the larger Department of Health, Education, and Welfare, already would be challenged to implement the ESEA as Johnson's team envisioned it. (The Department of Education, which now administers the ESEA and whose secretary is part of the president's cabinet, did not exist until 1980.) Still, Kennedy's persistence persuaded Johnson to allow his congressional allies to quietly insert language in the proposed ESEA that required school districts to submit evaluations of student progress to their states, which the states would collate and forward to Washington.

ESEA *

{ 1) $ for low income schools   3) Standards
  2) help (&) catch up   4) Accountability } } New NCLB
ASA

This initial attempt to use the ESEA to hold local schools and districts accountable produced a jumbled mess. Lacking effective tests or other measurement tools, and receiving unclear guidance from Washington on what information they should generate, districts reported results from a range of instruments. Within individual states, results were frequently incomparable across schools or districts. The tests also failed to produce information that would help state or federal officials determine whether federal aid was helping disadvantaged students to learn. Additionally, federal enforcement of these accountability measures was weak. Districts that simply ignored the requirement and reported no data never lost funds or felt other consequences. As education historian Diane Ravitch observed about these early attempts at accountability, "Eventually, Washington settled for assurances that the money would reach schools that enrolled poor children—no performance results required."[14]

In subsequent years, evaluations of Title I, the ESEA's major component that would eventually contain NCLB's school accountability requirements, found that school districts were ineffective at implementing testing systems to assess disadvantaged students.[15] Too often districts would use tests to draw inferences beyond what the tests could show. Additionally, when disadvantaged students took tests to gauge their academic progress, typically the tests examined only very basic skills. A focus on minimal levels of understanding suggested to Title I evaluators that communities were operating with relatively low expectations for disadvantaged students and higher ones for their more advantaged peers, whom districts seemed to believe more capable of learning challenging academic material. Using two sets of standards conflicted with the ESEA's goal of bridging the gaps in achievement between advantaged and disadvantaged youngsters.

In the Improving America's Schools Act (IASA) of 1994, federal policymakers seriously attempted to address the shortcomings of scattered testing and low expectations that had persisted after previous ESEA reauthorizations. But in 2001 legislators and Bush administration officials remained unsatisfied with the IASA's track record. Although it had required states to develop high academic expectations for advantaged and disadvantaged students, only eleven states had systems of testing and accountability consistent with the IASA's requirements by 2001. Partly because of its own capacity limits, but also delays at the state level, the Department of Education had reviewed these systems from only thirty-four states and the others were awaiting the department's judgment.[16]

Supporters of NCLB believed that part of the IASA's problem was that federal officials lacked the political will to enforce the law and incorporate tough consequences for schools and districts where disadvantaged students struggled academically. One reason why so many states were out of compliance with the IASA, the NCLB advocates believed, was that the Department of Education tended to offer timeline waivers to states that were slow to implement the law. In other words rather than punishing states for not meeting the law's requirements,

[margin note, handwritten] Early accountability as disorganized/inequitable

the department tended to work with the states by encouraging them to move forward, even if they were many years behind where they were supposed to have been.

Similarly, even though the IASA required states to test their students and gauge their progress in reading and math at least one time in grades three through five, six through eight, and ten through twelve, the law did not contain any clear consequences for schools making limited or no academic progress. The IASA's authors let states determine what should happen if a school's performance lagged. Critics at the nonprofit research and advocacy group The Education Trust, for example, noted the IASA's limits and the low expectations that it allowed states to maintain: "In the past, states had complete freedom in defining progress under Title I however they saw fit. But many states fell down on the job. Some set goals so modest that it would have taken more than a hundred years to see meaningful progress; one even defined 'progress' as not falling backward very far. In addition, many failed to measure and report the achievement of low-income and minority students."[17]

Compounding concerns about low expectations, weak accountability, and limited enforcement was evidence of persistent inequities between student groups. When NCLB's authors and their allies observed the nation's educational landscape, they saw powerful evidence that prior laws had fallen short. Most important, gaps in achievement remained noticeable and compelling across all years of the ESEA's history for which reliable data existed. Put simply, despite some progress that began to narrow some gaps, the nation's black and Hispanic students still scored consistently lower than their white peers. Similarly, students from families earning low incomes lagged behind students with middle- or upper-class backgrounds. These results showed that the nation was still far from eliminating gaps in achievement, one of the ESEA's principal objectives.[18]

Inequities in resources between advantaged and disadvantaged students also were apparent, especially to civil rights groups that had advocated for children with low family incomes and those who were racial minorities. Two resource problems were especially acute and persisted even with the ESEA. First, despite funding formulas in earlier ESEA reauthorizations that attempted to direct federal dollars toward districts serving disadvantaged students, evaluations of the law had shown that many needy students never benefited from these additional resources. For example, one study from the early 1990s found that nationwide 14 percent of high-poverty elementary schools received no money from the ESEA's primary funding component (then called Chapter 1 instead of Title I). Further, "one-third of the low achieving children (who score at the 35th percentile or below on reading tests) in elementary and secondary schools with poverty rates over 75 percent did not receive Chapter 1 services."[19] Efforts to improve targeting occurred with IASA, but those changes still failed to serve all the nation's disadvantaged students. One key reason was politics. By ensuring that

Title I funding was distributed widely across the nation, even in school districts with small disadvantaged populations, advocates could maintain political support for the program in Congress.[20]

A second persistent resource problem concerned teachers. By 2001 evidence had accumulated that teacher quality can have a powerful impact on student achievement.[21] Still, disadvantaged students and racial minorities were less likely than advantaged students and whites to have high-quality teachers. These differences existed no matter how one measured teacher quality, including the number of years teaching in one's subject, whether teachers had full versus emergency or temporary certification, or whether teachers had majored in or even taken courses in the subjects they taught.[22] Similar differences in qualifications also tended to exist for classroom teacher aides who were hired with ESEA funds. Especially in urban areas with concentrated poverty, few aides possessed college degrees and those employed typically received limited training.[23]

During its 1988 reauthorization, lawmakers incorporated into the ESEA a professional development program to help teachers improve their knowledge and skills. Supporters hoped that program implementers would reach out to teachers of disadvantaged students.[24] Although the program commanded relatively few funds compared with ESEA's Title I, it still received hundreds of millions of dollars per year. Evaluations suggested that these teacher development initiatives were lackluster and tended to support low-quality activities. Nor did they reach large numbers of teachers from disadvantaged communities.[25]

Inequities in achievement and resources motivated NCLB's advocates to promote a tougher approach. In the view of President Bush, leaders in the education committees on Capitol Hill, members of the business community, and writers at nonprofit groups such as the Citizens' Commission on Civil Rights, past ESEAs had not done enough to alter practices in states, school districts, and schools. Put differently, the ESEA may have collided with state and local institutions and practices, but the anticipated transformations had not materialized.

In contrast, other observers considered the accumulated data about student achievement and teacher quality and wondered if it was proper to blame past ESEA reauthorizations for these problems. Historically, the federal role in K–12 education had been to supplement, not replace, state and local efforts. Blaming federal policy for enduring inequities seemed unfair, some people argued, given that officials at other levels of government were primarily in charge of education. Also, federal funding for the ESEA had tended to fall short of what some groups, especially the nation's teacher unions and other advocacy groups, believed was needed. As these advocates suggested, it was unfair to blame the ESEA's mechanisms when they were never given a full chance to succeed.

Determining whether federal expectations and enforcement had been tough enough requires one to account for the limited authority that federal officials have wielded in education. Because the ESEA has always relied on state and local governments to carry out federal initiatives, federal policymakers have had to walk a fine political line. Leaders in the federal government have had difficulty demanding much from states and local governments because they had charged these levels with eliminating historically persistent problems, namely, massive inequities between student groups. Without state and local support, federal policymakers would be powerless to realize their ambitions. But giving the states and localities too much leeway meant that federal money would flow without clear results coming in return. Striking that balance of issuing demands but encouraging states and localities to support federal goals was administratively complicated, as federal education officials who implemented earlier ESEA reauthorizations had learned.[26] Thus, it is difficult to understand the ESEA's historic performance and the nation's more recent experience with NCLB without understanding how the United States governs education.

INSTITUTIONS AND POLITICS

The country's faith in the ability of education to solve pressing problems is matched by its desire for state and local control of schools. Since the nation's founding, the institutions and traditions of American federalism have tended to limit the federal role in classrooms. Despite the federal government's increasing interest and involvement in K–12 education, this persistent desire for state and local control has revealed itself in several ways. When asked in 2008, for example, who should have the greatest influence in deciding what a community's public schools teach their students, 46 percent of adults identified the local school board, 30 percent said state government, and 20 percent said the federal government.[27] That did represent a larger fraction favoring federal involvement than in 1980, when a poll asking the same question found 68 percent saying local government, 15 percent saying state government, and 9 percent identifying the federal government.[28] Even though respondents now appear more comfortable with a stronger federal role in schools, the overall pattern during the past three decades suggests people prefer state and local leadership.

One factor explaining public opinion is that states and localities have more developed institutions for governing education. Many state constitutions contain explicit and detailed sections outlining the state's responsibility for providing all citizens with access to quality schools. Those constitutions frequently establish several organizations, including state boards of education and state education agencies, that along with governors and state legislatures are charged with establishing free systems of public education. In contrast, readers can search long and hard, but they will find no references to education in the U.S. Constitution. Certainly, the Supreme Court has issued several rulings and Congress has passed several laws affecting the nation's classrooms, but those actions have flowed from interpretations about general powers and protections that the Constitution includes, not from specific language that grants to the federal government the authority to control the nation's schools.

Federalism / local control

governance

State constitutions describe educational guidelines, federal does not

Figure 1.1 K–12 Education Revenues from Federal, State, and Local Sources, 1974–1975 to 2006–2007

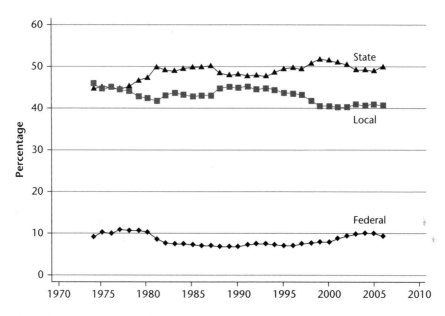

Note: Each data point represents the average percentage across all fifty states. "Local" sources represent revenues from local governments, intermediate sources, private gifts, and any tuition or fees from school patrons. Results are based on the author's calculation using data from the U.S. Department of Education, Common Core of Data (http://nces.ed.gov/ccd/).

The allocation of financial responsibility for education also reflects a balance weighted toward state and local levels. Figure 1.1 tracks the source of revenues for K–12 schooling across time. As the figure shows, since the 1970s states have assumed a greater burden of funding schools while local governments have contributed less. But collectively, state and local governments have nearly always accounted for more than 90 percent of the total. Despite important changes in federal policy, which increased the federal government's regulatory involvement in schools and districts, the fraction of federal contributions to K–12 revenues has remained quite stable, usually hovering around 7 to 9 percent per year since the mid-1970s.

State and local power over education has created a diverse patchwork quilt of approaches and institutions across the United States. Saying that the country has a "system" of elementary and secondary education overstates the degree of coherence that actually exists. Other nations that have more centralized governments and more developed social welfare systems, such as France and Japan, have vested much power over schools in their national education departments.

Local / State funds account for 90%+ os school funds

The resulting systems and subsequent experiences of French and Japanese students tend to be more structured and uniform compared with experiences in the United States. In the fragmented American setting, teaching, learning, and equality of opportunity for students can be quite different across schools owing to variation in state and local priorities and the bureaucratic systems that implement education policy.

As one example, consider the specific state-level institutions that govern education. All but two states (Minnesota and Wisconsin) have state boards of education, and every state has a state education agency. State boards and agencies have explicit responsibilities for governing a state's schools. The former are policymaking bodies that frequently determine teacher certification rules, the nature of state testing systems, the required content students must learn, and the courses students must take to graduate from high school. Some state boards have much power in these areas, but others do not. Leaders of state education agencies, often known as chief state school officers or state superintendents, are responsible for day-to-day administration of state and federal policies that affect schools. These state agencies also provide assistance and advice to entire school districts and individual schools, although their administrative capabilities vary. As the remaining chapters will show, that variation powerfully influenced NCLB's performance.

Interestingly, states have established different procedures to govern how chief state school officers and state education board members come to power. Governors in some states have much say over who runs the state education agency and who sits on the state board. The governor's power is more limited in other states, as where governors select board members but not the state chief. Even more disconnected are governors in some states who lack direct influence over selection of the chief or board members. A common, but by no means dominant, model is to have voters elect state board members and then to have the board select the chief. Other arrangements also exist, including some states where chiefs themselves are popularly elected. These paths to power for state education officials are relevant for understanding NCLB's impact because they illuminate part of the diverse institutional terrain on which federal policy operates.

Local variation also exists in everything from classroom practices to school and district capabilities to funding levels. Earlier, Figure 1.1 showed that on average state governments contribute roughly 50 percent and local governments 40 percent of the revenues that fund the nation's elementary and secondary schools. But as Figure 1.2 shows, within individual states the division of financial labor between state and local governments can vary greatly. At one extreme is Hawaii, where the entire state serves as a single school district. Local school districts, therefore, do not fund Hawaii's schools, and only a small fraction of school funding comes from local sources. At another extreme is Nevada, where local sources provide 66 percent of K–12 funds and the state itself provides 27 percent. In

Figure 1.2 State and Local Revenues for K–12 Education, 2006–2007

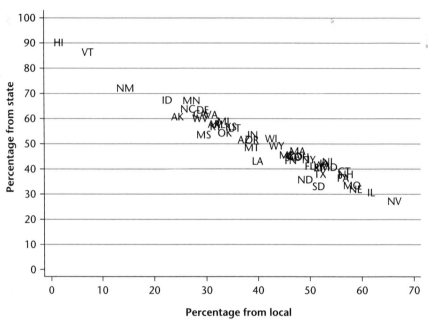

Note: "Local" sources represent revenues from local governments, intermediate sources, private gifts, and any tuition or fees from school patrons. Results are based on the author's calculations from U.S. Department of Education, Common Core of Data (http://nces.ed.gov/ccd/).

other states the balance resides somewhere in between. Often, state supreme court decisions have influenced the balance of financial power for education by ordering state legislatures to design schemes to improve funding equity.[29]

In addition to financial matters, local school districts also vary in their administrative organization and the conditions they face. Overall, there are roughly 14,000 school districts and 99,000 public schools in the United States. In some places such as New Jersey, which has 615 school districts, districts operate on highly localized scales and oversee few schools. New Jersey contrasts sharply with Florida, which has 67 districts, where each county operates as a single school district.[30] Further, states across the country, and those in the Midwest and West especially, often have rural districts that stretch across wide expanses of territory and serve relatively small numbers of students. That contrasts sharply with large urban districts such as those in Los Angeles, Chicago, Houston, and New York City, which serve tens of thousands of students, many of whom are recent immigrants who speak little or no English.

The diverse landscape of institutions that govern American schools and the overall nature of American federalism provide advocates on all sides of education debates with numerous venues in which to advance their policy and political agendas.[31] Given the potential consequences of schooling on the lives of children, and the billions of dollars spent on schools each year, it is no wonder that the politics of education can be intense.[32] Historically, at the national level scholars have tended to consider education an issue owned by the Democratic Party.[33] Those perceptions flow primarily from the Democrats' support, dating to the first ESEA, for federal programs and funding to support American students, and the Republicans' desires to rely on local communities or market forces to make decisions about teaching and learning. Despite those historical perceptions, the growing shift in popular debate from a focus on programs that support education to concerns over actual results has created additional space for Republican advocates to advance their own initiatives in national and state arenas. Passage of NCLB, with support from a Republican president who worked with leaders of both parties in Congress, illustrates as much.

Inside the Washington, D.C., beltway and out across the country, numerous organizations have formed to influence the political debates over education policy. Perhaps the most powerful in terms of raw political muscle, given the size of their membership rolls and their ability to raise money, are the nation's major teacher unions, the National Education Association (NEA) and the American Federation of Teachers (AFT).[34] Members of teacher unions reside in every congressional district in the United States, making them potent forces during election season, during which they overwhelmingly support Democratic candidates for office. Their large memberships are also powerful in lobbying campaigns in state capitals and on Capitol Hill. Finally, collective bargaining between teacher unions and local school districts, which produce teacher contracts, also has an important impact on local practices and the distribution of teacher talent, as subsequent chapters will show.

Finally, although teacher unions remain powerful, other groups also have joined the fray, which has changed the overall environment during the past two decades.[35] Chief among them have been members of the nation's business community, traditionally a Republican Party constituency. Like governors in state capitals, business leaders have increasingly supported efforts to hold schools accountable for results. Through groups such as Achieve, which emerged from a partnership between governors and business, industry leaders have pushed for raising standards and focusing efforts in subjects such as math, science, and technology. Think tanks and research institutes also have flourished. Since the rise of the Internet, especially, these groups have enjoyed more opportunities to gather data and distribute their analyses to wide audiences in federal, state, and local arenas.

COLLISION COURSE

In December 2001 members of Congress, anxious to improve education, passed NCLB and charged state and local governments with implementing it. After

President Bush signed the bill into law in January 2002, the statute prompted diverse reactions from its supporters, detractors, and neutral observers alike. Its most vocal advocates saw NCLB as a powerful engine to improve schools and eliminate inequities in educational achievement.[36] Some saw the law as a civil rights statute dressed up as an accountability system with inspiring ambitions but questionable mechanisms.[37] Others saw flaws in NCLB's main components but believed that targeted changes could correct those mistakes and, in turn, increase the chances of achieving its loftier goals.[38]

More vocal critics attacked the law from diverse perspectives. One group believed NCLB simply represented more of the same failed approaches that, since *A Nation at Risk* appeared, had been unable to promote educational excellence and equity. These critics suggested new approaches that would represent major departures from the system of testing and accountability that resided at the core of NCLB.[39] Those proposed changes included dramatic expansion of school choice. Others believed that NCLB represented an unrealistic effort, offensive to American federalism, that failed to account for the state and local capacities that would ultimately determine the law's success. Chief among such critics were members of the bipartisan National Conference of State Legislators, who were vocal critics during NCLB's development and after it became law.[40] Finally, other critics saw NCLB as a grand conspiracy designed to set up schools for failure, which would lead to the eventual elimination of public education in the United States.[41]

NCLB's well-established track record makes it is possible to assess the law's performance, competing claims about it, and the collisions it prompted. Regardless of one's political perspective, one thing is clear: After NCLB's passage, federal ambitions to push the nation's students to higher levels of achievement and to hold schools accountable for performance collided with the institutional environments in which NCLB operated. What happened as a result? Before answering that question, it is worth recognizing that collisions themselves come in several forms.

In general, all collisions concentrate energy at some point of impact, but their consequences can vary. Sometimes they provide enjoyment rather than pain, as anyone who has ridden bumper cars at an amusement park will attest. At other times they are abrupt and dramatic but seem to have no lasting effect. Sports fans have no doubt witnessed what appear to be bone-crushing hits between players in soccer, hockey, football, or rugby that, nevertheless, end in both players getting up as if nothing had happened. Some collisions are initiated with great precision and intentionality, as when billiards masters effortlessly execute seemingly impossible bank shots. Slight deviations of the cue angle, though, can create unintended consequences and end a player's turn. Outside of controlled environments, on the nation's highways, for example, collisions can be tragic and physically and emotionally devastating.

What about NCLB and the collisions it initiated in states and local communities? Based on the accumulated evidence, the law produced many results, rather than a clear single one. That is perhaps not surprising given the large ambitions of NCLB's authors and the diverse state and local settings where the law played out. Still, to preview the arguments to come, at least three broad positive results have ensued: The nation has become more attentive to concerns about achievement disparities between student groups; the technical capabilities of state and local governments have increased; and policy entrepreneurs have been able to leverage NCLB to push for important reforms.

Simultaneously, two negative effects have unfolded and affected the nation's ability to promote educational equity and excellence. Although some exceptions exist, by and large NCLB's implementation tended to produce practices that decreased academic quality and expectations in the nation's schools. Further, it expanded bureaucratic rules that often led policy implementers to focus their efforts on meeting technical rules. As a result, substantively important outcomes for schools and students suffered.

To investigate NCLB's implementation, ensuing chapters consider the law from several different perspectives, providing insights about its impact and the larger lessons it suggests. Chapter 2 examines how federal policymakers crafted NCLB. How, for example, did White House leaders and members of Congress attempt to align their ambitious goals with the state and local institutions that would be responsible for carrying out the law? What theories of accountability and administration and which specific mechanisms did federal lawmakers incorporate into the legislation? Analyzing the levers and logic residing at NCLB's core helps to answer those questions.

Chapter 3 focuses on the choices of system leaders in Washington and state capitals who were charged with overseeing the law's implementation. How did the compromises over NCLB that emerged during the lawmaking process influence federal and state officials, especially those in the U.S. Department of Education and state education bureaucracies? Some potential collisions between federal and state policy were in clear view during 2001. Others surfaced once federal, state, and local administrators began implementing NCLB. State officials found themselves in a pinch, given that they were agents of the federal government charged with making NCLB work in their individual states, but they were also overseers of their own local districts and schools. That sort of middle management position always puts state leaders in a challenging political and administrative spot. Fielding local requests while simultaneously attempting to align NCLB with preexisting state systems often moved state education agencies to ask Washington to adjust NCLB's requirements. In turn, federal bureaucrats decided where to bend and where to hold firm.

Chapter 4 considers NCLB's local impact, focusing especially on how the law labeled and affected schools that failed to meet annual achievement goals.

How did NCLB's content and the system leaders' choices influence how schools were judged and ordered to improve? A popular notion in education is that schools can resist external pressures for change.[42] The saying "This, too, shall pass" sums up the opinions of many educators and school principals regarding reform waves that have come and gone. If that pattern held, perhaps NCLB created much political controversy but few substantive changes in the critical tasks that classroom teachers perform each day. Alternatively, it could be that the law, much like its advocates anticipated, collided with school systems in transformative ways, helping local officials to initiate changes and improve educational opportunities and performance. Finally, collisions between these local institutions and federal ambitions may have been more negative, as the law's critics predicted, undermining potential progress that existed before NCLB.

Chapter 5 analyzes NCLB from the perspective of the nation's teachers. Ultimately, the law was supposed to be about more than the legal and regulatory choices of system leaders or the bureaucratic changes that schools and districts initiated in response to the law. Those activities were mere means to accomplishing the larger ends of improving educational opportunities and ultimately elevating student achievement in reading and math. Educators were central to achieving those primary goals. NCLB's highly qualified teacher provisions attempted to improve educational opportunities by guaranteeing that all students would learn from talented teachers. The law's other requirements created incentives and constraints that affected teachers' daily classroom tasks. How did NCLB affect the quality of the teaching profession and the classroom choices that teachers make each day?

Chapter 6 investigates how NCLB influenced the learning opportunities and achievement of students, especially those from disadvantaged backgrounds. Considering how NCLB affected the nation's young people is the most important element in judging whether, on balance, the collisions the law initiated were desirable. In the collision between federal ambitions and state and local institutions, did NCLB seem to increase overall student achievement and decrease gaps between the nation's traditionally advantaged and disadvantaged students? Just as one might have expected NCLB's effects to vary in schools and school districts, one also might have expected the law to affect students differently. The chapter begins by focusing on how NCLB affected learning opportunities for two traditionally disadvantaged groups that the law aimed to assist: students with disabilities and students learning English (or English-language learners). It then concludes by examining larger trends in student achievement across multiple states and years. That examination includes discussion of achievement gaps between advantaged and disadvantaged student groups.

Finally, Chapter 7 reflects on the broader lessons that America's experience with NCLB suggests. To what extent were the collisions that NCLB produced actually transformative and energizing, destructive and tragic, or something in between? What guidance does the law's track record provide for subsequent federal efforts in education? More generally, what can NCLB teach us about the degree to which the federal government can successfully hold state and local governments accountable for results? Despite a healthy and sometimes vocal skepticism about the federal government's ability to solve problems, citizens frequently turn to Washington when pressing crises and persistent inequities become intolerable.

It is an open question as to whether or not citizens should realistically expect federal officials to have the skills and institutional capacities to demand accountability from state and local governments and then have those policy implementers produce desirable results. That question is relevant not only in education but also in other areas. Can federal policymakers hold states or localities responsible for moving people from welfare to work? Are officials in Washington able to assure that local economic development choices will not unduly affect the massive underground aquifers or great rivers that flow across state and municipal boundaries? Can federal plans to protect public safety ensure that state and local governments will be able to efficiently and effectively respond to future natural disasters or terrorist attacks? Those issues and others, in addition to school performance, will remain salient for years to come.

Calls for greater accountability have echoed in the halls of government and on newspaper editorial pages in the United States ever since the nation's founding.[43] Across American history, few people have argued that governments need less, rather than more, accountability for results. But even as elected officials and ordinary citizens embrace accountability, few of them have spent much time studying the difference between simply demanding results versus creating administrative systems that can produce them. Issuing demands is simple, especially for politicians who have ready access to microphones and the airwaves. Developing workable yet demanding systems of accountability that produce educated students and high-performing schools is difficult and complex. The next chapter begins to show how the advocates of No Child Left Behind approached that tall task.

Demanding accountability vs. creating viable systems

Chapter

2

Logic and Levers
of NCLB

DURING PRESIDENT GEORGE W. BUSH'S TWO TERMS, Republicans
and Democrats battled in what some political scientists have considered one of
the nation's most polarized political times.[1] Amid such division, people may
forget that passage of the No Child Left Behind Act (NCLB) emerged from a
bipartisan effort involving the White House and leaders in Congress. That is not
to say that partisan posturing and fireworks were absent from the legislative debate
producing NCLB in 2001. Far from it. But in the end, as President Bush signed
NCLB into law in January 2002, members of both parties celebrated the victory.

In the White House, Bush and his team relied heavily on a lifelong Democrat,
Sandy Kress, to help shape and negotiate the president's plan with Congress.
Kress, a Texan who grew up in Dallas, had previously been an official in Jimmy
Carter's presidential administration and had campaigned for Democrats in state
and national elections. In the 1990s, Kress also served as a member of the Dallas
school board. In that role he eventually connected with Bush, who at the time
owned the Texas Rangers baseball club but held no elected office. The two men
clicked immediately, and their relationship continued after Bush became the
state's Republican governor in 1995. Although Kress had become "politically
ambidextrous" in working with Bush on education, his allegiance was to "Bush
and education, rather than to an overarching Republican philosophy."[2]

When Bush began his presidential run, he asked Kress to advise him on education. After the dramatic U.S. Supreme Court decision in *Bush v. Gore* gave Bush
the White House in December 2000, the new president again tapped Kress. This
time it would be to help him pass his education agenda. During the campaign
and in Washington, Kress's ideas were crucial in developing Bush's education
reform initiatives, in particular his ideas concerning testing and accountability.
The president's top domestic policy adviser, Margaret La Montagne (who eventually became Margaret Spellings, Bush's second education secretary), called Kress

"the primary front person" on education negotiations within the president's policy team and with elected officials and staff on Capitol Hill.[3] Interestingly, Kress's influence even appeared to overshadow Bush's own education secretary, another Texan, Rod Paige.[4]

In contrast to the smooth working relationship between Bush and Kress, the politics of NCLB on Capitol Hill were much feistier during 2001.[5] The year had begun with Republicans controlling the House and Senate by the narrowest of margins. That balance of power changed suddenly in the late spring when Senator Jim Jeffords of Vermont, a Republican and chair of the Senate education committee, left his party to become an Independent. Jeffords was motivated primarily by what he believed were the president's misplaced priorities. Rather than using large budget surpluses for a tax cut, Jeffords believed they should have been used to fund the federal commitment to special education.[6] Jeffords's decision meant that Republicans lost their majority status in the Senate, which led to Democratic senator Edward Kennedy of Massachusetts becoming the education committee chair. Given Kennedy's experience, stature, and close ties with traditionally strong education interest groups, especially the nation's teacher unions, the political dynamics surrounding the bill's debate shifted.

As the legislative process advanced through the spring and into the early fall, much of the heavy legislative lifting fell to John Boehner of Ohio, Republican chair of the House education committee; George Miller of California, the ranking Democrat on the committee; and, in the Senate, to Kennedy and Judd Gregg, Republican from New Hampshire and the ranking Republican on the Senate education committee. Those members, who became known as "the big four," played key political roles that helped the legislation advance.

On the Republican side Boehner and Gregg were instrumental in defending President Bush's agenda to fellow Republicans, many of whom could not believe that a Republican president was proposing to increase the federal role in the nation's schools. Conservatives in Congress were especially angry when Bush compromised by dropping his support for school vouchers—monetary subsidies that parents can use to send their children to public or private schools—to appease Democrats and win broader support for his testing and accountability plans. On the Democratic side Miller and Kennedy, both liberal stalwarts in their respective chambers, battled to convince fellow Democrats that the extensive testing in Bush's plan did not represent a wolf in sheep's clothing, merely designed to make the public schools look bad. Additionally, they lobbied the president to make a strong commitment to increasing education funding, a position that appealed to the array of interest groups in the Democratic coalition. Miller was also instrumental in pushing for added measures on teacher quality, an area where Bush and his team showed less interest.

Perhaps most ironic in the political machinations on Capitol Hill was the role of Senator Joseph Lieberman of Connecticut. Were it not for the *Bush v. Gore* decision, Lieberman would have been vice president, given that he had been Al Gore's running mate on the 2000 Democratic ticket. In 2001, Lieberman's status in the NCLB debate became elevated owing to his prior legislative experience on education and his influence among centrist Senate Democrats, who liked Bush's general ideas about testing, standards, and accountability. The presence of the Lieberman bloc combined with Gregg's advocacy with Republicans put pressure on Kennedy to urge his most liberal supporters to endorse or at least not openly oppose NCLB. Otherwise, Kennedy's ability to influence the final content of the bill and its funding provisions would have been compromised.

Despite the advocacy of Bush, Kress, the big four, and Lieberman, hammering out compromises between the House and Senate versions of the Elementary and Secondary Education Act (ESEA) reauthorization proved difficult into the summer and early fall. It was only after the September 11, 2001, attacks that the process regained traction and eventually produced NCLB's passage, in December. The result was a lengthy and complicated bill that preserved several existing programs, altered others, and incorporated new provisions for student testing, school accountability, and teachers. A looming challenge for NCLB, one that Capitol Hill and White House negotiators recognized, was that its success depended on the ability of states and local school districts to implement it well. While figures fluctuated from year to year, Kress recognized the federal government's tenuous position, given that it was only a "7 percent investor" in education (see Figure 1.1), while states and localities contributed the remaining 93 percent of funds for American schools.[7]

But if the federal government's financial stakes in education were low, its substantive stakes were incredibly high given persistent achievement gaps between students (the equity issue) and fears that the nation's economy would atrophy if achievement trends continued (the excellence issue). Politicians and advocates across the political spectrum had many concerns about the prior performance of the ESEA and its various reauthorizations. In designing NCLB, the law's authors attempted to address those prior difficulties while simultaneously brokering deals with their colleagues and interest group supporters that would satisfy their key concerns. Thus, like most complicated bills produced in Congress, the result was not based primarily on technical knowledge and evidence about which approaches would work best. Rather, it was shaped largely by the ambitions of federal policymakers and laws already in place, as well as the political context.

KEY PROVISIONS OF NCLB

The criticisms hurled at prior ESEA reauthorizations helped persuade the president and large majorities of congressional Democrats and Republicans to act in 2001. In reauthorizing the ESEA as NCLB, federal legislators increased the pressure on states, school districts, and schools to remedy gaps in student achievement and resources. After nearly four decades and several reauthorizations, the law's advocates hoped that NCLB's combination of requirements and funding would accomplish the lofty goals for education that had existed since Lyndon Johnson proposed the first ESEA in 1965. President Bush offered such an optimistic prognosis on January 8, 2002, at the ceremony where he signed NCLB into law. Among other things, he stated confidently, "As of this hour, America's schools will be on a new path of reform, and a new path of results."[8]

Whether the president's prediction would materialize depended on the proper functioning of NCLB's several moving parts. The law itself was quite lengthy and contained over fifty specific programs. Many were miniscule in budgetary terms. The most crucial programs and requirements, designed to eliminate inequities of achievement and resources, appeared primarily in Title I and Title II of the law. Collectively, the following four elements composed NCLB's substantive core: testing, adequate yearly progress, consequences for schools and districts, and teacher quality. The ensuing four subsections summarize those elements.[9]

Testing

Student testing linked to state-defined standards in key subjects was the main component of NCLB for determining whether schools were making necessary progress. Specifically, NCLB required each state to develop tests in three subjects: reading, math, and science. By the 2005–2006 school year, the reading and math tests were to be administered for students in 3rd through 8th grade and at least once for those in 10th to 12th grade. Science testing was slightly different. States had until 2007–2008 to begin conducting these tests, which needed to occur only one time each in 3rd to 5th grade, 6th to 9th grade, and 10th to 12th grade.

In addition to developing tests, states also had to define test scores that would designate whether a student was proficient in each subject. Those levels were commonly known as "cut scores." Students scoring above the defined score would make the cut and be deemed proficient, while those scoring below would not. Each year states had to define the percentage of students needing to be proficient in these subjects, such that by 2014 all students in each state—meaning 100 percent—would be proficient in reading, math, and science.

Importantly, to promote academic progress among disadvantaged students and to narrow achievement gaps between these students and more advantaged ones, NCLB required states to report school test results by student subgroups. For each school, states had to calculate the fraction of students scoring at proficient levels or better within the following groups: racial and ethnic minorities (e.g., black, Hispanic, Native American, and others), students from low-income families, students with disabilities, and English-language learners. It was possible for the student's scores to count toward more than one subgroup, depending on the student's characteristics. The scores of a black student who had a disability, for example, would count in two subgroups. In general, these scores were supposed to help state agency officials, local district officials and school staff, parents, and citizens to see whether individual subgroups, not just school populations as a whole, were achieving at proficient levels.

Also important, states needed to calculate subgroup results only for schools that had at least a certain number of students present. In all states, for instance, if an elementary school had 250 students, composed of 103 blacks, 145 whites, and 2 Hispanics, the school would not have to have its subgroup scores for Hispanics reported. Federal officials let the states themselves set these minimum group thresholds, known as "n-sizes." As later chapters will discuss, delegating that decision to the states would generate controversy when some states set their minimums so high that skeptics wondered if they were attempting to hide their schools' performance and avoid the law's consequences.

Adequate Yearly Progress

NCLB required states to use annual test results, in addition to some other measures to be discussed shortly, to determine whether individual schools and entire school districts were performing at acceptable levels. The law's adequate yearly progress (AYP) provisions defined how states were to make these judgments. Essentially, the process involved a few steps. It began with states setting annual goals that defined the fraction of students needing to score at proficient levels or better in reading and math. Although NCLB required the administration of science tests, science results did not factor into AYP calculations. The long-term goal was to assure that 100 percent of students would be proficient by 2014. (In practice, "100 percent" really meant nearly 100 percent, as exceptions to be discussed in Chapter 6 will clarify.) In the years leading up to 2014, schools and districts had to hit intermediate targets, too. For example, a state might have required 30 percent of students in each subgroup to be proficient by 2004–2005 and then increased the required percentage by 10 points per year (e.g., 40 percent proficient by 2005–2006; then 50 percent proficient by 2006–2007; and so on). Such a rate of progress would have enabled all schools in the state to hit the 100 percent target by the 2014 deadline.

Individual schools would miss AYP if any student subgroup did not have the required percentage of students scoring at proficient levels or better in reading and math, regardless of how the other subgroups performed. To illustrate, consider a hypothetical elementary school in a state that required 50 percent of students to be at proficient levels in reading and math by 2006–2007. Consider further that the school served students in kindergarten through 6th grade and had large numbers of black, Hispanic, white, and low-income students in each grade. Given the state's requirement, at least 50 percent of the school's students in each subgroup must score at proficient levels or better to meet the AYP goal. If at least 50 percent of the students in each subgroup scored at proficient levels on reading and all but one subgroup had at least 50 percent of students proficient in

Reading & Math Targets Set
Subgroups as a Factor
Attendance
Diplomas / HS Graduates

math, then the school would not make AYP. In short, based on NCLB's requirements, one subgroup scoring too low, regardless of how the others did, would be enough for the school to miss AYP. The law defined schools not making AYP as "schools in need of improvement" (sometimes shortened to "schools in improvement" or "schools in improvement status"), a label that could have important implications.

Test results in reading and math were the main factors determining a school's AYP status, but success on these exams was not the only factor. The others included a requirement that at least 95 percent of students across all tested grades and subgroups take state tests and another that student attendance levels for the year remain high. The participation and attendance requirements were intended to minimize the chance that schools would try to game the system by excluding students likely to score poorly. To truly leave no child behind, all children needed to participate. Finally, high schools had the additional requirement of demonstrating that a high percentage of students graduated with their diploma. Missing the attendance, test participation, or graduation requirements also would force a school to miss AYP, even if all students who took state reading and math tests scored at proficient levels or better.

As with individual schools, entire school districts were subject to the AYP system. To judge school districts, NCLB required states to use individual student test scores, test participation levels, attendance, and graduation rates to compute aggregate ratings for entire districts. Hypothetically, if a district were large enough, it could have some individual schools make AYP but the district as a whole could miss it. As in schools missing AYP, if overall district performance were too low, then the district itself would be deemed a "district in need of improvement" (or "district in improvement" or "district in improvement status"), with potential consequences.

In drafting NCLB, Congress included one exception to the AYP requirements, known as "safe harbor." This exception allowed a school to make AYP even if not all subgroups scored at high enough levels. Here is an example to illustrate how this exception worked. A school could benefit from NCLB's safe harbor provision if for particularly difficult subgroups it increased the number of students making proficiency by 10 percent from one year to the next. For example, imagine a school where 46 percent of students in one particular subgroup scored at proficient levels or better for 2006–2007, but for that year the state required 70 percent of students in each subgroup to be proficient. Assuming that all other subgroups exceeded the 70 percent threshold, without safe harbor the school would be in improvement status.

With the safe harbor provision, the school could make AYP if the subgroup with 46 percent of students proficient in 2006–2007 represented a gain of at least 10 percent from the 2005–2006 school year. If in 2005–2006, only 40 percent of students in this subgroup had been proficient, then 44 percent would need to be proficient in 2006–2007 for the school to satisfy the safe harbor requirement. In this example, the cutoff of 44 percent arises from taking 10 per-cent of 40, the percentage scoring proficient in the previous year, and then add-ing that number to 40.[10] Because 46 percent of students in this subgroup were proficient in 2006–2007, the school would have exceeded the 44 percent needed according to safe harbor. As a result, the school would have met its AYP require-ment even though not all subgroups had at least 70 percent of students attain proficiency. Importantly, schools still needed to have 100 percent of students reach the proficient level by the 2014 deadline. The safe harbor exception for any given year did not eliminate that ultimate NCLB requirement.

Consequences for Schools and Districts

Understanding what would happen to schools or school districts that missed AYP depends on a crucial distinction. By law NCLB required states to calculate AYP ratings for all schools and school districts. But NCLB's consequences for missing AYP applied only to schools or districts that received funding through Title I of NCLB, commonly called "Title I schools" and "Title I districts." As of 2006–2007, about 55 percent of schools and more than 95 percent of school districts received Title I funds.[11] As Chapter 1 explained, throughout its history, Title I of the ESEA has contained formulas that define how much money each state and school district receives under that part of the law. In general, the amount of poverty in a state and a district weighed heavily in determining how the federal government distributes these funds. Since the original ESEA of 1965, states and districts have had some discretion in determining how much Title I money individual schools receive; the formulas in Title I have not specified those precise amounts. Importantly, for accountability purposes, NCLB did not require any consequences to ensue for non–Title I schools and districts that missed AYP. Only Title I schools and districts failing to make AYP needed to take certain actions that the law defined. Consider next those consequences for schools and districts.

Table 2.1 outlines the consequences NCLB required for Title I schools that persistently missed AYP. These measures would begin after a school missed AYP for two consecutive years, after which the school would enter improvement status. Schools in their first year of improvement were required to allow their students to transfer to another school that had made AYP. That remedy was known as NCLB school choice to distinguish it from the variety of other school choice programs in operation around the country. After two years in improve-ment, schools needed to continue offering choice but districts also had to reserve part of their Title I funds to provide students with supplemental educa-tional services. Typically, those were after-school or weekend and summer tutor-ing activities (or sometimes combinations of all three). That extra help was

Table 2.1 Consequences for Schools Missing AYP

Years in a row missing AYP	Year in improvement	Consequences for the school
1	none	School put on watch.
2	1	School enters improvement status. Now must offer NCLB school choice.
3	2	Offer NCLB school choice and supplemental educational services.
4	3	Offer NCLB school choice and supplemental educational services; implement corrective action.
5	4	Offer NCLB school choice and supplemental educational services; implement corrective action; plan for restructuring.
6	5	Offer NCLB school choice and supplemental educational services; implement corrective action; and implement the restructuring plan.

Note: Adapted from the No Child Left Behind Act (Public Law 107–110), Section 1116.

provided by outside organizations, including for-profit and nonprofit groups, as well as by school district teachers or staff.

The consequences became more severe for schools that continued to miss AYP. A school entering a third year of improvement needed to initiate at least one corrective action while still offering choice and supplemental educational services. In general, corrective actions were intended to change some aspect of the school's daily functioning and may have included personnel and programmatic changes. Once a school entered a fourth year of improvement, all of the prior consequences were to continue and the school also needed to begin planning for more major restructuring. If the school remained in improvement for a fifth year, then it needed to implement that restructuring plan while continuing to implement the other NCLB-mandated consequences. Table 2.2 outlines the various options available for schools in either corrective action or restructuring. Schools did not need to adopt all of these actions to comply with NCLB; using one or a combination of several was acceptable.

Beyond these specific consequences for schools, NCLB also required entire school districts to make AYP. States needed to initiate improvement plans in Title I districts that failed to make AYP for two consecutive years. The districts were required to begin developing and implementing those plans within three months. At any point after that time, states had discretion to implement potentially tougher corrective actions for districts that were in improvement. However, the law required states to adopt those corrective actions in Title I districts that failed to make AYP for another two years. Table 2.3 outlines the various district-level consequences that could follow. They range from relatively mild

Table 2.2 Corrective Action and Restructuring Measures for Schools Missing AYP

Type of consequence	Corrective action (4th year missing AYP)	Restructuring (5th and 6th year missing AYP)
Personnel	• *Staff*: "Replace the school staff who are relevant to the failure to make adequate yearly progress."	• *Staff and principal*: "Replacing all or most of the school staff (which may include the principal) who are relevant to the failure to make adequate yearly progress."
Management	• *Decrease authority*: "Significantly decrease management authority at the school level." • *Outside expert*: "Appoint an outside expert to advise the school on its progress toward making adequate yearly progress, based on its school plan."	• *Contracting*: "Entering into a contract with an entity, such as a private management company, with a demonstrated record of effectiveness, to operate the public school." • *Takeover*: "Turning the operation of the school over to the State educational agency, if permitted under state law and agreed by the State."
Structure	• *Time*: "Extend the school year or school day for the school." • *Curriculum*: "Institute and fully implement a new curriculum, including providing appropriate professional development for all relevant staff, that is based on scientifically based research and offers substantial promise of improving educational achievement for low-achieving students and enabling the school to make adequate yearly progress." • *Organization*: "Restructure the internal organizational structure of the school."	• *Charter*: "Reopening the school as a public charter school." • *General*: "Any other major restructuring of the school's governance arrangement that makes fundamental reforms, such as significant changes in the school's staffing and governance, to improve student academic achievement in the school and that has substantial promise of enabling the school to make adequate yearly progress as defined in the State plan."

Note: Schools must implement corrective action after missing AYP for 4 consecutive years. Schools must plan for restructuring after missing AYP for 5 consecutive years and then implement those plans if they miss AYP for 6 consecutive years. Passages quoted from the No Child Left Behind Act (Public Law 107–110), Section 1116.

measures, such as strengthening the core academic program, to more dramatic actions, which could involve the state intervening to take over the school district or individual schools within it. As in corrective action and restructuring for Title I schools not making AYP, states could choose from among the various options for Title I districts in improvement.

Table 2.3 Consequences for School Districts Missing AYP

Improvement plan requirements to be completed by school districts

- *Strategies based on research*: Incorporate scientifically based research strategies that strengthen the core academic program in schools.
- *Student achievement focus*: Identify actions that have the greatest likelihood of improving student achievement.
- *Professional development*: Fund the professional development needs of the instructional staff serving the agency.
- *Achievement goals*: Include specific measurable achievement goals and targets for student subgroups, consistent with adequate yearly progress.
- *Assess needs and prior actions*: Address the fundamental teaching and learning needs in schools, and the specific academic problems of low-achieving students, including a determination of why the district's prior plan failed to increase student achievement.
- *Out-of-school activities*: Incorporate, as appropriate, activities before school, after school, during the summer, and during an extension of the school year.
- *Identify state and district responsibilities*: Specify the responsibilities of the state educational agency and the school district under the plan.
- *Parental involvement*: Include strategies to promote effective parental involvement.

Corrective action requirements for the state education agency to initiate in school districts

- *Funding penalties*: Defer programmatic funds or reduce administrative funds.
- *Curriculum and professional development*: Institute and fully implement a new curriculum that is based on state and local academic content and achievement standards, including providing appropriate professional development based on scientifically based research for all relevant staff that offers substantial promise of improving educational achievement.
- *Staffing*: Replace district personnel who are relevant to the failure to make adequate yearly progress.
- *School takeover*: Remove particular schools from the jurisdiction of the district and establish alternative public governance arrangements for those schools.
- *District takeover*: Appoint a receiver or trustee to administer the affairs of the school district in place of the superintendent and school board.
- *Abolition or restructuring*: Abolish or restructure the district.
- *Student transfer*: Authorize students to transfer from a school operated by the district to a higher-performing public school operated by another district, and provide students transportation (or the costs of transportation).

Note: Adapted from the No Child Left Behind Act (Public Law 107–110), Section 1116.

Teacher Quality

In addition to holding schools and districts accountable for academic performance, NCLB attempted to increase the quality of the nation's teachers. The law's authors believed that its testing and AYP requirements would bolster student achievement and close achievement gaps between advantaged and disadvantaged students. That view was central to the approach that President

George W. Bush and his allies offered during the legislative process. The advocacy of other key figures, in particular Democratic representative George Miller of California, a member of the big four, led to new teacher quality provisions in NCLB as well.[12] Miller and others believed that these provisions would help remedy the inequities in teacher quality that often divided advantaged and disadvantaged students.

The teacher quality requirements of NCLB were less complicated than the law's testing and AYP elements, but no less ambitious. To begin, NCLB defined highly qualified teachers as those who held at least a bachelor's degree; were fully certified to teach, or had passed a state licensing exam and held a teaching license (e.g., teachers not teaching on an emergency or temporary state credential); and were competent in the academic subjects that they taught. Teachers in what the law identified as core academic subjects needed to meet this standard. Those core subjects were English, reading or language arts, math, science, civics and government, history, geography, economics, the arts, and foreign languages. States were to guarantee that all teachers of core subjects were highly qualified by the end of the 2005–2006 school year.[13]

Depending on a teacher's grade level and experience, the law offered different paths for meeting the subject matter competence requirement. New elementary school teachers needed to pass a state test demonstrating their knowledge in reading, writing, and math. The law required new middle and high school teachers either to pass a state test in their teaching area, to have a college major in that subject, or to possess advanced graduate course work or credentialing proving their knowledge. Veteran teachers also could demonstrate their mastery in these ways, but they had another option, too.

To incorporate some flexibility into the subject area competence requirement in the highly qualified teacher definition, NCLB's authors allowed veteran teachers to meet what the law called a High Objective Uniform State Standard of Evaluation (HOUSSE). States were left to design their own particular approach to HOUSSE, which could include, among other things, requiring veteran teachers to show they possessed relevant course work in their teaching areas, had completed substantial professional development activities in their area beyond formal classes, or had a track record of producing students who achieved at high levels.

THEORIES OF POLICY ACTION

Clearly, NCLB was a complicated law with numerous moving parts. Why did its supporters expect such a massive undertaking focused on test-based accountability, performance of student subgroups, and teacher quality to work? Answering that question requires taking a step back and considering the theories of action that motivated NCLB. A theory of action is simply a larger rationale that provides the logic for why certain policy actions should produce desired results.[14] The reason why pulling policy lever "A" should produce result "B" is a causal connection that a policy theory would help to explain.

For example, in economic policy one school of thought holds that governments should run deficits to encourage productive commercial activity during slow economic times. This view, known as Keynesianism for its principal founder, John Maynard Keynes (1883–1946), assumes that when economies flounder and even stagnate, government is really the only institution in society that can intervene to help spark consumer demand. By using short-term transfers of money and credit to unemployed persons and struggling businesses, governments through these expenditures, Keynesian theory maintains, will rejuvenate an underperforming economy. The $787 billion economic stimulus package that President Barack Obama pushed for and Congress passed early in 2009 contained several provisions based on Keynesian assumptions.

Every policy, no matter how large or small, embraces some theory or theories that suggest why the policy should produce desirable results. Whether policy theories are right or wrong depends on how they perform in the real world.[15] Assessing their accuracy can sometimes be complicated, especially when a single policy embraces multiple theories, which may or may not be consistent with one another. Those potential contradictions may arise from compromises that emerge during the legislative process as lawmakers make deals and split differences to build majorities and pass their initiatives. The resulting policies sometimes emerge with internal contradictions or tensions that may challenge civil servants in federal, state, and local government bureaucracies—the people charged with implementation—to achieve the policy's primary objectives.[16]

To understand the logic motivating NCLB's key parts, consider the law's theory of accountability and its theory of administration. These two dimensions reveal the important working assumptions that the law's supporters embraced. In other words, these supporters had a theory of accountability in mind for why testing, subgroup performance, and consequences for missing AYP should motivate schools to improve. They also embraced a theory of administration that suggested who should be responsible for implementing the law's various provisions. Examining NCLB's theory of accountability and administration also helps to identify some of the law's internal tensions that the legislative process produced. Those tensions created subsequent implementation challenges for bureaucrats across levels of government and teachers in the nation's schools.

NCLB's Theory of Accountability

Since the late 1980s and especially into the 1990s, state and federal policymakers have become increasingly interested in educational accountability. Depending on the context, accountability in public policy can assume many different forms.

Most generally, to hold some person or institution accountable for results means that one can properly assign credit for policy successes and blame for policy failures. Simply observing a government agency's actions, such as how much money a school district spent on reading programs, without being able to link spending to key goals, such as increases in reading achievement, would make it impossible to say whether the agency made positive, negative, or negligible contributions to students' reading skills. Similarly, it may be possible to observe certain outcomes—tests may show how well students understand math—but several things may prevent one from connecting those results to specific policies or practices.

One reason why educational accountability became popular was that for many decades before the 1980s public schools had operated as classic "coping organizations," to borrow a term from political scientist James Q. Wilson.[17] In coping organizations, school principals and district leaders—the formal overseers of a community's schools—have difficulty observing what teachers do on an hourly or even a daily or weekly basis. They also cannot assess how much students are learning. In other words, to use Wilson's terms, both outputs (the teachers' work) and outcomes (student achievement) were not very visible to principals and district leaders. For most of the history of American education, a popular saying held that once a teacher closed the classroom door, it was anyone's guess what was happening in there. NCLB's theory of accountability attempted to change that situation by focusing on two elements: (1) measurement and transparency of results and (2) consequences for performance.

Consider measurement and transparency first. A key part of NCLB was its requirement that students take tests in reading and math every year during 3rd through 8th grade and at least once in high school. The results would then be reported at the school level, broken down by student subgroups, made publicly available, and examined to see if schools were meeting the law's goals of increasing achievement and decreasing gaps between groups. The subgroup data would provide valuable information to help advance the law's equity objectives. Knowing how individual groups performed would prevent overall school averages from obscuring the fact that schools might be leaving behind students who were economically disadvantaged or members of racial minorities, among other groups.

In essence, NCLB's testing and reporting provisions created a particular type of school report card to see if schools were accomplishing the achievement goals that the law's authors had identified. Prior to NCLB's passage, a comprehensive study of organizational report cards by political scientists William Gormley and David Weimer found that school report cards had been a popular policy tool. In fact, in the mid-1990s thirty-five states had some sort of individual school-level reporting system. In most of these states, laws made these report cards available to parents and the general public.[18]

As Gormley and Weimer explain, advocates of organizational report cards find them valuable tools because they help to reduce two kinds of information asymmetries, or differences, that exist for schools and other public organizations.[19]

Measurement → Consequence
(Transparency)

One form of asymmetry exists within an organization. An example is the challenge that school principals face in knowing what is occurring in their schools' classrooms. Teachers, in contrast, have a much better gauge of daily progress and the pace of learning because they work alongside their students. By requiring schools to produce annual report cards, school principals would have better information about how well their students were performing. Also, principals would be better positioned to alter school policies to improve their students' chances of success.

A second type of asymmetry that organizational report cards help to minimize is that of information differences between school employees and school overseers. This asymmetry applies to the relationship between external officials—be they elected representatives on local school boards, in the state legislature, and Congress or bureaucrats in local, state, or federal agencies charged with monitoring schools—and the principals and teachers who work in schools. (One might also consider parents to be external overseers, although typically they lack formal authority over a public school's operations.) Without good information on school performance, these external overseers cannot know which schools are struggling or excelling. When report cards work, they enhance accountability by enabling internal managers (e.g., principals) and external overseers to improve school-level processes, reallocate resources to meet pressing needs, refocus managerial attention on pressing concerns, and enhance school missions by providing personnel with goals on which to refocus their efforts.[20] Of course, making such smart reforms depends heavily on the skills of school managers and features of the political environment in which the school operates. In short, administration is not merely a technical exercise immune to political considerations.

NCLB's requirement for states to gauge annual progress and generate school report cards, through calculating AYP results, flowed from theories of performance measurement and continuous organizational improvement. Many authors writing about private and public sector organizations have examined these issues.[21] In the public sector much of this work frequently falls under the label of the New Public Management, of which "performance measurement has become one of the main tenets."[22] The basic assumptions of performance measurement draw heavily on a similar logic that parallels what students commonly learn as the scientific method.[23] In a laboratory, scientists gather data to test hypotheses about the world. Those test results can lead to refined hypotheses and new insights or broader theories about why we observe certain natural phenomena, such as patterns in the weather and the migration of birds. The key for science to progress, then, is for researchers to seek information, examine it rigorously, and in light of the evidence be willing to adjust their ideas about how the world operates.

Theorists and advocates for the New Public Management have drawn on the scientists' approach to experimentation in developing ideas about how to improve public organizations, including schools.[24] In education the view holds that one must gather school-level performance data each year to know whether school practices—the "hypotheses" that school officials make about what they believe will enhance student learning—are producing desired results. If the results fall short of stated goals, then performance data can inform a search for better practices. Measurement in subsequent years, then, can help determine whether these reforms have produced the expected outcomes. As long as measurement occurs each year, the logic goes, schools will be better positioned to identify effective and ineffective methods of instruction or management.

If measurement and transparency composed the first assumption of NCLB's theory of accountability, then consequences for performance were the second. The law's AYP requirements for schools and districts in improvement status were the concrete manifestation of this second assumption. The law's authors believed that measurement and transparency alone were limited. There would be no guarantee that needed changes would occur without consequences for schools that failed to achieve key goals. In short, the view held that when data revealed poor performance, concrete actions must follow. That connection between measurement, transparency, and consequences would help ignite a sense of urgency among school and district officials to make needed changes and improve student learning.[25] Of course, the assumption about changes that would occur depended on school overseers and personnel mustering the political will to initiate reforms that were difficult and uncomfortable, especially for adults working in the school (e.g., see Tables 2.2 and 2.3).

One way to understand NCLB's internal logic is to consider the contrast between what one political scientist and education policy scholar, Frederick Hess, has called "nice versus mean" accountability.[26] A system that required only measuring and reporting of results would be a nice approach, Hess argues. With nice accountability, the system would rely on schools and districts themselves to act appropriately when results were subpar. Public shaming or embarrassment may ensue in such a system, which could prompt action, but the accountability system would require no particular measures.

The nice approach contrasts with mean accountability, in which school and district officials know that clear and sometimes even painful consequences will follow if performance falls short of specified goals. Recall that one criticism of the Improving America's Schools Act (IASA) of 1994 was that it required measurement and transparency but let states determine what should happen as a result. NCLB's supporters believed that the accumulated evidence showed that such an approach was too casual and did not seriously push the nation to foster educational equity and excellence. NCLB's supporters were convinced that a nice approach to accountability would not produce the kind of jarring collision with state and local systems that conditions required. A more aggressive and tougher approach was needed.

"Nice" w. "Mean"
Accountability

The assumption that accountability policies will be more effective when they embrace clear and compelling consequences is consistent with prior research on what political scientists call principal-agent theory.[27] Work in this area considers relationships between a boss, known as the principal, and the boss's subordinate, the agent. In its most basic form, a principal-agent relationship exists when a principal hires an agent to perform some work that the principal cannot complete alone. A contract is an agreement that defines the relationship between principals and agents, laying out their respective responsibilities. Research using principal-agent theory suggests that principals must take their agreements with their agents seriously or else agents know they can violate them without any penalty. Critics of the ESEA's track record believed that the federal government's unwillingness to enforce the law's requirements created this type of dynamic because states and local school districts could fail to comply with certain ESEA provisions yet continue to receive federal funds.

Principal-agent theorists have identified two types of consequences that can motivate agents to fulfill their end of the contract. Positive consequences provide rewards, while negative consequences assess penalties. For individuals, bonus pay would be an example of the former, while the threat of losing one's job or being demoted would represent the latter. In considering the consequences associated with the AYP system of NCLB, it is important to note that the law's authors stressed penalties for school and district officials failing to make required progress, rather than rewards for those who succeeded. Generally speaking, the remedies for schools and school districts in improvement required these institutions to lose some autonomy over resources and internal operations, as Tables 2.1, 2.2, and 2.3 showed. Further, it is also interesting to note that NCLB contained no consequences for individual students who performed poorly or well on state exams. In other words, consequences were to ensue for schools and school districts that missed AYP; in contrast, NCLB would assign no penalty to a student who did not try hard to succeed on state math and reading exams, nor would it reward students who did exceptionally well.[28]

Taken together, measurement and transparency of results along with consequences for performance made up the core of NCLB's theory of accountability. But what did the law say about how that theory would be put into practice? In other words, there are many different arrangements that could implement accountability as NCLB's authors envisioned it. To understand which approach NCLB's authors selected, one must consider the law's theory of administration.

NCLB's Theory of Administration

Education economists Charles Clotfelter and Helen Ladd have described two approaches to hold organizations, including schools, accountable for performance.[29] One approach relies on market forces in which consumer preferences and choices determine which organizations succeed. Education reform proposals to expand school choice with voucher programs to fund private education or charter schools, which are public yet operate with freedom from many regulations affecting traditional public schools, are examples of this method of accountability. In those instances, the ultimate measure of a school's success would be the extent to which it could attract students. Parents would evaluate data about the school; talk with other parents to glean insights about teachers, administrators, and school offerings; and ultimately decide whether they thought the school met their own personal standards. *(Market)*

The other major approach to accountability that Clotfelter and Ladd describe is to construct governmental administrative systems for monitoring and oversight. Rather than exclusively relying on individuals and their choices, these systems require the construction of more elaborate government bureaucracies, rules, regulations, and performance goals. Civil servants, guided by laws and regulations, would be the ones judging organizational performance in that approach. In such a setting, schools would be accountable to not only individual parents but the political community as a whole.[30] *(Gvt)*

While NCLB's theory of administration incorporated an aspect of market forces by providing transfer options to students in schools that consistently missed AYP, the law primarily relied on governmental administrative systems to hold schools accountable. Based on NCLB's content, the law's authors assumed certain things about how accountability is likely to be administered in the American federal system. On one hand, with NCLB the federal government wanted to promote accountability for academic performance, but on the other hand state and local governments still retained much power over schools. How did NCLB's theory of administration attempt to balance those two issues? Examining prior research on standards-based reform, federalism, and intergovernmental relations helps to reveal the main features of the law's theory of administration.

A major part of NCLB's administration involved the implementation of its testing provisions, which built upon the IASA of 1994. In that prior ESEA reauthorization, President Clinton and Congress required states to develop standards in reading and math. Those were to guarantee that disadvantaged and advantaged students alike would meet high academic standards. NCLB's authors still required states to develop reading and math standards, but they made the testing requirements more stringent by requiring states to administer reading and math tests annually in 3rd through 8th grade and once in high school. Put differently, in the language of standards-based reform, NCLB and its predecessor law required states to develop policy in three areas. First, states needed to develop content standards, which defined what students need to know and be able to do for key subjects and grades. Second, they needed to develop exams to see how well students learned this required material. And third, they had to

State Rules

market vs. government forces

establish cut scores to define how well students needed to perform in order to make a score deemed proficient or better.

In theory, one could imagine many different administrative arrangements that might possibly implement such a system of standards-based reform. People could have their national government develop standards and exams and then require all schools across the country to administer them. This practice would follow what other nations, such as Japan and France, have designed for their own education systems.[31] One could also rely on nongovernmental professional associations of educators, rather than governments themselves, to design standards and exams. In the United States, for example, the National Council of Teachers of Mathematics (NCTM), a national group of math instructors at all levels, has developed detailed expectations for students in each grade. It would be possible for a government simply to adopt such standards based on what the educators within particular fields determined was important.[32] As a final example, a country could decide to allow states or local school districts to develop their own content standards and, if desired, accompanying exams, which they could administer to their students each year. That approach and its ensuing content would likely reflect the priorities of smaller communities of leaders, especially if local districts could write their own standards and tests. Across the United States today, some school districts have developed content standards for particular subjects. In the Detroit Public Schools, for example, citizens and school leaders have decided that it is important for students to have in-depth study of African and African American history because the vast majority of the city's students are black. The school district has developed standards and curriculum materials in those subjects to help guide local teachers.[33]

In weighing how to administer standards-based reform with NCLB—using national, state, local, or nongovernmental approaches—federal policymakers favored focusing on the states. NCLB's requirements avoided national or locally developed standards and instead made states the key administrative actors that would carry out the law's standards and testing requirements. Specifically, NCLB required each individual state to develop content standards, exams, and cut scores for proficiency that would apply to all of the state's schools. Importantly, even though NCLB was a federal law, it did not establish federal expectations for students in reading and math, nor did it instruct federal bureaucrats in the Department of Education to write exams that all students would take. Instead, it simply required that students take tests in certain grades and certain subjects but left state leaders the task of developing the standards and administering the exams.

In essence, NCLB's authors did not create a uniform national system of accountability for K–12 education. Rather, lawmakers envisioned the creation of fifty different systems, one for each state, in which reading and math content and the level of mastery demanded of students could differ across state lines. Within any one state the expectations would be identical. For example, all 4th graders in

Illinois would have to master the same reading and math content at the same level to reach proficiency. But 4th-grade students to the north in Wisconsin could have different reading and math expectations, including different standards, different tests, and different cut points that defined proficiency. Consequently, it would be impossible to compare Wisconsin's 4th-grade reading scores with those from Illinois because the expectations and exams would be different.

Further, schools in each state would still have to make AYP, but again, whether schools achieved it or not would depend on state expectations and definitions of proficiency. Based on NCLB's theory of administration, one would predict that states with lower expectations would likely have fewer schools missing AYP, while states that expected more would have more schools entering improvement status. The enforcement of consequences for schools that missed AYP also fell to the states. Just as NCLB did not create a system where federal bureaucrats would write student exams, no individual school in the United States was subject to direct federal control if it missed AYP. Federal law did specify the consequences that would ensue when schools or school districts missed AYP (see Tables 2.1, 2.2, and 2.3), but NCLB also required the states themselves to administer their accountability systems to ensure that these consequences would occur. Schools and school districts were directly accountable to the states, not the federal government. The states were to work within the federal government's framework of AYP that NCLB prescribed.

NCLB's heavy reliance on the states suggests a few things about the law's theory of administration. First, in passing NCLB, federal lawmakers needed to confront the reality that even though they had much license to argue for increasing accountability in K–12 education—favoring equity and excellence were not controversial—they lacked the capacity to design and implement such a system on their own. That fact reflects Sandy Kress's point from this chapter's opening about the federal government being a "7 percent investor" in American education. Given the relatively small federal investment in education, national policymakers routinely borrow from state administrative capacities to make federal education policy work. The country is simply too vast, the number of schools and districts too large, the reach of the Department of Education simply too limited, and the nation's system of education governance too fragmented for Washington policymakers alone to design and implement a system to hold the nation's tens of thousands of schools accountable for performance. Although several Republicans in Congress preferred an even more decentralized approach, based on expanding school choice for students and encouraging solutions that were developed in local communities, the majority opinion favored continuing the long-standing ESEA tradition of relying on the capacities of state education agencies to administer federal policy.[34]

Second, even if the federal government did possess the capacity to administer standards and testing with NCLB, in relying heavily on states, the law's authors implicitly recognized an important general principle about policy implementation.

The literature on federalism, public policy, and administration tends to show that initiatives will be more successful when governments or bureaucracies charged with carrying them out have power to make important implementation judgments.[35] Making local schools or school districts responsible, as some Republicans preferred in the NCLB debate, would affirm this principle even more. But having local communities develop standards and exams would re-create the same problems from the 1960s that the ESEA's original authors experienced in their failed attempt to incorporate expectations for performance into the law. Having the states impose a degree of uniformity on local districts and schools would help federal officials avoid that problem. In theory, having states as the key administrators of NCLB would keep decisions more local but not so local that the system would be incoherent. A key issue, which later chapters will assess, is whether federal officials made valid assumptions about the state capacity available to implement the law.

Federalism, Capacity, Decentralization

POLICY THEORIES IN TENSION

In studying NCLB's theory of accountability and its theory of administration, readers may begin to recognize tensions between the two. Those tensions affected the collisions between NCLB and the state and local systems charged with carrying it out. Consider two particular tensions that will return as recurring themes in later chapters. First, NCLB's supporters believed that prior ESEA reauthorizations suffered from weak enforcement. That failure required a new approach, they argued, to make the federal government a tougher principal, better able to oversee its agents in states and local districts. The law's theory of accountability reflected that desire. In contrast, the law's theory of administration, which reasoned that states should shoulder much responsibility for implementing the law, seemed to undercut the federal government's ability to be tough. If the institutional and political realities of American federalism meant that Washington needed to defer greatly to the states' judgments and initiatives for NCLB to succeed, then it would become harder to force the states to act as federal leaders preferred. In other words, by providing the states much discretion to develop standards, exams, and student expectations, federal policymakers weakened their own hand in the relationship.

A second tension becomes clear given what scholars of public administration have learned about implementation of systems designed to hold organizations accountable for results. The management reforms mentioned earlier suggest different roles for principals and the agents they are attempting to hold accountable. According to what New Public Management scholars call "liberation management," for example, principals will enjoy more success when they set clear goals and then turn loose their agents to determine the most effective methods for achieving them.[36] In other words, principals should not care how their agents achieve the goals (assuming their methods are legal, of course), only that

Balance of federal vs. State implementation
undermined NCLB?

the goals be achieved. While the principal is still responsible for determining the goals, the agents are liberated because they have freedom to choose how to accomplish them.

Taken together, however, NCLB's theory of accountability and its theory of administration represent an inverted form of liberation management. The law reversed the roles that liberation management theorists and scholars of policy implementation suggest principals and their agents should play. In crafting the law, federal leaders allowed those at lower levels of the system to set the goals. Certainly, NCLB did say that 100 percent of students needed to be proficient by the year 2014. But the law allowed states to define the substantive content of what *proficient* meant. States determined the content standards that indicated what students should know and be able to do. States also wrote the tests to gauge student progress. And finally, states identified the cut scores for these exams, which determined whether students were deemed proficient.

Further, instead of letting states determine how to fix persistently troubled schools, federal policymakers imposed a specific approach—the law's system of AYP and ensuing consequences for schools or districts in improvement status— that all states needed to follow. Certainly, NCLB afforded states and local school districts that repeatedly missed AYP some flexibility, given that multiple options existed for schools and districts in improvement, especially at the corrective action or restructuring stages. But still, the requirements for public school choice and supplemental educational services, including the order in which they needed to occur, were quite specific. Also, the law was relatively detailed about the range of acceptable corrective actions and restructuring measures, with one important exception, which later chapters will discuss. Advocates of liberation management or performance management would have preferred to let lower levels of government sort out those details.

In short, the inverted division of responsibility for establishing goals and policy implementation in NCLB created the potential for federal officials to micromanage the policy details and focus on administrative processes, leaving them little power to substantively influence academic performance. Put differently, if federal administrators in the Department of Education have no power to determine whether the academic progress of a state's schools is real or acceptable, then those administrators will focus on matters over which they do have some control, namely, whether states have followed the procedural rules that the law and department regulations have established. The federal-state relationship then becomes focused on discussions about state adherence to procedures, which is something that management theorists and scholars of policy implementation have predicted can produce counterproductive rather than transformative collisions.[37] When procedures take center stage, it becomes difficult for public administrators across levels of government to implement laws while focusing on larger substantive goals, such as having all students become knowledgeable in crucial subjects.

* * *

Passing NCLB represented a major success for President Bush and members of both parties in Congress. Long-standing political concerns and views of American federalism, such as the tradition of state and local control of curriculum and teaching, kept some options such as federally developed standards and tests off the negotiating table from the start. The most liberal advocates during NCLB's construction favored expanding federal programs and funding with few consequences for schools that failed to improve. Those on the conservative end of the spectrum supported trimming back federal programs and empowering local communities and students to make wise educational choices.

In 2001 the political decision of President Bush and leaders in Congress to focus on standards and testing occupied what appeared to be a well-established middle ground in the national debate over how to improve American education. The prior ESEA reauthorization of 1994 had helped to spur the state standards movement. Across the country, governors, members of the business community, and groups such as the Citizens' Commission on Civil Rights and The Education Trust had embraced the use of standards and testing to encourage educational equity and excellence. In attempting to construct NCLB in a way that appealed to these wide-ranging constituencies, and other groups as well, federal legislators designed several mechanisms, grounded in theories of accountability and administration, that they assumed would improve teaching and learning across the country. The next chapter begins examining that assumption by considering how system leaders in Washington and state capitals implemented the law.

System Leaders
Implement the Law

ALONGSIDE THE POTOMAC RIVER just south of the nation's capital sits Mount Vernon, George Washington's historic estate. On January 9, 2002, the day after President George W. Bush signed the No Child Left Behind Act (NCLB) into law, Secretary of Education Rod Paige went to the first president's home to address a conference of federal education officials and roughly two-thirds of the nation's state education chiefs. According to Paige's staff, it was the first time that a secretary of education had convened such a meeting. The gathering gave federal and state system leaders a chance to begin assessing each others' hopes, worries, and priorities at the beginning of what NCLB's most optimistic supporters characterized as a new era for educational accountability in America. The meeting also began to suggest some of the collisions that NCLB would create as state implementers attempted to understand this latest reauthorization of the Elementary and Secondary Education Act (ESEA).

After promising that the upcoming year would be one of "dramatic change," Paige offered remarks reflecting the internal tensions between NCLB's theories of administration and accountability.[1] On one hand he attempted to reassure state education department leaders that he would construct a productive relationship with the states. "I invited you here tonight not to give orders, but to offer my help in a bold mission," he said. "Those of us from the Department of Education want to help you implement the Act [NCLB], and we want to hear about your needs, your concerns, and your suggestions. I am serious about the partnership, and very sincere in the statement that we are in fact in this together. Our success is dependent upon one another."

In his very next breath Paige noted how he would aggressively implement the act. Just as classroom teachers often attempt to set a strong tone as school begins, the secretary did the same at Mount Vernon in saying that "No Child Left Behind is now the law of the land. I took an oath to enforce the law, and I intend to do that." Drawing on his teaching and coaching experience, Paige reasoned,

"When students beg their teachers to extend deadlines, the choice between discipline and compassion can be very difficult. But if states ask me to extend deadlines, they will be asking me to make a choice between the needs of children and the flaws of the system. . . . When choosing between kids and the system, I choose the kids." Then, in a clear reference to the perceived inadequacies of prior ESEA enforcement, he added, "And if anyone comes to me to appeal for a waiver from the federal requirements, I hope to be very pleasant as I firmly say, not in this century. Not in this country."

The state chiefs, coming from different political perspectives and whose schools enjoyed varying levels of educational success, reacted positively but also cautiously. Iowa's chief, Ted Stilwill, was enthusiastic. "I thought this meeting was going to be about rules and regulations," he said, "but instead it has been about values, principles and commitment, which was what I needed to hear." Kentucky's Gene Wilhoit echoed those sentiments. Simply holding such a meeting with the state chiefs, Wilhoit explained, was "a positive sign." He and North Carolina chief Mike Ward were both confident that Paige and his assistants would incorporate state feedback as they crafted the all-important regulations that would clarify NCLB's expectations and instruct federal, state, and local education officials on how to implement its provisions. "I am confident that Paige will involve us in the rule-making process," said Wilhoit, while Ward added, in addressing the secretary directly, "The details matter the most if we are going to implement this legislation. I'm encouraged by your willingness to meet and negotiate those details." And Susan Zelman, Ohio's state superintendent, welcomed partnering with Washington, saying optimistically, "I think all the chiefs are willing to say that it's doable." [2]

Reactions were not uniformly positive, however. Andy Tompkins of Kansas, while generally supporting the law, was frank in predicting that he and other state leaders "are always going to scream about federal intrusion—that is the American way." Shortly after the Mount Vernon meeting, interviews with officials in forty-five states reflected some optimism but also worries over NCLB's key elements. [3] Of greatest concern were the deadlines for administering annual tests and for having highly qualified teachers in all classrooms by 2005–2006. Fears also existed that federal accountability requirements would not mesh well with pre-existing state systems, some of which had operated for several years and had taken many more years to develop. Even early in 2002, state system leaders worried that once they and their federal counterparts began implementing NCLB, the ensuing collisions would be counterproductive rather than transformative.

STATE LANDSCAPES AND CAPABILITIES

Given NCLB's theory of administration, it is most accurate to say that the law created different sets of collisions in each state, which reverberated after 2002, rather than one uniform and immediate jolt across the country.[4] Three major state-level factors influenced the nature of those collisions: first, the way that preexisting state education systems interacted with NCLB's requirements; second, the willingness of state education leaders, including the chiefs just quoted, to embrace tough expectations for schools so that students would learn rigorous content and schools and districts would feel pressure to improve; and third, state capabilities to implement the law, especially its demanding requirements regarding testing and school accountability. Consider these three factors in turn.

First, baseline conditions in the states illustrated their diverse points of departure as they began implementing this latest ESEA reauthorization. Although in accepting federal funds under NCLB the states agreed to meet the law's new expectations, much of NCLB's content built on the Improving America's Schools Act (IASA) of 1994. That prior ESEA reauthorization required states to expect all students to meet the same high state-defined standards, to evaluate students with tests aligned with those standards (but in fewer grades than NCLB, remember), and to report test scores by student subgroups. Successful implementation of NCLB depended on the states having already fulfilled those requirements.

In early 2002, collectively the states were far from achieving those earlier IASA milestones. A study from the General Accounting Office (later, Government Accountability Office; GAO) found that in March 2002 only seventeen states were complying with the testing requirements from the IASA. The GAO discovered that states faced the biggest problems in aligning tests and standards and in having systems that tested all students and then reported results by student subgroup. The GAO concluded that "because the majority of states have not met the requirements of the 1994 law [the IASA], many states may not be well positioned to meet the deadlines for implementing the additional requirements in the 2001 legislation [NCLB]."[5]

Baseline state policies in testing revealed some of the diverse approaches that existed across the country. As President Bush signed NCLB into law, for example, only nine states had testing of the sort that NCLB required: aligned with state standards in reading and math and administered in 3rd through 8th grade, plus once in high school.[6] Some states, such as Colorado, were relatively close to meeting the requirements. Others had farther to go. Kansas, for example, possessed the required reading tests for 5th, 8th, and 11th graders and the math tests for 4th-, 7th-, and 10th-grade students. In Pennsylvania the state had proper tests only for 5th, 8th, and 11th grades; however, that state's education secretary, Charles Zogby, did note that at least 70 percent of the state's districts administered "nationally norm-referenced tests in grades 3, 4, 6, or 7."[7]

Even though NCLB required states to develop state exams, Pennsylvania leaders hoped federal administrators in the Education Department would allow the state to use a combination of state and local tests. System leaders in Louisiana faced a similar situation. They hoped that federal administrators would allow

Different Baselines
Different Conditions
Different Readiness
} Disparate Implementation

them to use nationally developed tests that they could show were aligned with state standards. "If not," said Rodney Watson, an assistant state superintendent, "it would require major changes in state policy and perhaps state statute." Further, he worried, "We could have tremendous backlash, primarily because we are showing a positive trend in terms of student performance."[8]

Figure 3.1 summarizes the number of tests that states needed to develop just as NCLB implementation began. The figure shows that only five states were completely ready, while some were quite far behind. In fact, eighteen states needed to develop ten or more tests—including seven states that needed seventeen—by NCLB's 2005–2006 deadline.[9]

Interestingly, the states facing the greatest early difficulties were not always those that needed to develop several new tests. States with quite developed systems of standards, testing, and accountability also faced challenges, sometimes even major ones, as NCLB's implementation began. As Jack O'Connell, California's state superintendent, noted, "The states that were ahead of the No Child Left Behind ballgame have had the most difficult time implementing this."[10] In such states NCLB collided with preexisting systems that usually had relatively

Figure 3.1 Tests States Needed to Develop by NCLB's 2005–2006 Deadline, as of
            March 2003

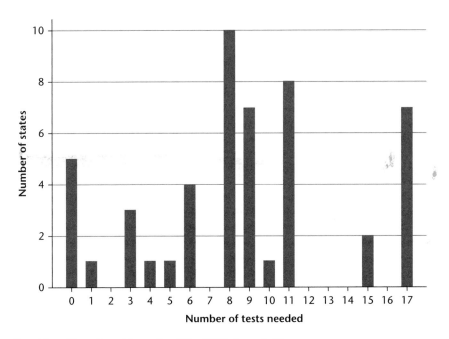

Note: Adapted from General Accounting Office (2003, Appendix III).

established track records and reasonable levels of political support. Adapting those conditions to NCLB's accountability expectations fostered frustration among some state system leaders. Missouri's state education department spokesman Jim Morris captured such worries in noting that because the state was in the process of implementing its own accountability system, state leaders were "very concerned about, in effect, changing horses in midstream."[11]

State development of NCLB-required accountability also created the potential for schools, districts, parents, and the public to receive mixed messages.[12] That could occur when schools made high marks from preexisting state accountability systems yet missed adequate yearly progress (AYP) based on the new federal expectations in NCLB. Some states, in developing their own school ratings and report cards prior to NCLB, used sliding scales based on letter grades or numerical scores. Those differed from the either-or system of NCLB, in which a school either made or missed AYP, with no intermediate levels.[13] NCLB did not necessarily require states to dismantle their preexisting accountability systems, only that they maintain a system that conformed with NCLB. States could comply by creating a new system from scratch, consistent with what NCLB demanded, adapting an old system to meet NCLB's requirements, or simply maintaining a dual system of accountability where schools were rated by an approach that state system leaders preferred as well as by a method consistent with NCLB.

Florida's experience illustrated how dual systems of accountability unfolded in practice. That state's accountability system prior to NCLB assigned schools letter grades from A to F based on their performance. Importantly, the Florida system did not evaluate schools based on student subgroups, as NCLB required. Rather, the state's grading system assigned points to schools if they improved from the prior year and especially if they increased achievement among the lowest scoring 25 percent of students in the school.[14] When evaluations of the state's schools for 2002–2003 appeared, reports showed approximately 87 percent of Florida schools did not make AYP, although many excelled on the state's letter grade system. Across the state roughly 22 percent of schools earning an A did not make AYP.[15] Overall, 69 percent of schools were in the A or B category, while only 6 percent made a D or F.[16]

Other states, including North Carolina, California, and Arizona, reported similar differences between marks based on preexisting state accountability systems versus the new ones required under the AYP framework.[17] State system leaders often argued that their own approaches were better. A common complaint was that state system leaders believed the NCLB approach over-identified schools as needing improvement. Defenders of NCLB responded by saying that such discrepancies often revealed that the neediest students were still falling behind and that without the attention that NCLB had sparked, state leaders would feel less pressure to respond.

Conflicts w/ state systems (report cards) & NCLB Report Cards

In addition to baseline conditions, a second major state-level variable influencing the collisions from NCLB was the degree to which state system leaders embraced demanding expectations or relatively easier ones. While NCLB required states to administer annual tests, rate schools for AYP, and have 100 percent proficiency in reading and math by 2014, it allowed states to resolve several issues that would ultimately determine NCLB's impact. These issues included how much and how well states required their students to know their subjects and how much annual improvement they expected of their schools.

One crucial point to reiterate is that NCLB did not create "national standards" for students, teachers, or schools. Rather, it created a set of administrative process requirements—provisions for testing in certain grades and the approach to calculating AYP being prime examples—that states needed to follow to hold schools accountable. It was the states' job to define the substance that would guide those processes. In other words, by defining content and performance standards, states determined what students needed to know and how well they needed to know it. Similarly, working from the broad federal requirement for highly qualified teachers, states were left to set specific criteria to decide which teachers met the standard. While NCLB required all teachers in core subjects to be fully certified, for example, each state determined what full certification meant. In sum, NCLB did not create a uniform set of specific academic standards for students, teachers, and schools, even though it did require the states to follow various procedural requirements, described in Chapter 2, to hold schools accountable for academic results and to guarantee that teachers were highly qualified.

State flexibility to make important substantive decisions prompted criticism that some state system leaders were not demanding enough of their students, teachers, and schools. The language of NCLB evoked a certain image that disadvantaged and advantaged students alike would be meeting high standards, that all teachers would be knowledgeable and expert performers in the classroom, and that schools would be improving so that all students would be proficient in key subjects by 2014. The reality, according to the states' critics, was that many states perhaps met the letter of the law but nevertheless violated its spirit by using NCLB's flexibility to lower their expectations of students and teachers.[18] State choices, then, had the effect of buffering the potentially transformative collisions that the law's authors had hoped to create.

As NCLB's implementation unfolded, state critics cited certain evidence to support their claims. Regarding student expectations, observers pointed to the differences between state test results and results from federal exams in reading and math, known as the National Assessment of Educational Progress (NAEP). All students do not take the NAEP tests, which are administered by the National Center for Education Statistics at the U.S. Department of Education and overseen by the National Assessment Governing Board. Rather, they are taken by

Varying levels of rigor between states (teacher qualification / assessment)

samples of students every couple of years and allow one to draw inferences about student achievement at the national level, for individual states, and for a handful of very large school districts. Unlike the tests that states developed to meet NCLB's requirements, NAEP test results are comparable across states and across time. In fact, the NAEP is the only widely administered test that allows for such comparisons. That is why it is frequently called the "Nation's Report Card." [19]

One analysis found large discrepancies when it examined state test scores for 2004–2005 and the 2005 NAEP results. For example, based on state tests, 89 percent of Colorado's 4th graders were proficient or better in math, but only 39 percent achieved proficiency based on NAEP standards. Similarly, 88 percent of North Carolina's 8th graders achieved proficient marks or better on the state's exams, but only 39 percent did so on the NAEP.[20] These and similar results moved some people to argue that states had low academic expectations for their students. As one critic of NCLB and state behavior noted, demanding that students become proficient but letting states define what proficiency meant was "like a parent demanding that her child get a 95 percent on her next math test but then saying she can take the test in calculus, or algebra, or arithmetic. States have maximized their scores by defining proficiency down. That foils the law's core goals of encouraging excellence and holding schools accountable for achieving it."[21]

Whether lagging NAEP scores reflected state shortcomings or other factors prompted spirited debates during NCLB's implementation. State advocates correctly noted there was nothing in NCLB mandating that state tests must conform to the NAEP's expectations. Thus, the divergent results could exist simply because state exams addressed somewhat different areas of study. Because no clear consensus existed about the appropriate grade level for introducing certain topics in math or reading, it was not surprising that states picked different approaches. As a consequence, those state choices influenced their state's NAEP score.

Other evidence suggested that even if dissimilar content produced some score differences, state expectations also were a factor. One study from the federal Education Department attempted to map state standards from 2005 onto the NAEP to see if state tests were more or less demanding than the federal one. The task involved looking at what each state expected in reading and math and then comparing those expectations with the NAEP. By lining up the NAEP against each state's expectations, researchers could evaluate them both on a similar metric. By analogy, the process was much like developing a system to convert temperature from Fahrenheit to Celsius. This exercise showed that states varied widely in how much they expected their students to know to be proficient in reading or math. Importantly, the study found that most states defined proficiency at a level that was below the NAEP "proficient" standard, and further, in some states students could make proficiency by scoring below the NAEP "basic" standard.[22]

An additional source of state criticism came from how states set cut scores for their exams, which determined how high students needed to score to make proficiency. During NCLB implementation, some states changed these cut score levels.[23] Those shifts meant, for example, that in one year a test score of 75 percent correct was required for 5th graders to be proficient in reading, while 5th graders in later years would need to make only a 70 percent score for proficiency. In one sense those changes were perhaps unsurprising given that so many states needed to develop multiple tests in several grade levels to meet the law's requirements. As states wrote and rolled out their exams, and refined their understanding of how preexisting exams worked, it would have been reasonable to expect some trial and error as state policymakers adjusted their systems based on real world experience.

Researchers found that as states redefined their cut scores, sometimes states lowered the bar rather than raised it. Most states kept cut scores constant after 2002, but according to one report, among states that made changes, "twice as many states have seen their tests become easier in at least two grades as have seen their tests become more difficult."[24] In Wisconsin, for example, a change made in 2003 lowered cut scores in twelve out of fifteen tests administered to state students at the time, which were being used to fulfill NCLB's requirements. The state superintendent, Elizabeth Burmaster, and researchers at the University of Wisconsin defended the changes by arguing that they were more realistic than where previous cut scores had been set.[25]

A third and final important variable affecting the collisions between NCLB and state institutions was state capabilities to implement the law's requirements. Dating to the original passage of the ESEA in 1965, federal education policy had relied on state capacity to help achieve federal objectives. But for much of their history since the 1960s, and even still today, state education agencies have operated primarily as compliance-oriented organizations. In other words, despite being charged with implementing education policy in a state, these agencies have tended to possess little expertise in actually working on substantively important education initiatives, such as the development of standards, curriculum, and tests. Instead, their main purpose has been to distribute state and federal money to local communities and then monitor to ensure that those dollars have been spent appropriately. Although the agencies in some states improved their capabilities during the 1980s and 1990s, they still remained relatively weak and focused mainly on compliance-oriented work.[26]

The capabilities of state education agencies were especially important because those bureaucracies and the state chiefs who lead them, many of whom attended Secretary Paige's meeting at Mount Vernon, were the key overseers of NCLB across the country. The logic motivating NCLB's theory of administration assumed that states, and, in particular, state education agencies, were the best positioned to make the law work. Much of the day-to-day heavy lifting associated with the law's implementation fell to state education bureaucracies, which occupy a challenging administrative and political spot because they must respond

States set up for compliance rather than in-depth implementation

(i.e. designing/scoring tests)

to federal overseers but also remain attentive to the school districts and schools that they govern. Recall, too, that chief state school officers are elected officials in some states, making them especially vulnerable to criticism from state-level interests—namely, teacher unions and members of the business community, who pay careful attention to state policy. Several aspects of NCLB's implementation revealed much variation in state abilities to carry out the law's demanding provisions.[27]

Perhaps the most difficult charge that state agencies needed to administer was NCLB's annual testing requirement. That involved creating standards, exams, and cut scores, but also much more. These exams also needed to be scored, which could be challenging and expensive when standardized tests contained short-answer or essay questions. Further, states needed to maintain large data warehouses that enabled them to organize, evaluate, and generate reports to determine whether schools made AYP. And they needed to communicate those results in a timely, comprehensible fashion for schools, teachers, parents, and students.

Managing the administrative tasks associated with annual testing proved challenging for several state agencies, in particular, because they typically did not actually write and score state tests. Rather, state agencies usually contracted out that function to one of the few large testing companies that dominate this industry in the United States. That relationship between state agencies and the test companies created added pressure as more states sought assistance from these contractors to meet NCLB's requirements.[28] Even before NCLB became law, a GAO study noted that errors from testing contractors had created problems for preexisting state accountability systems. In some states inaccurate scoring required students to enroll in summer school classes or mistakenly labeled schools as not making required progress.[29]

In examining shortcomings in contractor performance, the GAO also noted that lax state oversight was a source of these problems. The authors explained that although "almost all states" hired contractors to score state exams, "16 of these states reported that they did not monitor the scoring done by the contractor. Most of those who did monitor the scoring reported they did so by selecting a sample of answer sheets to compare with the contractor's results to ensure their accuracy."[30] Such sampling might have allowed a state to maintain a general level of quality, but absent a process that validated each and every score, mistakes on individual student exams could slip through.

Scoring and reporting accurate results in a timely manner could be challenging when state data systems were relatively weak. For example, NCLB required states to break down scores by student subgroups to rate schools for AYP. But because state data systems often relied on local school districts or students themselves to report information such as student race or ethnicity, data that the testing companies received and used to compute subgroup scores were sometimes inaccurate. In one extreme case involving scoring and administrative errors, Illinois state leaders delayed releasing scores from the 2005–2006 school year until the spring of 2007. That meant that schools' AYP ratings, which were due by the start of the 2006–2007 academic calendar, were developed after the second semester had already begun.[31]

One study of all fifty states for the 2004–2005 school year found that nearly all states took well into the summer or early fall to compute final test scores and AYP determinations. Only five states had finished scoring spring exams and made AYP calculations before the start of August. Those delays meant that most schools did not know their official AYP status until just as the 2005–2006 school year was beginning.[32] Similar delays occurred the following year, when many states added new exams in order to have their accountability systems fully operational and consistent with NCLB's requirements.[33]

In addition to administering annual testing requirements, state education agencies faced new oversight responsibilities that stressed their capacities even more. One specific area that created such administrative work was NCLB's supplemental educational services provisions. Schools in their second year of improvement status were required to offer students supplemental educational services, which typically amounted to additional tutoring beyond the regular school day. NCLB required states to maintain a list of these providers and to monitor them to guarantee they were offering quality services and that districts were properly implementing the program. One early question that emerged after President Bush signed NCLB was how effective the state education agencies would be at carrying out these oversight tasks. At the time, an assistant state superintendent in Louisiana, Rodney Watson, noted that the monitoring requirements for supplemental educational services "moves a state agency into a whole different arena that we may not be equipped to handle."[34]

As implementation unfolded, a GAO study of state actions during the 2005–2006 school year found that states made progress in some areas but still experienced difficulties overall. States had increased their efforts to visit local communities to evaluate providers of supplemental educational services and monitor district actions. Some states had also begun surveying local parents and principals to help them assess provider performance. In general, the GAO concluded that state oversight was still weak in several areas. Among other things, the GAO noted the following: "Approximately three-fourths of states reported that they are experiencing challenges evaluating SES [supplemental educational services], including designing methods for determining sufficient academic progress of students, having the time and knowledge to analyze SES data, and developing data systems to track SES information." Further, the GAO analysts explained that "only a few states had drafted or completed an evaluation report addressing SES providers' effect on student academic achievement, and no state had produced a report that provided a conclusive assessment of this effect."[35]

In addition to the general task of administering annual tests, and the narrower one of overseeing supplemental educational services, state education agencies faced a major capacity challenge in deciding how to assist the thousands of schools that missed AYP and thereby entered improvement status. Using state resources and working through local school districts, NCLB required state education agencies to assist struggling schools so they would make AYP. A major challenge for state agencies was that the sheer number of schools in improvement status continued to grow as NCLB's implementation unfolded. Based on results from the 2007–2008 school year, approximately one-third of public schools in the nation, nearly 30,000 in all, failed to make AYP.[36] Among that total, over 3,500 had consistently missed their yearly progress targets and were facing corrective action and potential restructuring. In some states the numbers were quite high, as in South Carolina, where 80 percent of schools missed AYP for 2007–2008. Even before the numbers of schools in improvement reached these heights, state agencies had struggled to provide assistance to all schools that were entitled to it.

FEDERAL EFFORTS

As NCLB rolled off the legislative assembly line, enthusiasm for its provisions ran high in Congress, the White House, and the Department of Education.[37] Such a bipartisan legislative success helped raise the spirits of many federal policymakers. It is an understatement to say that 2001 was a challenging year in Washington. Bitter partisan battles over President Bush's tax cut plans divided Democrats and Republicans. As Chapter 2 noted, such disputes even led Republican senator James Jeffords to leave his party, which returned control of the Senate to the Democrats. Then the September 11 attacks rocked the nation to its core and sent the country hurtling down the path toward commencing major military action in Afghanistan. Thus, successful passage of NCLB in December 2001 helped federal officials to reassure themselves, and the country as a whole, that better days were likely ahead despite their political differences and a national catastrophe.

NCLB's implementation began in earnest after President Bush signed it into law in January 2002. As news of its becoming law fanned out across the country, the president and his top administrators, including Paige and his assistant secretaries, emphasized that federal officials were committed to faithfully implementing it. A common theme during the legislative process in 2001 was that earlier ESEA reauthorizations had not achieved their goals partly because federal officials lacked the political will to be strong enforcers. Bush and his surrogates hoped to signal with their words and actions that they were serious and that state system leaders should be, too.

During the fall of 2002, Paige sent what some observers considered a warning shot to states that appeared slow to embrace NCLB. Responding to states' complaints that the federal Education Department had not issued the timely guidance states needed to implement the law, the secretary responded with a sharply worded letter to state education chiefs. In addition to praising states that had made progress, Paige noted that delays or policy gamesmanship would be unacceptable. "Some states have lowered the bar of expectations to hide the low performance of their schools," he said. According to Paige, that was "not worthy of a great country." Those who would embrace such tactics, Paige scolded, "are the enemies of equal justice and equal opportunity. They are apologists for failure. And they will not succeed." [38]

That same fall Eugene Hickok, who served in several high-ranking posts in the Department of Education during Bush's first term, called state critics of NCLB "guardians of mediocrity" who were committed to a culture in American education that had proven to be ineffective.[39] The following year, in February 2003, he noted that he would willingly listen to genuine concerns about the challenges NCLB created, but he also cautioned that some of the law's critics would be satisfied only if the law were dismantled. "A lot of the people who say they support it support it in concept only," Hickok said, before noting, "They're really people who want to amend the law to kill it." [40] Later that spring he brushed off critics who claimed that NCLB was underfunded, pointing out that funds were adequate; he reminded critics that "the color of change is not always green." [41]

In some instances the administration backed its tough talk with concrete enforcement actions. In May 2003, Secretary Paige made good on his promise to hold states to key timelines when he ordered the withholding of nearly $800,000 of NCLB administrative funds from Georgia. A provision in NCLB required that ninety days after it became law, no state with unfulfilled prior obligations under NCLB's predecessor law, the IASA, could request additional time. Georgia's problem was that it was unable to implement certain end-of-course exams, so it asked for extra time beyond what the Clinton administration had granted. In a letter to Georgia officials, Paige wrote that "by not administering these end-of-course assessments this school year, Georgia has violated the terms of its timeline waiver," and that NCLB prohibited him from granting additional time. He had no choice but to penalize Georgia for noncompliance. While the penalty did not directly affect schools—the $800,000 was for administrative activities in the Georgia Department of Education, not teaching in local districts—it sent an important symbolic message. Prior to Paige's action, the Department of Education had never penalized a state financially for failing to fulfill an obligation under the ESEA.[42]

The tough approach to implementation that the administration had promised appeared to pay early dividends when the president and Secretary Paige described the law's progress at a press conference on June 10, 2003. In a Rose Garden ceremony at the White House, President Bush reminded the audience that when he took office, only eleven states were complying with the IASA. But owing to the efforts of federal and state system leaders, Bush was pleased to report what he called "an historic milestone of accountability." Just that morning, the president

State vs. Federal → "Tough Approach"

said, Paige had finished approving the NCLB-required accountability plans from the states. The result was that all fifty states, along with the District of Columbia and Puerto Rico, had approved plans in place. The president noted that in contrast to prior ESEA implementation, these approvals meant that "every state, plus Puerto Rico and the District, are now complying with the No Child Left Behind Act after one year." [43] In his own remarks Paige added, "The extraordinary efforts of the states have laid the foundation for education improvement and accountability. The reforms of No Child Left Behind mean that, for the first time in history, every child in every school in every state in this country will have an education accountability plan for them—and accountability means results." [44]

A careful look at the state's plans and the Education Department's actual approvals, however, shows that the president and the secretary overstated the states' progress in carrying out NCLB. [45] In short, just as in federal implementation of past ESEA reauthorizations, Bush and his team gave states credit for anticipated rather than actual progress. Evidence for that claim comes from the accountability plans that the states submitted for approval. Specifically, as part of developing their accountability systems, NCLB required states to explain how they would fulfill thirty-one specific requirements. These included elements to show how the state's accountability plan would incorporate all schools and districts, how it would calculate AYP to incorporate data disaggregated by student subgroups, and how the state knew that its approach would produce valid and reliable decisions. [46] In the documentation states submitted, they indicated for each of these thirty-one elements whether a final policy existed for the element, whether a policy had been proposed but was not yet approved, or whether the state was still developing a policy.

If the accountability plans were as complete as Bush and Paige had suggested, then all states should have reported that final policies existed for each required element. A tally of the data in the reports, though, showed that only eighteen states had final policies for all required elements. [47] Put differently, thirty-two states still had work remaining in at least one area. Some states had much work, indeed. For example, twelve states lacked final policies on twenty-one or more of the thirty-one total elements. Among the items that states failed to complete, the most challenging were those that focused on calculating AYP, a core element of NCLB's theory of accountability. Despite these numbers the president and secretary still called state plans complete. What they were really doing was calling the plans complete, conditional on the states finishing work on the remaining areas. Their praise was essentially equivalent to a teacher giving a student's ten-page paper a provisional grade of A, even if the student had completed only a detailed outline and written the paper's introduction. The student would keep the A as long as he or she actually wrote an excellent paper.

The content of these initial state accountability plans and the response of federal system leaders in the White House and the Education Department illustrated some of the enduring challenges that federal administrators faced as they attempted to get tough with their state counterparts. It is easy to promise tough enforcement and jarring collisions to prompt reforms, but it is more difficult to deliver them. Approving state plans in a high-profile Rose Garden ceremony when much work still remained was one way for federal leaders to build political capital with the states and to help the states embrace NCLB's theory of accountability. Such an approach was at odds with federal promises to be a strict principal, carefully monitoring and holding state agents accountable for obeying the law. In addition to approving state accountability plans, federal implementation actions in two other areas revealed how federal system leaders found it difficult to remain tough in the face of subsequent implementation challenges. These areas were the administration of NCLB's teacher provisions and the handling of state requests that the federal Education Department waive certain parts of the law and its regulations.

Federal enforcement of NCLB's highly qualified teacher requirements challenged federal administrators in many ways. To be highly qualified based on NCLB's definition, states had to guarantee that teachers in core subjects possessed at least a bachelor's degree, had full state certification, and were knowledgeable in the subjects they taught. The law also included a deadline that teachers needed to meet these standards by the end of the 2005–2006 school year. As NCLB's implementation progressed, critics pounced on how the Department of Education handled its responsibilities for enforcing these provisions.

Perhaps most vocal among the department's critics was The Education Trust, a Washington-based research and advocacy organization that promotes setting high academic expectations and eliminating inequities between advantaged and disadvantaged students. The Education Trust strongly supported NCLB, especially because it promised to shine a light on educational disparities—regarding both academic achievement and access to excellent teachers—between student groups. In a brief report appearing in August 2003, over eighteen months after NCLB's passage, The Education Trust's authors criticized the department for what they perceived as inattention to the highly qualified teacher issue.

In particular, the authors noted an important contrast. After NCLB became law, they contended, "Paige's team at the Department has acted as if it believed that better accountability, alone, will bring about better achievement. The teacher quality provisions of NCLB have been at various times ignored, misinterpreted, and misunderstood. There is too little focus on these important issues and widespread confusion about what they mean." The department's administrative effort devoted to the states' testing and AYP policies had produced "reams of federal guidance interpreting the accountability provisions of NCLB," but on teacher quality, the authors argued, "Questions from the field, if answered at all, are often answered with confusing and/or conflicting 'advice.'"[48] Secretary Paige's inattention, they concluded, had produced state implementation and reporting with inaccurate data, or no data at all, on teacher quality.

A follow-up report from The Education Trust in December 2003 noted, for example, that some state definitions of "highly qualified" seemed impermissible under the law. Further, even though those flawed definitions produced inaccurate reports about the status of teachers and their qualifications, Secretary Paige seemed to let this shoddy work slip by without any consequences. In noting that the Education Department had penalized Georgia (and subsequently Minnesota) for failure to comply with NCLB's testing provisions, The Education Trust concluded, "Through its inaction, the Department signaled that failure to collect or report honest teacher quality data would be overlooked. . . . These decisions send a clear message to the states about the Department's priorities. Sadly, producing good data about highly qualified teachers has not been among them." [49]

Other sources tended to confirm The Education Trust's concerns. Two reports from the GAO, one in 2003 and another in 2005, indicated that states needed clearer guidance from the federal government about how to meet NCLB's teacher quality requirements. The first report noted, "It is important that states have the information they need as soon as possible in order to take all necessary actions to ensure that all teachers are highly qualified by the 2005–06 deadline." [50] The latter report indicated that the Department of Education began its monitoring of state implementation of the highly qualified teacher provisions only in June 2004. [51] As of July 2005 it had done monitoring visits in twenty-nine states, but had completed only twenty monitoring reports. In other words, before 2004 states received some guidance and advice, but no external check, from the federal government to guarantee that they were properly executing the law.

The lack of federal feedback meant that by the summer of 2005, more than half of the states were waiting for either a monitoring visit or receipt of a monitoring report. Given the state implementation problems that existed, the GAO offered an important caution about the numbers that states had produced to indicate whether their teachers met NCLB's requirements. Owing to problems in data collection and reporting, the GAO concluded in 2005, less than one year before all teachers needed to be highly qualified, that "until these data issues are resolved, state reports on their status in meeting the teacher qualification requirements [of NCLB] should be viewed as preliminary." [52]

Finally, a Department of Education analysis of teacher quality, issued in 2009, also reported state frustrations with the advice that the department had offered on the highly qualified teacher requirements. One common refrain was that the department's guidance "has been all over the board." One state official also remarked that because the federal department frequently adjusted expectations for NCLB's highly qualified teacher provisions, "trying to predict things on our end is hard." [53] Part of those difficulties involved developing state policy—but also then communicating it to local districts and teachers.

Clearly NCLB's passage dramatically increased and altered the workload of federal education administrators in Washington. Past research on policy implementation has shown that when facing challenging decision-making environments, bureaucrats react in somewhat predictable ways in order to prioritize critical tasks and break down complex problems into simpler parts.[54] One way to set priorities in government agencies is to consider the priorities of bureaucratic overseers, namely the elected officials who are responsible for monitoring agency behavior. Given that perspective, which is based on the same logic of principal-agent theory discussed in Chapter 2, it is important to remember that NCLB's highly qualified teacher provisions were never atop the Bush administration's education agenda. The president's original proposal for NCLB focused on testing and school accountability and said nothing about highly qualified teachers. Those provisions became part of the law during the legislative process as administration officials negotiated with congressional leaders, especially Democratic representative George Miller, a member of "the big four" that helped pass NCLB in Congress. Thus, less aggressive attention from the president and his top education administrators was an unsurprising outcome given their greater desire to focus on testing and school accountability.

Stricter enforcement of the law's highly qualified teacher provisions also would have prompted broader political battles between system leaders and teacher union representatives. During the legislative process that produced NCLB, the American Federation of Teachers (AFT) and the National Education Association (NEA) invested much effort to ensure that the law would protect teachers' rights, especially those in states where collective bargaining was allowed to determine teacher contracts. Strict implementation of NCLB's teacher provisions would have led to some teachers being reassigned out of their current subjects and potentially into other district schools. Such outcomes would have clashed with local teacher contracts that defined the terms of teacher employment. It is likely that state system leaders refrained from aggressive implementation in part because of union advocacy in the states.

Given that teacher quality was not a top Bush administration priority, the action and rhetoric of federal officials did little to provide state system leaders with political cover to more strictly implement those parts of the law.[55] If anything, comments from the administration sometimes made things more difficult for state leaders. In February 2004, for example, Paige commented in a private meeting that the National Education Association (NEA), the nation's largest teacher union, was a "terrorist organization." With the September 11 attacks still fresh in people's minds, when the secretary's statement became public, it angered union supporters across the country. Some people called for Paige to resign. While apologizing for his remark, Paige nevertheless dug in his heels and argued that the opposition of union leaders, but not individual teachers per se, was undermining NCLB's implementation and sacrificing opportunities for the nation's students.[56]

Despite vowing to push forward even with union criticism, the administration's priorities led the Department of Education to back down on NCLB's requirement that teachers be highly qualified by the end of the 2005–2006 school year. In a letter to state education chiefs dated October 21, 2005, Secretary of Education Margaret Spellings, who had replaced Paige earlier that year, attempted to reassure state leaders by promising "that States that do not quite reach the 100 percent [highly qualified teachers, or HQT] goal by the end of the 2005–06 school year will not lose federal funds if they are implementing the law and making a good-faith effort to reach the HQT goal in NCLB as soon as possible." [57] She then explained that in moving forward the department would monitor the states to ensure they were using a proper definition of a highly qualified teacher, presenting required information to the public and parents, reporting data accurately and completely, and making certain that disadvantaged children had fair access to high quality teachers. States that fulfilled those process requirements but still lacked highly qualified teachers in required subjects would have until 2006–2007 to meet the requirement.

Almost two years later, in a follow-up letter dated July 23, 2007, Spellings noted that no state had met the highly qualified teacher deadline of 2005–2006.[58] She also appeared to extend the revised deadline beyond 2007 by reiterating that she would not penalize states as long as they possessed approved plans and were progressing toward NCLB's overall teacher quality objectives. She further promised a new round of monitoring and explained that the department still had concerns, now more than five years into NCLB's implementation, that the teacher quality "data we receive from States are not always as accurate as they should be." Thus, the existence of plans, improved data collection, and detectable progress toward meeting the highly qualified teacher goal, rather than accomplishing the goal itself, became the department's expectation. That was a far cry from the assurances of Paige and other administration officials who early on promised to enforce all of NCLB's deadlines.

Looking beyond the highly qualified teacher issue, federal leaders in the Bush administration entertained dozens of requests from state system leaders to alter or waive NCLB's requirements in several other areas. These requests essentially asked the federal Education Department to allow the states to implement NCLB in ways that could conflict with the actual law itself or the department's regulations governing its implementation. Such requests are quite common, in education and other areas. When NCLB became law, department leaders, especially Secretary Paige, promised to faithfully enforce its provisions. That meant no waivers would be forthcoming. Assistant Secretary of Education Ray Simon restated that view in early 2005 when he noted that if the department offered waivers, then "we will be back in ESEA, the 'we didn't mean it law.' We don't want a generation of children 'waived away' from academic excellence." [59]

As federal system leaders, including Simon, Paige, and Spellings, discovered, however, keeping their promises to strictly enforce NCLB was easier said than done. The prior discussion about state accountability plans and the highly qualified teacher requirements illustrated as much. Like past rounds of ESEA implementation, Education Department officials continued to receive state requests for regulatory changes or waivers and, as in the past, they adapted the law's implementation. Those adjustments revealed yet again how the division of labor in the American federal system can alter the collisions that occur when federal officials attempt to hold states and local school districts accountable for educational results.

Most notable among those adjustments were periodic changes in federal regulations that governed NCLB's implementation. Bush education officials and their allies in Congress succeeded in repelling state requests to change the actual law; no legislated changes occurred between 2002 and 2008, a notable accomplishment. Secretary Paige, though, did alter federal regulations in light of the implementation experiences of state and federal system leaders. Four key changes occurred between December 2003 and March 2004, for example. First, Paige allowed states additional flexibility in how they tested and held schools accountable for students with the most severe cognitive disabilities. NCLB itself did not specifically address these students' particular needs, and the department's regulations allowed states to give these students alternative assessments. In other words, a 6th-grade student with severe disabilities could take a reading test designed for 2nd graders. But to calculate AYP for individual schools, only 1 percent of students could have these alternative assessments count as proficient or advanced for their grade level.[60]

A second regulatory change, announced in February 2004, addressed how schools could test students classified in the English-language learner (ELL) subgroup. Before the regulatory change, these students were to take the same exams as their peers and their test performance would count toward AYP. State and local officials noted a paradox that these requirements created: schools with an ELL subgroup would almost never be able to make AYP. The reason was that students were in this group because, by definition, they did not understand English well enough to receive all of their instruction in regular classrooms. It would be almost impossible for such students to pass a state test in reading. The regulatory changes that Paige issued allowed states to exempt these students from testing during their first year in school. When rating individual schools for AYP, the changes also enabled states to count these students in the ELL subgroup for up to two years after they demonstrated English proficiency.

Secretary Paige announced the third and fourth regulatory changes in March 2004. On March 15 new rules provided teachers working in certain geographic areas or in certain subjects with additional flexibility in meeting NCLB's highly qualified teacher requirements. In particular, in rural communities, which make

Legislation is implemented & monitored cases are priorities

up approximately one-third of the nation's school districts, teachers who taught several different subjects received more time to meet the requirements, as did science teachers who taught multiple subjects, such as biology, chemistry, and physics.[61] Interestingly, those changes, which gave ground on the teacher quality issue, came less than one month after Paige had remarked that the NEA was a terrorist organization.

In a final round of changes, announced March 29, the secretary allowed states to average student participation rates over three years when they calculated AYP for schools. Thus, to meet the AYP requirement that 95 percent of students participate in testing, it would be acceptable if a school had, for example, 94 percent, 94 percent, and then 97 percent of students participate, because the average would be 95 percent. The rules also prevented schools from suffering on their participation score if students missed tests because of a documented medical emergency.[62]

The willingness of federal system leaders to alter NCLB's regulations in response to state and local feedback contrasted with Paige's approach to state waiver requests. Some observers had wondered if the regulatory changes were at least partially motivated by a political need to defuse state concerns about NCLB as the election season approached. Still, as Paige promised at Mount Vernon, during the 2004 presidential and congressional campaigns, the secretary refused to grant any waiver requests, and none had been granted by the end of Bush's first term. That changed, though, during Bush's second term after Margaret Spellings replaced Paige as education secretary.

Shortly after becoming secretary, in April 2005, Spellings announced what she called a new "common sense" approach to implementing NCLB.[63] She essentially promised to states that if they could show that their students were making academic gains, then she would be willing to grant them additional flexibility. Such concessions could include waiving some of the law's regulatory or statutory requirements. Spellings summarized her view by noting, "It is the results that truly matter, not the bureaucratic way that you get there. That's just common sense, sometimes lost in the halls of the government."[64]

In the ensuing months Spellings promised and began granting the states more flexibility. In September she announced that she would grant the first NCLB waiver, allowing Virginia to reverse the order of NCLB's school choice and supplemental educational services remedies in four districts where schools were missing AYP. Other waivers would follow, including a few later that year that enabled several large urban school districts to provide supplemental educational services to their own students, even though the districts themselves were not making AYP.[65] Many state system leaders praised these decisions, but others, including former assistant and deputy education secretary Hickok, were more critical. Paige's former colleague in the department wondered why Spellings, who held a key post in the Bush White House from 2001 to 2004, had fought

Waivers / lack of penalties

to deny Paige the ability to exercise the same discretion and flexibility that she was now using. Further, Hickok questioned some of Spellings's decisions and believed that she had exceeded her authority. He accused her of wrongly overriding key mandates in the law, including areas where Paige and his team had refused to compromise.[66]

STALLED EXTENSIONS

Amid NCLB's daily implementation challenges, federal system leaders also thought how to extend the law's influence and redesign some of its key features. For example, in his 2005 State of the Union Address, President Bush announced plans to expand NCLB with added reform initiatives for high schools. Specifically, the president proposed creating a new program to provide states with funds to help increase graduation rates among at-risk students. The proposal also included new requirements that high school students take annual tests in 9th, 10th, and 11th grades, rather than the existing NCLB requirement that students be tested at least once during high school.[67]

In addition to promoting high school reform, the president also desired to reauthorize NCLB on schedule. During the reauthorization process, which for NCLB was due in 2007, lawmakers in Congress would essentially open up the law for new debate and adjustments, just as they had in 2001 when passing NCLB as the latest reauthorization of the ESEA. Despite the president's ambitions, his high school reform agenda quickly lost momentum, as did the NCLB renewal effort. Even though the law required an overhaul, Congress failed to reauthorize it during 2007 and 2008. President Barack Obama and the new Congress followed in similar fashion, leaving the law untouched during 2009.

Why did momentum for Bush's high school agenda and the NCLB reforms fail to gain traction? Scholars of policy agenda setting have offered several explanations for why issues rise and fall on the nation's agenda. One theory posits that policy advances are likely to occur when popular understandings of current problems become linked to specific policy proposals in the right political environment. That intersection creates a window of opportunity for policy advocates to push their reform agendas forward.[68] Another view, focusing on agenda setting in the context of American federalism, argues that when federal system leaders pass laws that rely heavily on state implementation, responses from state system leaders can alter or derail federal officials' plans.[69] In that view agenda setting is tied to the back-and-forth dynamics that unfold between system leaders in Washington and those in state capitals. Both of these theories are useful for understanding why President Bush's high school reform plans and the scheduled NCLB reauthorization failed to advance.

One major issue that upset several members of Congress and system leaders in the states was President Bush's budget for NCLB. Liberal legislators on Capitol

Hill, including key Democratic leaders such as Senator Edward Kennedy and Representative George Miller, argued that the administration had failed to honor its commitments. That left the law underfunded, they argued, even as its demands for testing and consequences for struggling schools intensified. Miller, for example, wrote to Paige on January 8, 2004, to criticize the administration's NCLB funding priorities, a position he underscored in a subsequent report he issued in April. The report, titled "How the Bush Administration Has Failed in Funding and Implementing the Historic Law," argued that from 2002 to 2004, NCLB was underfunded by $17.1 billion, an amount that would rise to $26.5 billion were the president's budget request for 2005 to become law.[70]

Three years later, in February 2007, Miller pressed harder when the president proposed using savings realized from other program cuts in order to provide more funds for NCLB. "The cuts in this budget for students with disabilities and for young children are reprehensible and undermine the efforts of students and teachers who are working hard in classrooms across the country," Miller said.[71] Those criticisms persisted into the 2008 presidential campaign as well. On the stump Barack Obama, then a U.S. senator from Illinois, often referenced NCLB by saying that one of its major problems was that in trying to leave no child behind, the administration had "left the money behind."[72]

State system leaders, including governors, legislators, and chief state school officers, joined the chorus in arguing for more funding during the law's early years and as reauthorization approached.[73] Some states produced estimates of the state revenues required to implement NCLB, money that they believed Washington should have provided. Compounding state financial challenges were the national economic downturn in the early 2000s and then the meltdown of the housing and financial sectors in 2007 and 2008. Both of those economic blows sent state tax revenues plummeting, even as the number of schools missing AYP and subsequently eligible for additional state assistance under NCLB continued to climb.

Members of the administration mustered data and shot back that the law was appropriately and adequately funded. In a letter to Senator Kennedy dated February 24, 2004, Secretary Paige defended the president's first-term budgets by arguing that funding for programs in NCLB had increased almost 43 percent over what had existed when the president assumed office. For the Title I program specifically, NCLB's primary funding stream, Paige explained, "President Bush has requested more for Title I than the previous administration did during its entire eight-year term." Further, the secretary argued, "with the flexibility added by NCLB, states, districts, and schools can spend the money more freely than ever so long as they do what works to improve student learning and achievement." He also criticized state system leaders who, he said, had failed to spend appropriated funds in a timely fashion; millions of dollars in aid remained in the federal till simply waiting for states to use them. Later that spring Paige told

Was NCLB funded appropriately?

members of the National School Boards Association, "In my view, as well as several independent experts, the law is fully funded."[74]

Findings from a GAO report helped the administration to rebuff some critics, especially state system leaders who claimed that NCLB was an unfunded mandate that required major state action without offering financial resources. The GAO, echoing findings from the nonpartisan Congressional Budget Office, reported that according to a key federal law, the Unfunded Mandates Reform Act (UMRA), NCLB was not an unfunded mandate. The reason, according to the GAO, was "if the requirements on nonfederal parties [for example, states or local school districts] arise from participation in a voluntary federal program or are a condition of federal financial assistance, as was the case with No Child Left Behind, those requirements are not considered federal mandates under UMRA." In other words, because states did not have to participate in NCLB, by accepting federal funds they were implicitly agreeing to abide by its mandates.[75]

The reality revealed some truth on both sides of the debate. Paige was correct that education funding had increased when compared with the Clinton years. But it was also true that the president's budget requests were still much lower than NCLB had authorized, especially for the law's principal funding stream, Title I grants to local school districts. As Figure 3.2 shows, NCLB had authorized the Education Department to spend increasing amounts on Title I, expanding the department's budget authority from $13.5 billion in fiscal year 2002 to $25.0 billion in fiscal year 2007. In comparison, the president's requests never approached those numbers during his two terms in office and, interestingly, neither did congressional appropriations. Thus, Paige was right that funding had increased. His critics also were right that a shortfall existed if one compared actual funding requests and appropriations with the authorized levels. Further, although NCLB technically was not an unfunded mandate based on UMRA, observers wondered, then, how to interpret Section 9527(a) of NCLB, which stated, "Nothing in this Act shall be construed to authorize an officer or employee of the Federal Government to . . . mandate a State or any subdivision thereof [e.g., a school district] to spend any funds or incur any costs not paid for under this Act."

Section 9527(a) of NCLB eventually became the basis for a federal lawsuit filed by nine school districts in three states (Michigan, Texas, and Vermont), along with the NEA. The suit claimed that the federal government could not force states to comply with NCLB's mandates unless more funding was forthcoming, regardless of the UMRA definition of an unfunded mandate. After losing in federal district court, the school districts and the union appealed to the U.S. Court of Appeals for the Sixth Circuit. In that venue a three-judge panel issued a 2–1 decision on January 7, 2008, and agreed with the school districts' claims. But that did not settle the dispute.

Figure 3.2 Funding for NCLB Title I, Part A, Grants to Local Education Agencies

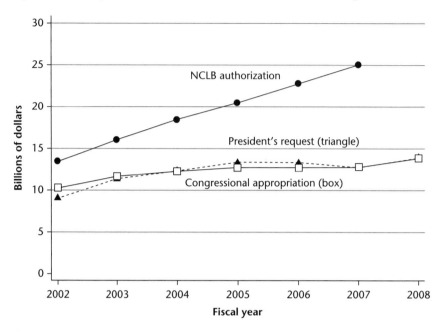

Note: From No Child Left Behind Act (Public Law 107–110), Section 1002, for NCLB authorization. U.S. Department of Education Budget History Tables for president's request and congressional appropriation available at www.ed.gov/about/overview/budget/history/index.html.

The court then decided to rehear the case *en banc,* meaning that all sixteen judges of the Sixth Circuit Court of Appeals would participate in proceedings. That full panel of judges heard the case on December 10, 2008, and the court issued its ruling on October 16, 2009. The court's decision was a complicated opinion that ran almost 100 pages. In the end eight judges voted to affirm the lower court decision and eight voted to side with the school districts and over-turn it. As a result of the split decision, the lower court decision remained in force, meaning that the school districts were obligated to comply with NCLB, despite any funding shortfalls that they believed existed.[76] The school districts and the NEA appealed the decision to the U.S. Supreme Court, but the high court announced on June 7, 2010, that it would not hear the case.

In addition to disagreements over funding, party politics also managed to slam shut any windows of opportunity that might have existed to reauthorize NCLB and advance Bush's high school proposal. The political environment that helped make NCLB possible in 2001 was dramatically different in 2008. The splitting of the political coalition (described in Chapter 2) that pushed for NCLB's original passage meant that the reauthorization and Bush's high school proposals faced opposition across the political spectrum. Much resistance came from members within the president's own party. Many conservative Republicans had voted for NCLB in 2001 to help the president secure one of his primary domestic victories and to stand by Bush in the wake of the September 11 attacks. Those votes were also politically smart at the time, given that Bush had enjoyed record high approval ratings.

But in 2007 and 2008, with Bush suffering in the polls, conservatives felt little need to help the president push forward his education agenda, which privately they had never fully embraced back in 2001. In fact, some Republicans even overtly pushed back against the president and his second-term education priorities. In March 2007 a group of more than fifty Republican members of the House and Senate introduced a bill to allow states to opt out of NCLB's requirements. The group included legislators who had supported NCLB in 2001 and who were party leaders in the House, such as Roy Blunt of Missouri, the minority whip, and the Republican chief deputy whip, Eric Cantor of Virginia. Such a proposal, if passed, would have cut against the president's priorities by eviscerating the law's accountability mechanisms.[77]

Criticism even emerged from some of Bush's former Education Department appointees. Those critics included Hickok and Bryan Jones, who was general counsel in the department during Bush's first term. Jones noted, "There has been disappointment among conservatives like me" that the federal education bureaucracy had grown too strong. "Those of us who consider ourselves federalists believe that at some point, the federal government needs to step back and vest states and local authorities with the power to get to the original goals of No Child Left Behind."[78]

One reason why conservatives went on the offensive was that they feared Bush would rebuild alliances with Democrats—by 2006 the majority party in both houses of Congress—and expand federal funding and control of education even further.[79] But those fears were misplaced. The oceans of goodwill that enabled Bush to work with liberal stalwarts such as Miller and Kennedy had dried up as the president's second term marched forward. Persistent Democratic complaints about funding, described earlier in this section, drove the president further away from his former allies, even as early as 2002.

Miller recalled, for example, that on the heels of the law's passage, the president proposed a budget with funding levels much lower than Democrats had expected. "That just really poisoned the well," he remembered.[80] It also boomeranged to derail Bush's reauthorization goal. When the president's ally in the House, Republican John Boehner of Ohio, tried in 2007 to assure Miller, then chairman of the education committee, that more funding would emerge if Miller could get the president the reauthorization, Miller responded dismissively: "I bought a horse from that man once. . . . I'm not going to buy another horse from him."[81] By the end of 2007 draft proposals for the reauthorization had circulated but no bill had been introduced in either the Senate or the House.

Complaints across the political spectrum unfolded against the backdrop of the 2008 campaign season, which began in earnest during 2007. Although the wars in Iraq and Afghanistan, along with health care reform, dominated the campaign discussion, the political debate made clear that NCLB had become a tainted brand, attached to the president's name. That led Republican and Democratic members of Congress to lend sympathetic ears to constituents who complained about its mandates. Presidential contenders, while supporting the law's broad aims, also hurled criticisms. Democratic senator Hillary Clinton of New York, a challenger for the Democratic nomination, even suggested that she would "end" the law because it was "just not working." That was good politics for Democrats especially, argued Tad Devine, a Democratic strategist. "There's a grass-roots backlash against this law. And attacking it is a convenient way to communicate that you're attacking President Bush."[82] With Bush's approval at such a low ebb, Democrats in Congress were unwilling to revive the president's political fortunes by spending their own time and effort to deliver him a parting victory on high school reform or a reauthorized NCLB.

* * *

The efforts of federal and state system leaders described in this chapter reveal especially well how administering NCLB at high levels of government posed several technical and political challenges. Federal promises to strictly enforce the law collided head-on with the realities confronting state-level implementers across the country. It was one thing to say that requirements would remain stiff but yet another to follow through, especially when much of the overall success of NCLB was out of the hands of federal officials and instead depended on effective and faithful implementation in state capitals. Federal and state capacity deficits were becoming more evident as the law's implementation deepened. Political tensions also became more apparent as the annual budget process, election campaigns, and the law's major implementation milestones arrived and passed.

While federal and state system leaders worked to address or sidestep some of the challenges that NCLB posed, local communities across the country faced challenges of their own. With increased scrutiny and accountability requirements came new political and administrative challenges for local district and school officials. Things became especially more complicated for those schools that failed to make AYP. The next chapter considers NCLB from the perspective of those local officials who managed the day-to-day implementation of the law in the nation's diverse communities.

4

Schools and Districts under the Microscope

JUST WEST OF INTERSTATE 75/85 IN ATLANTA, GEORGIA, on the corner of Lynnhaven Drive and Metropolitan Parkway, sits Capitol View Elementary School. Its student body is nearly 100 percent black, and over 80 percent of the students qualify for free or reduced-price meals under the federal school breakfast and lunch program.[1] Although the school's neighborhood is becoming revitalized, strip clubs and prostitutes have previously operated in the area. Given Capitol View's profile and location, those driving by may leap to the stereotypical conclusion that it is simply another urban school churning out many children with little or no chance of graduating from high school and attending college. But reaching such conclusions would be unfounded. Capitol View is, and has been, a top elementary school in Atlanta and in the entire state of Georgia. In 2008–2009, almost 97 percent of the school's black students scored proficient or advanced on state exams in reading, and 99.5 percent scored similarly in math.[2]

"High expectations" and "no excuses" are how Capitol View teachers and administrators have explained why the school produces such strong results. But high test scores have not come at the expense of boring or watered-down instruction. The curriculum includes project- and concept-based learning, hands-on experiences, and a commitment to teaching literacy and reading skills in all subjects, including science and math. Capitol View's instruction specialist, Trennis Harvey, noted that with high expectations all children can learn. That view led him to support the ambitions of the No Child Left Behind Act (NCLB) authors. "If you're poor, you may not have access to trips to Paris," said Harvey, "but you can still learn. One thing that No Child Left Behind has done is to say that schools have got to teach all children. You can't take Johnny and throw him in a corner because he's not getting it. Schools have to teach Johnny, too."[3]

Almost 400 miles northeast of Capitol View, in Fayetteville, North Carolina, sits T. C. Berrien Elementary. Like its counterpart in Atlanta, when NCLB's implementation began, Berrien was serving a student body that was overwhelmingly black (nearly 100 percent) and low income (over 90 percent of students qualifying for free or reduced-cost meals). Jacqueline McLeod became Berrien's principal in 2002 and began observing classes and teachers to decide, in her words, "who could do the job."[4] Given McLeod's strong reputation, several outstanding local teachers transferred to Berrien to work under her leadership.

As principal, McLeod also had high expectations. She required students who did poorly on the state's exams to complete additional work during vacation breaks and to attend remedial sessions at school. When a fraction of the students arrived for those initial meetings, she reacted this way: "I told the bus drivers, 'Find the rest.' We spent the morning calling homes." By the end of the week, "I had them all," she remembered.

In June 2003, when state test results arrived, Berrien had made great improvements over the previous year. The school's scores climbed eleven points, which helped it earn a state award and $1,500 bonuses for its teachers. But the celebration ended abruptly. Despite its strong improvement and state recognition, Berrien had missed its adequate yearly progress (AYP) goal. The school had 66 percent of students scoring proficient or better in reading and math but North Carolina's threshold requirement to make AYP that year was 68 percent, so the school missed its target.[5] Because it was the second consecutive year that Berrien missed AYP, the school's parents had to be notified of their right to transfer to another school. Those results led Don Jones, an eight-year teaching veteran and a 5th-grade teacher at Berrien, to sum up his frustrations about NCLB by saying: "This school is the best I've ever seen it. The feds are sending the wrong message to teachers, parents, and students."

After 2001, NCLB initiated collisions with local district and school practices and in the process affected the incentives to which local officials, principals, and teachers responded. As the previous chapter showed, implementing NCLB proved challenging for federal and state system leaders who wrestled with the policy details. But it was local educators, in schools such as Capitol View and Berrien, who had to translate those policy requirements into concrete actions. For them NCLB's collisions hit much closer to home because they experienced the law's impact firsthand. As policy implementers, they had perhaps as much say over what NCLB meant in practice as federal and state system leaders profiled in the previous chapter.

Scholars of policy implementation have long noted that frontline employees in government bureaucracies ultimately make the choices that determine how policies will take shape. The opening phrase in the lengthy subtitle to Jeffrey L. Pressman and Aaron Wildavsky's important book about 1960s economic development programs, *Implementation,* is "How Great Expectations in Washington

Are Dashed in Oakland."[6] The implication, which the authors' analysis supports, is that agreements among system leaders may stoke enthusiasm for policy but they do not guarantee success. One should not overlook the impact of ground-level implementation decisions, especially in the American federal system, where power is fragmented across state and local institutions. Choices on the ground are crucial for understanding why the collisions that a policy prompts will be energizing and transformative, wasteful and destructive, or perhaps something in between. Education historians David Tyack and Larry Cuban have made a similar point in arguing that reforms sometimes change schools, but schools can also change reforms, even major ones such as NCLB.[7] This chapter examines those on-the-ground collisions as schools and districts addressed the law's AYP requirements, in particular its consequences for schools in improvement.

JUDGING SCHOOLS AND DISTRICTS

Adequate yearly progress was NCLB's mechanism for judging schools and school districts. It created the potential for major collisions between federal priorities and local institutions. As Chapter 2 explained, schools receiving Title I dollars that failed to make AYP were required to implement a series of actions. That link between judgments followed by concrete consequences emerged directly from NCLB's theory of accountability. Simply measuring school performance and then hoping the results would motivate needed changes were not enough, argued the law's supporters. Tougher accountability, in which consequences followed inadequate performance, was needed to create jarring, transformative collisions that fostered a sense of urgency to improve.

Determining whether a local school made AYP partially depended on the nature of the school's student body. Recall that NCLB required schools to attain state-defined levels of achievement for students in all subgroups. By definition, then, schools with more diverse student bodies would have more groups needing to perform well each year. At the extreme a school with all subgroups defined in the law would be required to demonstrate required progress in several different areas. Table 4.1 illustrates the details by comparing two hypothetical elementary schools, Washington Elementary and Jefferson Elementary.

The table itself represents a rough version of the organizational report card that state system leaders used to rate schools for AYP. Schools were required to have at least 95 percent of each subgroup participate in annual testing and have other specified percentages achieve proficiency each year. (More discussion of the required proficiency percentages follows.) Because Washington and Jefferson are both elementary schools, NCLB would not have required them to report a graduation rate—only high schools did that—but in addition to test participation and proficiency levels, they would have been evaluated on overall levels of student attendance.

Table 4.1 AYP Calculations for Two Hypothetical Elementary Schools

Variable included in AYP Student subgroup testing	Math tests		Reading tests	
	% tested	% proficient	% tested	% proficient
All students	W J	W J	W J	W J
Asian	W	W	W	W
Black	W J	W J	W J	W J
Disabled	W	W	W	W
Economically disadvantaged	W J	W J	W J	W J
English-language learner	W	W	W	W
Hispanic	W	W	W	W
Native American	W	W	W	W
White	W	W	W	W
Other school-level indicators	Attendance rate—W J		Grad. rate—Not applicable	

Note: In this example Washington (W) has enough students to have all subgroups represented, while Jefferson (J) has only the "all students," "black," and "economically disadvantaged" subgroups. The graduation rate indicator applies only to AYP calculations for high schools.

As Table 4.1 shows, Washington is a much more diverse school than Jefferson, which means more subgroups would need to participate in annual testing and perform at required levels. In fact, Washington represents the most extreme case: a school with all subgroups represented in large enough numbers (i.e., with large enough "n-sizes") that all subgroups would be included in the school's AYP calculation. As a result Washington would need to perform adequately in thirty-seven different areas. In contrast, Jefferson Elementary has only enough students to represent two subgroups (black students and economically disadvantaged students). Jefferson may have students of other races or backgrounds, but they are present in small enough numbers that for purposes of calculating AYP, their results would be incorporated into only the "all students" category, not as individual subgroups. Consequently, Jefferson contrasts sharply with Washington because the former would need to report and adequately perform in thirteen different areas to make AYP, not thirty-seven.

Although Table 4.1 focused on two hypothetical schools, readers should remember that entire school districts were rated for AYP as well. District ratings incorporated the same data points as those that appear in Table 4.1, but results were aggregated across all of a district's schools. Thus, even though some schools may not have been rated for particular subgroups because their populations did not meet or exceed required thresholds—as is the case for Jefferson—those subgroup proficiency levels may have been reported at the district level. Such reporting would have occurred if the district as a whole had a large enough n-size in the subgroup.

How high did the proficiency percentages presented in Table 4.1 need to be for a school to have made AYP? Those levels depended on the intermediate goals that state system leaders had set for their schools and districts. NCLB required that 100 percent of students across all subgroups demonstrate proficiency in reading and math by 2014 and for those scores to be used in AYP calculations. But the requirements for each year preceding that goal depended on how states designed their accountability systems to meet NCLB's expectations.

Figure 4.1 illustrates three different scenarios from hypothetical states A, B, and C.[8] Notice that all eventually required 100 percent of students to be proficient. But their paths to that point differed. The straight line represents state A, which expected schools and overall districts to demonstrate increasing, but equal, annual gains in the percentage of proficient students in each subgroup. State B expected proficiency percentages to increase but at uneven intervals. Some years required no gains at all, in fact. State C represented a case where expected gains were back-loaded. In other words, proficient levels could be relatively low early on, but then large gains needed to occur just prior to 2014.

Debates existed over these varying state trajectories of improvement.[9] Some observers criticized plans such as state C's, suggesting that states putting off most gains until later were betting that NCLB's requirements would have changed by then. Testing expert W. James Popham, for example, described such rapid

Figure 4.1 Hypothetical Trajectories for School Improvement

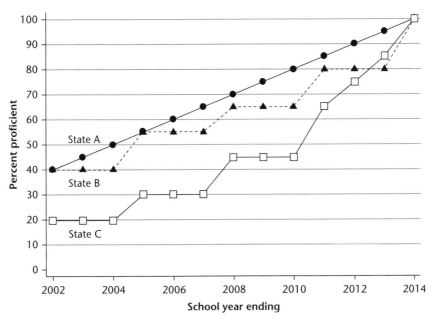

Note: "Percent proficient" refers to the percent of a school's students in each subgroup required to score at proficient levels or better on annual math and reading exams. For other examples, see Government Accountability Office (2004c) and Sunderman (2007).

expected gains on the eve of the 2014 deadline as "altogether unrealistic" and designed to "reduce early school failures."[10] Defenders responded that establishing these systems takes time. Reed Hastings, president of California's state board of education, offered that rationale in arguing, "We believe that we'll have significant improvement between now [2003] and 2007, but even more steep after that, once we have all the infrastructure developed."[11] A state only just developing its accountability system would be a case in point, these defenders suggested. Offering more time to help acclimate students, teachers, and principals while simultaneously allowing state leaders more time to troubleshoot the system was a reasonable approach, not an attempt to play games, they said.

As NCLB's implementation unfolded, increasing numbers of schools failed to make AYP. Initial reports after 2002–2003, the law's first year, showed that approximately 28 percent or nearly 26,000 of the nation's schools missed AYP.[12] A smaller number, about 6 percent, had failed to make required progress for at least two consecutive years and had thereby become schools in need of improvement.[13] Among schools in improvement status, those receiving money under NCLB's Title I program needed to implement the law's required consequences (see Table 2.1), which varied depending on how many consecutive years the school had missed AYP. As one might expect, the numbers during 2002–2003 varied dramatically by state. Alabama, for example, had only 5 percent of its schools miss AYP, while Pennsylvania had 34 percent and Florida had 76 percent.

Over time the number of schools missing AYP grew, including those missing for multiple years, which meant that more and more schools entered improvement status. Based on state test scores from the 2007–2008 school year, preliminary results showed that approximately 35 percent of schools nationwide missed AYP. (Variation across individual states was comparable to the 2002–2003 results appearing in the previous paragraph.) For the 2008–2009 school year, approximately 18 percent of the nation's schools were in some stage of improvement. District-level percentages were similar. For 2008–2009, approximately 16 percent of the nation's school districts had entered improvement status for missing AYP at least two consecutive years.[14]

One factor that drove up the number of schools missing AYP was the increasing number of students needing to attain proficiency, as illustrated in Figure 4.1. More schools had difficulties making AYP as states required higher percentages of students to score at proficient levels. In Vermont, for example, increasing expectations was one factor that led the percentage of schools missing AYP to jump from 12 percent in 2006–2007 to 37 percent in 2007–2008, more than a threefold increase. California also experienced a large, although not as steep, increase, going from 34 to 48 percent of schools missing AYP across those years.[15]

As more schools fell short of yearly performance targets, NCLB's consequences for Title I schools collided with local operations and priorities. After entering improvement status, several schools had to provide their students with opportunities to transfer to schools whose students had achieved adequate yearly progress, as well as to offer students supplemental educational services, or, for schools having missed AYP for several years, to engage in potentially major corrective actions or restructuring. These requirements sparked a growing chorus of critics who questioned whether AYP was a valid instrument for judging school performance. If AYP was the major tool that NCLB relied on to create transformative collisions, then it may have been ill suited to the task. Before looking further at the law's implementation of NCLB's consequences for schools in improvement, consider some of the debate over whether AYP was useful in helping to distinguish between effective and ineffective schools.

In a few different papers, economists Thomas Kane and Douglas Staiger offered powerful statistical critiques of the law's AYP system.[16] At the most basic level AYP was designed to produce regular judgments about schools based on quantitative information, primarily test score performance. The assumptions were that schools with greater numbers of students scoring at proficient levels were doing something well, and schools where students were scoring below proficiency needed improvements. Kane and Staiger noted, however, that a school's test score results could vary for several reasons unrelated to its actual academic performance.

Two main factors can render a school's scores quite volatile. The first is year-to-year changes in student cohorts. As the authors argued, "The average elementary school contains only 68 students per grade level. With a sample this small, having five particularly bright students (or a few students with undiagnosed learning disabilities) in any one year can lead to large fluctuations in a school's test scores from one year to the next."[17] The second source of volatility is random factors that may influence a school's performance on test day. A particularly hot afternoon combined with faltering air conditioners, noisy construction outside a school building, or an unusually disruptive student can all rattle the test takers' concentration, influencing their individual scores and the overall scores for the school. One result of such test score volatility is that small schools, with few total test takers, are particularly susceptible to swings in performance from one year to the next. As a result small schools tend to be overrepresented among a state's highest and lowest performers.

Kane and Staiger's critique was especially relevant to the debate over whether states were setting appropriate n-sizes for student subgroups.[18] Recall that if n-sizes were too small, based on thresholds determined by a state, then a particular subgroup's scores would not factor into a school's AYP calculation. Rather, those students' scores would simply be accounted for in the overall proficiency level of the entire school. Critics had asserted that some states set n-size thresholds so high that they were intentionally trying to hide the performance of individual subgroups. Concerns over protecting students' privacy, which could be understandable if a school had only a few students in a subgroup, for example, could not justify setting minimum n-sizes at high levels. Privacy clearly was not the issue for states with n-sizes at 45, or 50, or even 75 students, which some states had set. The law's supporters wondered if states were trying to avoid the law's consequences by setting thresholds so high. The statistical arguments provided by Kane and Staiger suggested that valid technical concerns regarding measurement also could be involved.

Additional criticisms persisted about why AYP was technically weak at judging school performance. Some, in addition to Kane and Staiger, argued that schools with many subgroups were particularly vulnerable to missing AYP because with more groups, the argument went, the school would have a greater chance of failing.[19] In a hypothetical school, if one assumed that each subgroup in a given year had a 90 percent chance of scoring at required levels or better, a school with two groups represented would have had an 81 percent chance of making AYP, while one with six subgroups would have had only a 53 percent chance.[20] Other critics argued that NCLB unfairly ignored massive inequalities that lead some children to arrive at school hungry, ill, and unsure of where they might be sleeping that night. It was unrealistic to avoid accounting for these harsh realities by expecting all students to perform at the same levels, the critics explained.[21]

Even when students experienced strong gains, as they did at T. C. Berrien Elementary, discussed in this chapter's opening, NCLB still may have cast their performance in a negative light. If a teacher's 5th-grade class were reading at a 1st-grade level, and the teacher's instruction helped increase their achievement to 3rd-grade standards (making two grade levels of progress in a single year), the school still would have been vulnerable to missing AYP, because students probably would have performed poorly on the 5th-grade test. That led some AYP critics to argue that schools should receive credit for growth in student achievement, in addition to whether students tested at grade level. Allowing states and local school districts to experiment with different ways to address these issues, the critics said, rather than subjecting all to the strict and uniform approach of AYP, would have helped bolster the law's credibility in the eyes of teachers and other school officials.[22]

Supporters of AYP responded that despite its flaws, it helped state and local administrators, and parents, make valuable judgments about school performance. One of the law's most worthy contributions, these supporters noted, was its requirement that states report data and that schools demonstrate progress for all student subgroups. This point echoed the sentiments of Trennis Harvey, Capitol View Elementary School's instruction specialist who was quoted in this chapter's opening pages. Before NCLB, The Education Trust argued, "Old accountability systems allowed schools and districts to be deemed successful even while groups of students—often low-income and minority students—were not getting the education they deserved."[23] Countless examples of disadvantaged schools achieving beyond expectations, these advocates continued to point out, proved that poverty or other inequalities were not absolute barriers to helping all students achieve at high levels.

Further, AYP's supporters explained that safeguards in NCLB addressed some of the critics' technical concerns. In calculating AYP, for example, states were allowed to measure school progress using two- or three-year rolling averages. In other words, to determine whether a school had made AYP for 2004–2005, a state was allowed to average the school's proficiency levels from 2002–2003, 2003–2004, and 2004–2005. Using additional years of data, rather than a single snapshot each year, was one simple, albeit not perfect, way to address the effects of annual test score volatility. Also, NCLB's safe harbor provision, described in Chapter 2, was partly designed to give schools credit for growth of student achievement even if all students in all subgroups were not scoring above state-determined thresholds. Safe harbor allowed a school to make AYP if it decreased the percentage of students within subgroups missing proficiency by at least 10 percent over the previous year, even if the percentage of students proficient in the current year fell below the state's requirement. Safe harbor was especially valuable for schools with many subgroups, which tended to be more vulnerable to missing AYP.

Disagreements over how effective NCLB was at judging schools have important implications for NCLB's theory of accountability. If school report cards contained statistically invalid, misleading, or dubious information, then, as scholars have shown, they would be a poor basis for promoting change and continuous organizational improvement, core goals of the performance management movement.[24] School administrators and teachers who considered AYP a poor measure of actual school conditions would have had little motivation to initiate changes, thus creating an effect opposite that the NCLB's authors had intended. In general, report card systems that fail to inspire confidence are unlikely to foster transformative change. Conversely, in some communities advocates recognized that AYP was not a perfect approach, but nevertheless they embraced it and the information about student subgroups that it made transparent. In those instances local school officials, teachers, and parents used school report cards to promote needed changes that they believed would improve their schools, some of which had struggled for many years to meet their students' needs.

Debates between AYP's skeptics and advocates persisted during NCLB's implementation and raised important technical issues for subsequent ESEA reauthorizations to consider. Despite those ongoing disagreements, thousands of schools across the nation missed AYP, including some for several consecutive years. A crucial assumption of NCLB's theory of accountability was that reporting school performance would not be enough to ensure improvement. Schools needed to face consequences if inadequate performance continued. One way to understand how those consequences played out in practice is to consider them in two categories: (1) choice and supplemental educational services and (2) corrective action and restructuring. The former were designed to foster competition among schools, while providing parents and students with additional options. The latter two, corrective action and restructuring, were intended to foster concrete organizational changes in schools.

CHOICE AND SUPPLEMENTAL SERVICES

School choice and supplemental educational services came early among NCLB's consequences. After a school missed AYP for two consecutive years, it became a school in need of improvement. Once that happened, in the first year of improvement status students became eligible for NCLB school choice, which allowed them to transfer, with transportation included, to another public school that had made AYP. If a school missed AYP for another consecutive year, it had to offer its low-income students (not all students) supplemental educational services, which typically took the form of extra tutoring in reading or math.

While states played an important supportive role in implementing choice and supplemental educational services, local school districts were the main organizations that administered these two activities. Districts were required to reserve up to 20 percent of their Title I Part A funds (a major funding stream in NCLB) to cover associated administrative costs, transportation expenses for students exercising choice, and tutoring fees for supplemental educational services. Complaints that choice and supplemental educational services would hurt districts financially emerged from this requirement because districts did not receive extra money to cover those costs. Although states needed to develop a process to certify supplemental educational services providers and maintain a list of those earning approval, local school districts were responsible for working with providers to enroll students, monitor student achievement gains, and ensure that providers were offering instruction consistent with state standards. NCLB also required districts to notify parents when their children became eligible for choice or supplemental educational services.

After NCLB's adoption, thousands of students took advantage of its choice and supplemental educational services options, but few participated relative to the number of students eligible. Participation in NCLB's school choice option remained quite low during the years after 2002. Various studies examined nationwide participation rates and typically found that they hovered around 1 to 2 percent of eligible students each year.[25] In contrast, participation rates were higher for supplemental educational services and grew over time. Early take-up rates were relatively low, at approximately 7 percent of eligible students during 2002–2003, according to one study, which also reported that the number nearly tripled by 2003–2004, when it grew to 19 percent. Other estimates pegged participation rates at roughly 17 percent in 2004–2005. By 2005–2006 estimates ranged from around 20 to 23 percent, before dropping by other counts to under 15 percent by 2006–2007.[26]

Student participation varied by district. For instance, one study estimated that in Richmond, Virginia, participation in supplemental educational services consistently rose, growing from approximately 10 percent of eligible students using them in 2002–2003 to more than 43 percent in 2006–2007. Other districts saw surges and declines. Chicago and New York, for example, saw eligible participants rise from 8 to 43 percent and 13 to 41 percent, respectively, from 2002–2003 to 2004–2005, before declining to around 25 percent in each district for 2006–2007.[27] Local decisions about implementation influenced these participation levels. As a result, NCLB's school choice and supplemental educational services provisions did not foster the kind of transformative collisions that their advocates had hoped. In many cases the presence of choice and supplemental educational services had a minimal impact on the daily experiences of most schools and children. On balance they created relatively weak consequences for schools missing AYP.

District officials across the country received criticism for not embracing choice and supplemental educational services with more enthusiasm and diligence.[28] Among the leading complaints was that some districts seemed to make implementation decisions designed precisely to limit rather than expand the number of students using these two options. Such accusations focused on two main arguments.[29] The first was that some districts were ineffective at notifying parents about their options. Some parents did not learn of their ability to transfer or to sign up their children for supplemental educational services until just before or even after the school year had commenced. Even when parents learned of these options, sometimes the letters describing them were difficult to understand. Some letters were loaded with technical jargon, for example, so some parents may have had trouble simply knowing what was available.

A second point that critics put forth was that districts sometimes established difficult application processes for students eligible for choice and supplemental educational services. Some local letters, for example, failed to mention how to enroll or whom to contact for more information. That created an additional hurdle for parents wishing to pursue these options. For example, Eugene V. Wade, president of a supplemental educational services provider, complained, "The sign-up is so arduous. That's where the bottleneck is." For example, he continued, "A parent said to me, 'I have an easier time going down to the [department of motor vehicles] and getting a driver's license than getting my child tutored under SES [supplemental educational services].' And he's right." Overall, critics noted that these implementation experiences revealed that NCLB did not create strong enough financial incentives for districts to make choice and supplemental educational services widely available to eligible students. In fact, as some providers suggested, the incentives minimized participation. "On one hand," according to another provider, "you're telling [districts] they're under the gun to tell parents" about their options, "but on the other hand, if the money is not spent [on supplemental educational services or choice], [the districts] can keep the money."[30]

Although some local officials may have intentionally tried to undermine the use of choice and supplemental educational services while still technically obeying the law, other factors beyond districts' control, namely the fragmented nature of educational governance in the United States, complicated even the most diligent local efforts to administer and implement these two measures.[31] First, it was impossible for districts to notify parents in a timely manner if states themselves were late in notifying districts about which schools made AYP. Even though districts were ultimately responsible for informing parents about their options, district officials could not provide accurate information until states had determined which schools were in need of improvement. Mary Kusler, assistant director of government relations for the American Association of School Administrators, a group representing thousands of principals and superintendents, noted that her members "can't provide timely and accurate notice [to parents] if the state doesn't give us timely and accurate notice of what the test scores are. States have been dramatically late over the past six years."[32]

Second, local notifications to parents suffered when districts received poor advice from higher levels of government. For example, to facilitate NCLB's implementation, federal and state system leaders developed guidelines and model letters for districts to use to notify parents when a child could transfer to another public school or use supplemental educational services. Local districts complained, though, that federal guidelines required so many elements that it was difficult to write a concise, coherent letter without technical jargon. Further, some examples offered to districts either were inaccurate or seemed more like cheerleading pieces. One model letter that state officials in West Virginia designed to help their districts notify parents of NCLB school choice led with this opening paragraph: "West Virginia's public schools have been working hard to improve the performance of our students in reading, writing, and mathematics. On state tests, most students are scoring well and are achieving mastery in these core subjects. Our schools have shown that they can and will rise to high standards." Another model letter's opening paragraph, from Connecticut officials to their school districts, simply said: "Our school is committed to providing all students with an excellent education. (SCHOOL NAME) has strong, dedicated teachers, who want to help your child succeed."[33] This sort of advice made it difficult for districts to craft effective letters that met legal requirements. The result was that parents receiving the letters could have been confused about their options.

Finally, even when districts worked hard to promote NCLB's options to families, parental preferences may have prevented more students from taking advantage. This was especially relevant for NCLB's school choice provision. Studies found, for example, that even when schools entered improvement status, some parents still expressed confidence in their child's school or were reluctant to transfer their child because the student's choices may have been in distant neighborhoods.[34] In other districts parents may have had several school choice programs available even before NCLB became law. In places where NCLB school choice was one of many options, it was unsurprising that few parents chose to transfer their children.

For example, one study of Miami-Dade County, one of the largest school districts in the nation, found that parents had five school choice programs they could consider, in addition to NCLB's school choice option.[35] During the five years from 2002–2003 to 2006–2007, NCLB's choice provision was one of the district's least popular, even though approximately one-fifth of all Miami-Dade students exercised school choice in some way. With so many students choosing, it was hard to claim that Miami-Dade officials stiffly resisted school choice—the district even operated an office to manage these multiple-choice programs—despite the low numbers choosing under NCLB's provisions.

In addition to state delays, the quality of advice from federal or state education officials, and parental preferences, local conditions interacted with NCLB's requirements and affected the implementation of choice and supplemental educational services. Officials in large urban districts argued it was difficult to administer NCLB's choice option when many district schools missed AYP. Under these conditions where existing school capacity was limited, they often asked a simple question: Which schools were these students supposed to choose? With few seats available in district schools making AYP, their choices were necessarily limited. Local officials complained that they could not accommodate large numbers of students requesting transfers. Federal education officials responded that local capacity issues were an invalid excuse for denying students the opportunity to use NCLB's school choice provision. Reconfiguring existing schools to create new programs, negotiating with neighboring districts to accept students who wanted to exercise choice, or experimenting with on-line education with nonlocal providers were all options that federal officials suggested.

Local districts frequently responded that the federal suggestions were infeasible options for a variety of reasons. For example, without the state's backing, and perhaps promises of some reward for participating, it was difficult if not impossible to coax neighboring districts to accept large numbers of students wishing to transfer. Even within a district where many schools were in improvement status, schools making AYP may have resisted accepting large numbers of new students for fear of creating overcrowded conditions where learning would be difficult. Further, schools might worry that an influx of new students from poorly performing schools would bring down the overall performance in their new school, making the new school vulnerable to missing AYP.[36]

Local conditions of a different sort sometimes placed school district officials in the tightest of spots, as when NCLB conflicted directly with other laws or directives that districts needed to follow. Florida's experience provides two examples, the first of which comes from its Polk County school district. During August 2006 district officials discovered that offering NCLB school choice to the 2 percent of district students who requested it would have led the district to violate a Florida constitutional amendment, approved by voters in 2002, that limited class sizes. The ensuing overcrowding from transfers would have forced some students to attend classes larger than the state constitution allowed. In deciding which requirement to violate—NCLB or the state constitution—the school district's attorney, Wes Bridges, quipped, "We have to make a choice—which spanking hurts worse." [37]

A second example, which illustrated how districts could find themselves pulled between competing federal institutions, arose in the Pinellas County school district during 2004. In that year the school district's attorneys determined that to implement NCLB school choice, the district would have had to violate a federal court order from 2000. That order, the latest in a round of desegregation decisions involving the county that stretched back to 1970, was intended to maintain appropriate race ratios and capacity requirements in the district's schools. The local school board's lawyer, John Bowen, argued that the district should obey the court's decision and not, as the Department of Education had requested, honor NCLB school choice. "The federal Department of Education does not have the authority to redirect a federal judge to change an order that has been duly entered," he explained. [38] The federal judge overseeing the district agreed, and in the end the federal Education Department rescinded its request that the district renegotiate the order with the federal court to accommodate student transfer requests.

In sum, as implementation of NCLB's school choice and supplemental educational services options unfolded, several factors influenced the law's collisions with local districts and schools. Most studies of these two options have considered only the actions of government officials, be they federal and state system leaders or local district administrators. Fewer studies have considered how NCLB school choice and supplemental educational services influenced student achievement. The limited take-up rates of school choice and the challenge of finding comparison groups of students make it difficult to assess the academic impact of that NCLB option. [39] But a growing body of work has analyzed the achievement effects of supplemental educational services.

On balance the findings have appeared somewhat positive, and authors have consistently called for more studies to investigate possible effects. Evaluations have generally shown that parents have been satisfied with the supplemental educational services their children have received. [40] Several studies have found some quantifiable academic gains but not consistent ones across student groups, subjects, or ages.[41] For example, one Department of Education study of nine large urban school districts, completed by the RAND Corporation, found statistically discernible gains that appeared to grow as students received supplemental educational services for more than one year.[42] One review of studies on supplemental educational services and achievement in Chicago, Los Angeles, and Minneapolis found mixed results. Chicago's evaluation found the most statistically consistent, albeit small, gains, while the others generally reported little or no improvement.[43]

CORRECTIVE ACTION AND RESTRUCTURING

Schools receiving Title I funds that missed AYP for several consecutive years were required to implement more dramatic changes. Whereas NCLB school choice and supplemental educational services provided options for students, corrective action and restructuring focused directly on school operations. Once a school missed AYP for four consecutive years, and thus entered its third year of improvement status, the law required it to implement corrective actions. Missing AYP for five consecutive years prompted planning for restructuring, and if the school missed AYP yet again, it was required to implement its plan. The law's corrective action and restructuring requirements, described in Chapter 2 and summarized in Table 2.2, required schools to make organizational changes that might include replacing school staff, adopting a new curriculum, altering overall school governance, or, among the most dramatic restructuring options, closing the school and reopening it with new staff and leadership or having the state take over the school.

As the law was designed, NCLB's authors intended its restructuring requirements to be more dramatic than corrective actions or other typical school improvement activities. Restructuring was supposed to force dramatic collisions with local practices and administrative routines in schools that persistently missed AYP. The goal was to get local district employees to take a hard, self-reflective look at their practices before initiating major changes. Schools would move out of restructuring status only if they made AYP for two consecutive years. Interestingly, NCLB and its accompanying federal regulations and guidance from the federal Education Department never outlined consequences for schools that missed AYP even after they entered restructuring.

Like NCLB's school transfer and supplemental educational services provisions, the law relied heavily on local school districts to administer corrective action and restructuring. Choosing from NCLB's required menu of options, districts were to identify corrective actions or restructuring approaches and guarantee that schools implement them. As the ultimate providers of education in a state, the law allowed state education agencies to become more deeply involved in helping districts execute their plans. States were required to assist their districts and struggling schools, funded through NCLB's various grant programs, but with the exception of restructuring that involved direct state takeover of a school, the actual design and implementation of corrective actions or restructuring were left to local communities.

Unlike corrective action or restructuring for schools, which were primarily administered locally, NCLB did require states to become much more engaged when entire school districts missed AYP. Remember, states were required to calculate AYP for individual schools and for whole districts based on the same fundamental measures of student achievement in reading and math, participation in state testing, elementary school student attendance rates, and high school graduation rates. States also were to initiate improvement processes when districts that received Title I funds missed AYP for two consecutive years. Districts were required to develop and execute those plans within three months, but states retained the power to become more deeply involved in implementation. If a district failed to make AYP for two more years, then it would enter corrective action and states were required to implement one of several possible measures. Table 2.3 described those measures, including financial penalties, personnel and curriculum changes, or, most dramatically, state takeover of the entire district.

Paralleling the number of schools required to offer student transfers or supplemental educational services, the number in corrective action and restructuring increased as NCLB's implementation deepened. Because it took a few years for schools to enter these latter stages of improvement, and because several states were slow in establishing their accountability systems, districts and schools in several states had little experience with NCLB's corrective action and restructuring requirements in the early years of NCLB. In 2004–2005, for example, an estimate reported by the Government Accountability Office (GAO) showed 1,047 schools in corrective action and another 1,065 in restructuring. But that same year 8 states had no schools in corrective action and 21 had no schools either planning for or implementing restructuring.

Those numbers more than doubled by 2006–2007. By then the GAO reported 2,330 schools in corrective action and 2,179 either planning for or implementing restructuring. Estimates from researchers at *Education Week* showed that for 2008–2009, approximately 2,200 schools were in corrective action, down from 2006–2007, but the number in restructuring more than doubled again to over 5,300.[44] The *Education Week* researchers also reported that for 2008–2009, approximately 90 school districts had reached the corrective action stage of improvement.

Analyses have shown that schools reaching corrective action and restructuring possessed several common characteristics that distinguished them from other schools receiving Title I assistance not reaching these stages. Title I schools in corrective action or restructuring were much more likely to be in urban areas and to serve students from families with low-incomes or who were racial minorities. The GAO's analysis of data from 2005–2006, for example, found that only about 25 percent of Title I schools were in urban school districts but nearly 66 percent of Title I schools in corrective action or restructuring were urban.

The numbers based on student characteristics were even more imbalanced. The GAO estimated that schools in corrective action or restructuring had 96 percent of their students as members of racial or ethnic minorities, while only 37 percent of all Title I students were members of those groups. A similar but less imbalanced pattern held when the GAO analyzed income; 83 percent of students in the corrective action or restructuring schools were from low-income families compared with 54 percent overall in Title I schools.[45] Those findings paralleled conclusions from state-level case studies conducted in California, Georgia, Maryland, Michigan, and Ohio by the Center on Education Policy.[46]

The latter study also revealed the challenging circumstances facing some schools. For the 2007–2008 school year, the Center on Education Policy found 187 California schools were in their seventh year of improvement status (that is, they had missed AYP for eight consecutive years) and another 10 were in their eighth year of improvement. Maryland had 14 and 20 schools and Georgia had 9 and 10 at these respective stages.[47] Looking ahead, and anticipating greater difficulties as more students were required to score at proficient levels or better, some California officials predicted that by 2014, the year NCLB required universal proficiency in reading and math, all of the state's 6,063 Title I schools would be in restructuring.[48]

With corrective action and restructuring taking hold in communities across the country, and with even more districts and schools poised to join these ranks, researchers began examining how these consequences affected daily school conditions. Despite the major changes that words such as *corrective action* and *restructuring* implied, in practice, studies consistently found that districts and schools adopted detectable but far-from-dramatic changes. That result suggested that despite relying on strong consequences for poor performance, NCLB prompted less jarring collisions than its authors had expected, even in schools and districts missing AYP for several years. The implementation experiences in local communities revealed the tensions between NCLB's theory of accountability, which required that the federal government be a strong principal willing to mete out strict consequences for poor performance, and its theory of administration, which left many implementation decisions to local district leaders.

Typical implementation tended to stress a few approaches that prompted some noticeable changes in schools but fell short of what a lay observer might have considered dramatic reforms. For example, a popular corrective action measure was to introduce an outside expert, sometimes called school improvement coaches or turnaround specialists, to help diagnose school problems and develop solutions. These experts typically were educational consultants, former expert principals or teachers, and sometimes state education agency personnel. Other schools in corrective action reorganized certain aspects of their structure. These included altering schedules so teachers could work and plan together, shrinking class size, and creating schools or programs within schools, which could foster smaller, more personalized learning environments.[49]

Among schools in restructuring, the vast majority implemented customized reforms, taking advantage of NCLB's open-ended restructuring option that allowed schools to adopt "any other major restructuring of the school's governance arrangement that makes fundamental reforms" (see the bottom-right cell in Table 2.2). The GAO estimated that for the 2005–2006 school year approximately 40 percent of schools in restructuring used this open-ended option. Other studies found much higher numbers. A synthesis of case studies from five states (California, Georgia, Maryland, Michigan, and Ohio), for example, reported that for 2006–2007, schools in restructuring used the "other" option between 86 and 94 percent of the time. Only a handful of schools in these states had replaced large numbers of staff, entered into contracts with external providers, or closed and then reopened as a charter school. No schools in restructuring had been taken over by the state.[50]

These case studies, which also examined several individual districts and schools, found local officials reporting that the schools' "official federal restructuring strategy was not their primary strategy for improvement; instead, they used the any-other [restructuring] option to implement a variety of district- and school-based strategies."[51] A common practice among schools in restructuring, for instance, was to expand how data were gathered to monitor student achievement. Also, schools themselves began administering their own periodic standardized assessments, in advance of annual state testing, to help teachers identify students' strengths and weaknesses.

Buchanan Elementary School, in Grand Rapids, Michigan, began implementing its restructuring plan during 2004–2005, in what researchers described as a "classic story" of a school using NCLB's open-ended restructuring option.[52] As implemented, the improvement plan did not change school staff or school governance. Rather, it incorporated an external review team, changed the school's instructional approach, intensified the use of data, and added full-day kindergarten. The data measures represented an especially big change, noted Buchanan's principal, Roberto Garcia. The plan required teachers to review data four times per year with one another and another three times with Garcia. Still, researchers studying the school noted, "The changes at Buchanan are hard to distinguish from the 'school improvement' measures under way at thousands of public schools nationwide," including thousands that were not in restructuring.[53] Garcia even admitted that some of the strategies described as restructuring were already in progress even before the school formally entered NCLB's restructuring status.

Although changes frequently occurred in schools reaching corrective action and restructuring, some studies questioned whether NCLB's requirements were being met. By the GAO's estimates, a small number of schools did not implement required corrective actions. Their analysis found that approximately 6 percent of schools fell into this category. The GAO visited one such school where the principal indicated it had not adopted any corrective actions—although technically required to, based on NCLB—because the district offered no input on what the school should do and, subsequently, the state education agency approved the school's improvement plan without requiring any changes.[54] Further, among schools reaching restructuring, approximately 40 percent had not implemented any official restructuring activities, even the open-ended "other" option that NCLB allowed. The GAO's analysts did conclude that reform initiatives were under way in about half of these schools and that while some may have been legitimate restructuring measures, other efforts appeared more like corrective actions rather than restructuring. That finding echoed others from a Department of Education report published the previous year.[55]

Despite what appeared to have been limited efforts to implement more intense corrective actions and restructuring, some local district and school leaders used NCLB to gain leverage to push forward more dramatic changes. In these communities, NCLB helped prompt collisions that the law's advocates had hoped would produce powerful school transformations. The state case studies cited earlier from the Center on Education Policy, for example, did conclude that most restructuring avoided making major structural changes. But still, the analysis also showed that among schools in restructuring in 2006–2007, 13 percent of California schools and 12 percent of those in Maryland replaced large numbers of staff as part of school restructuring plans.[56] In other states and communities, local school leaders such as Joel Klein in New York City and Michelle Rhee in Washington, D.C., pushed for major changes in staffing and school operations with help from the leverage that NCLB made available. Mayor Adrian Fenty had handpicked Rhee to be Washington's school chancellor after he assumed most of the control of the community's schools. With the mayor's help she initiated major changes in the district, including controversial moves to close or combine some schools, frequently wielding powers flowing from NCLB.[57]

Milwood Magnet School in Kalamazoo, Michigan, was one such place where federal law was a major catalyst for Principal Kevin Campbell's preferred restructuring approach. "Without NCLB," Campbell said, "we probably wouldn't have gone to this extreme. Most schools change principals, and that suffices in terms of meeting a restructuring claim even though they really aren't changing anything; they're just reshuffling. But I told my superintendent," he continued, "'I don't want to be in this environment for ten years. You have federal law behind you, and you can use it.'"[58] Restructuring at Milwood included firing the prior principal, whom Campbell replaced; formally closing the school and requiring all staff to reapply for their jobs, most of whom ended up teaching elsewhere; and establishing major curricular changes that reverberated across the entire school. Campbell called the changes "ugly" but necessary to improve the school's broken culture "that was very much into control, rules, and punishment as a way of trying to maintain order."[59] It remained an open question, even several years into NCLB's implementation, whether dramatic changes at Milwood or similar experiments in other communities would help students to achieve at higher levels.

While assertive and opportunistic leadership produced some major corrective action and restructuring in such places as Milwood, New York City, and the nation's capital, those changes were not the norm between 2002 and 2009. At least three factors help to explain why NCLB's corrective action and restructuring requirements, on balance, did not produce the dramatic changes that its authors and supporters had anticipated. First, NCLB's content and the choices of federal system leaders contributed to this result. Most prominently, NCLB's open-ended restructuring option provided much room for local communities to maneuver. Critics of that option termed it a "loophole" that neutered the law's intended effects. Supporters responded that local conditions were so variable that no federal law could have enumerated all relevant or useful restructuring options.[60]

Also, federal involvement in guiding or monitoring restructuring was limited. The federal Education Department offered minimal guidance to address key restructuring questions, including, for example, the number of years a school could continue using a particular restructuring strategy before improvements must occur.[61] Nor did the department monitor whether individual schools in corrective action or restructuring actually implemented required strategies. In their reporting to the federal government, state system leaders simply needed to indicate in general terms which strategies were under way in the state. That did not include a school-by-school breakdown of the changes or whether districts were fully complying with the law. As a result, the GAO concluded, the department lacked "information on which action was taken by each school, whether schools are taking actions at all, and whether or not states have taken any actions against schools or districts for failure to comply" with NCLB.[62]

Second, state and local capabilities limited the intensity of the interventions that schools and districts initiated. Even in communities that supported aggressive action, state law, conditions in state education agencies, and ground-level situations complicated the enactment of major changes. NCLB's restructuring options, such as the state taking over a school or closing schools and reopening them as charter schools, did not override state law on these matters. In other words, if a state forbade takeovers or lacked a charter school statute, then those restructuring options were unavailable.

As more schools entered the later stages of improvement, states and local districts also struggled to muster the capacity needed to provide advice and help. In a state such as California, for example, with hundreds of schools in restructuring and others nearing that stage, "that taxes the capacity of the whole school change industry," noted University of California, Berkeley professor Heinrich Mintrop.[63] Simply identifying schools and districts for improvement was one task made relatively easy by NCLB's AYP requirements, but then actually knowing how to reform them was not always obvious. One state education official in Iowa agreed, explaining that "looking at the overall curriculum, instruction, and assessment for a district is a demanding task that doesn't fit well with the time frame dictated in the federal legislation [NCLB]." A North Carolina official added that providing assistance is a major challenge because "There are not enough staff members at the state level to address the needs in all the districts/schools in need of improvement."[64]

Local capacity limits compounded these state-level problems and blunted the impact of corrective action or restructuring interventions. NCLB assigned to school districts primary responsibility for corrective action and restructuring. Some districts were unable to deliver all of the assistance that NCLB required, such as data analysis to help schools identify areas of need; the identification and implementation of specific instructional and teacher professional development strategies to improve student achievement; and careful budgetary analysis to help schools direct resources to underfunded areas. According to a GAO study, 42 percent of schools in corrective action and restructuring during 2005–2006 did not receive all that districts were obligated to provide, although nearly all schools received at least some assistance.[65] Another study found that large-scale staffing changes were difficult restructuring measures to implement in schools with bad reputations or in communities that prospective teachers avoided. When major restaffing was attempted in these schools, principals and district officials often spent so much time over the summer hiring new people that little time remained to plan for other restructuring activities before school began in the fall.[66] Sometimes district leaders themselves were at a loss as to what to do, which made partnering with their state agencies difficult. One state official in Connecticut explained how school principals usually were "trained to be managers, and not instructional leaders." That was important because "it is difficult [for the state] to assist with systemic change in school districts when the leaders in the district do not have the technical skills to lead large-scale organizational change."[67]

A third major factor accounting for why corrective action and restructuring measures were sometimes limited was politics. In effect political disagreements with NCLB and resistance to its measures sapped some of the potential energy that the law's advocates believed was crucial for reforming schools that repeatedly missed AYP. Some state officials, for example, simply refused to take over a school, even if state law allowed it. The reason was their philosophical disagreement with doing so. Proposals for such takeovers also prompted brutal political fights.

Maryland's state superintendent of schools, Nancy Grasmick, found much resistance when she tried to exercise the takeover option in 2006. Her announcement that the state intended to take over eleven Baltimore schools that were in restructuring prompted a major battle among state system leaders. Even though Maryland state education officials had a history of making aggressive interventions—in 1999 they contracted with a private provider to run three struggling elementary schools in Baltimore—their attempts in 2006 failed. The Maryland state legislature, at the prompting of representatives from Baltimore, passed emergency legislation that prevented Grasmick from wielding this power. The schools in question also received additional time to improve.[68]

Local politics were equally intense, especially when restructuring measures involved firing existing teachers and administrators and hiring new ones, introducing private providers to run struggling public schools, or converting a traditional public school to charter school status. As the authors of one set of restructuring case studies concluded, rather than major change, "Instead, local leaders face incentives to take more incremental, symbolic actions that may amount more to 'spinning wheels' than to true forward motion. While NCLB may place one fairly light weight on the scale in favor of substantial change, it will often not be sufficient to outweigh the heavy load on the other side."[69]

The power of local teacher unions and the content of teacher contracts were major forces that limited the reach of NCLB's most demanding restructuring measures involving personnel or school operations.[70] At the state level unions have used their influence to resist the development of laws that facilitate the opening or development of more charter schools. Those laws have limited the charter school restructuring option in many states. Locally, in many districts where teacher unions can collectively bargain (and even in places where collective bargaining does not occur), teacher contracts contain often elaborate process requirements that prevent dramatic changes in school staffing.

After NCLB became law, union officials recognized the potential for NCLB to collide with the prerogatives of their members. In 2002, for example, the national office of the National Education Association (NEA) advised its local union affiliates to press for the following language in subsequent teacher contracts: "Without the agreement of the Association [local union] the Employer [school district] shall take no action to comply with ESEA, as amended [by NCLB], . . . that has an adverse impact on any bargaining member."[71] Arguably, closing a school and forcing its teachers to reapply for their jobs would be the sort of adverse impact that the NEA had in mind in suggesting this contract language.

Other teacher contract provisions and union activities affected the reach of NCLB's restructuring. Seniority provisions in contracts often protect teachers from being transferred to other district schools and also mean that the last hired will usually be the first fired when schools are shut down or major staffing changes are proposed. Interestingly, one reason why the case of restructuring in Kalamazoo, discussed earlier, unfolded as it did was due to language in the local teacher contract. As Principal Campbell explained, in Kalamazoo the teacher contract had "favorable language for magnet schools that allows them to staff by matching credentials and interests with the focus of the school."[72] The contract language enabled the district to bypass seniority concerns, giving it and Campbell more flexibility in hiring teachers to staff the newly constituted school.

Union supporters frequently have defended contract provisions and other union actions that have been critical of NCLB.[73] They have argued that the law's collisions with state and local practices unfortunately undermined efforts needed to improve school conditions and student achievement. Further, they suggested that the AYP mechanism and the specific measures NCLB required of schools missing AYP, especially corrective action and restructuring, were mainly the result of political bargains and compromises, rather than a serious study of the evidence about school improvement. Finally, they questioned why reformers placed so much faith in principals and school district leaders, who would be leading corrective action or restructuring efforts, rather than teachers themselves who work in classrooms each day.

As with the research on NCLB school choice and supplemental educational services, most research to date on corrective action and restructuring has considered policy implementation, not the effects of policy on student achievement. The few studies on school effects that do exist have discovered two consistent findings, although more work is needed before reaching definitive conclusions. First, researchers have been unable to relate specific corrective action and restructuring measures to changes in a school's AYP status. In other words, schools that adopted one particular measure required by NCLB, or a combination of measures, seemed no more likely to leave improvement status than schools that adopted some other set of measures.[74] Second, and more positively, schools with more complete implementation appeared to do better. According to GAO estimates, "[O]ver a third of schools that fully implemented a corrective action or restructuring option made AYP, as opposed to 16 percent of schools that had mostly or partially implemented improvement activities," regardless of what those activities were.[75] Summing up the challenges involved, Maryland's state superintendent Grasmick noted the difficulties of finding the right mix of strategies for any given school. "No one has the answer. It's like finding the cure for cancer," she conceded.[76]

RURAL DYNAMICS

No Child Left Behind was a bold federal attempt to improve educational opportunities and outcomes in America's schools. That broad ambition included the thousands of rural districts and schools across the country. Although much emphasis in the policy debate and research literature on NCLB implementation has focused on relatively large school districts, especially those with diverse student populations, NCLB's authors extended the law's reach beyond urban communities. The measuring stick of AYP, and with a few exceptions the law's highly qualified teacher provisions, also applied to rural schools in the Rocky Mountains, the Great Plains, and the remote deserts of the Southwest, just as they did in the nation's bustling urban centers.

Some of NCLB's rural critics charged that its authors developed the law without their particular situations in mind. Such oversights, these critics argued, shortchanged rural communities of valuable resources while simultaneously offering few realistic reform paths for rural schools in need of improvement. One rural advocate, for example argued that "NCLB is basically a suburban-urban law. In general, the law is insensitive to many of the needs and problems of rural schooling. It tends to overlook the reality of rural places."[77]

Nevertheless, thousands of rural districts and schools across the country were subject to NCLB's provisions. More than 80 percent of the nation's students attend schools in what the federal Education Department considers nonrural settings. Still, 28 percent of the nation's schools and 56 percent of its school districts are in rural parts of the nation.[78] These rural areas tend to have three common features that influenced NCLB's implementation.

First, rural schools and districts are geographically distant from major population centers. That places them out of easy reach of important public, nonprofit, and private institutions that are instrumental in assisting suburban and urban districts with their schools in improvement. Republican senator Mike Enzi of Wyoming, who briefly served as chair of the Senate education committee in 2005 before Democrats reclaimed the chamber in 2006, noted, "We have a population of 493,000 people, and our state has 400 miles on a side. The average town that I visit is about 250 people. It is a long way between those towns."[79]

Second, rural schools and districts frequently reside in challenging geographic locations. Thus, sheer distance from urban settings is compounded by the terrain in rural areas, which may include coastal islands, dusty deserts, and high mountains. Not only are these places distant from population centers, but also rural landscapes and harsh climates can compound that isolation. Traveling to and within these districts can be extremely difficult, especially during the winter months when school is in session.

Third, rural districts and schools tend to be administratively thin. In some communities the district superintendent may also be the high school principal and middle school math teacher. Lacking large central offices, rural districts have fewer curriculum specialists and staff who can help teachers learn effective instructional techniques or help the entire district win competitive federal and state grants to fund needed local initiatives. North Carolina's state schools superintendent, June Atkinson, noted that this poses unique challenges because rural districts tend to have "Jacks- and Jills-of-all-trades in the central office," not narrow subject-matter or reform specialists.[80]

One major source of the rural critique of NCLB was that its AYP mechanisms, the core of its approach to accountability, were ill suited to operate in rural settings. Two matters were most relevant. The first was the AYP system for rating schools. The second was the set of required consequences (choice, supplemental educational services, corrective action, and restructuring) for schools consistently missing AYP. NCLB's rating approach that relied on annual testing and progress for student subgroups seemed inappropriate in many rural schools. Many of these schools were quite small, which meant that AYP ratings may have failed to work for a couple of reasons. In some cases schools simply had too few students to be rated. If a school lacked a minimum number of total students or students within particular subgroups, thresholds that state system leaders set to fulfill NCLB's mandates, then it was not rated for AYP. For some rural states that category of non-ratable schools represented the majority of their schools.[81]

In other cases rural schools may have had enough students to calculate AYP numbers but the schools were still quite small in comparison. That made their year-to-year test scores vulnerable to all of the volatility problems the first part of this chapter discussed. The academic performances of small schools tend to change each year, sometimes dramatically. Those changes occur because test averages based on small numbers of students can be volatile for reasons unrelated to actual learning.

Further, although most rural schools and districts tend to have few student subgroups, the vast majority contained enough low-income and disabled students for these subgroups to count, if not at the individual school level at least at the district level.[82] Guaranteeing appropriate accommodations during testing for students with disabilities was difficult for rural schools. Given the multidimensional roles that rural teachers and administrators frequently play, it was no wonder that several of these communities possessed neither the staff to proctor extended exam periods nor the technology that these students might have needed. The alternative of transporting these students outside the district on test day, where they could have taken their exams with appropriate accommodations, also may have been too costly.[83]

Another element of the rural critique of NCLB, beyond the ability to rate rural schools' progress, was regarding the law's consequences for schools that frequently missed AYP. Those consequences were difficult or impractical to implement in rural settings. NCLB's school choice and supplemental educational services requirements had limited utility, for example. With some districts containing only one elementary, middle, and high school (or even one school building that contained all students in grades K–12), and there being large distances between home-district schools and those in neighboring communities, rural students typically had no real transfer options if their schools missed AYP.

The geographic remoteness of these schools also made them relatively unattractive venues for supplemental educational services providers to offer their assistance. This was especially true of for-profit providers, who may have seen it as a losing financial proposition to establish facilities or staff in rural districts that may have had only a handful of students sign up. In one rural district, the GAO found that students needed to travel three hours to reach the site of their district's supplemental educational services provider.[84] By 2007, for example, Wyoming had approved a total of three providers to offer supplemental educational services, but according to the state's superintendent, Jim McBride, "none of these [service providers] have shown real promise in addressing the needs of our struggling districts." The implication, which he suggested in a letter to Senator Enzi, was that solutions would not likely come from these providers but rather from "aggressive staff-development activities, community support, and technical-assistance visits from my staff."[85]

Case studies of NCLB implementation in rural Colorado and Kentucky districts made similar assessments. The latter concluded that "NCLB's choice and SES [supplemental educational services] provisions will play, at best, only a marginal role in these [geographic] areas."[86] Nevertheless, the perception of how important choice and supplemental educational services were for fostering student achievement did not differ much between rural and nonrural districts. For example, according to a 2007 survey of a representative sample of districts, 7 percent of rural districts and 6 percent of nonrural ones said that supplemental educational services were either very important or important for improving student achievement in reading. But in math, interestingly, rural districts were slightly more willing to offer praise; 11 percent of rural districts said that supplemental educational services were helpful for that subject, compared with only 7 percent of nonrural districts.[87]

The prospects of rural schools benefiting from dramatic corrective actions or restructuring measures seemed limited as well. The most aggressive approaches, such as closing down entire schools and reopening them with new staffs or as charter schools, were simply impractical to many observers. Montana's state superintendent, Denise Juneau, explained that the state's rural context meant that it was "challenging for many communities and the state to support the public schools we currently have, much less encourage the duplication of infrastructure a charter school would mean in most communities."[88]

Replacing all teachers could be nearly impossible given the general difficulty that rural districts have in recruiting new staff, even under favorable operating conditions. Some teachers certainly crave rural living, at least for a while or until they can obtain teaching jobs in higher-paying urban or suburban districts.[89] But if a school were to seek wholesale replacements, which would include hiring teachers to teach multiple subjects beyond their areas of expertise (a common characteristic of rural schools), it would be likely that most schools would have trouble hiring enough staff. Those staffing issues compounded difficulties associated with NCLB's additional requirement that schools needed to employ only highly qualified teachers in core subjects. Changes to federal regulations in 2004 gave rural districts additional flexibility for meeting these requirements, in particular for teachers who covered multiple subjects. Still, despite that flexibility, teachers may have been reluctant to seek employment in a district where they would not be considered highly qualified.

Rural districts and schools had difficulty implementing even some of the less dramatic corrective actions or restructuring options. One reason was the lack of district staff to help in such projects. Lacking homegrown personnel to take on these additional duties, and facing the difficulty of developing working partnerships with distant universities or other organizations that could assist in school turnarounds, it was no wonder that rural schools experienced challenges. In studying a related matter, the need to hire highly qualified teachers, the GAO found, for example, in one state that "it was also not cost-effective for higher education institutions to send their representatives to these districts to offer training on-site, given a very small number of staff in small rural areas."[90]

On-line or distance learning opportunities could sometimes overcome the limits of geographical isolation—for corrective action and restructuring but also for the provision of supplemental educational services—and some districts used these strategies with much success. But these technical solutions were not always feasible or reliable.[91] Harsh weather conditions or challenging physical terrain, common in rural areas, sometimes made it difficult to establish consistent Internet connections. These solutions also increased demands on limited district staff who would have to develop the additional competency of servicing computers and computer labs for this purpose. On-line supplemental educational services may have been less helpful for some struggling students who desperately needed face-to-face time with a teacher to master difficult lessons.

Along with NCLB's AYP mechanisms and consequences, federal funding levels for the law prompted criticism from rural school officials. Those leaders echoed the concerns of their urban and suburban counterparts, and state system leaders, that the federal government had underfunded NCLB. But their critique went even further. Rural advocates pointed out that in attempting to direct financial help to the neediest schools, a laudable goal these advocates agreed, NCLB's authors operated with a major blind spot that shortchanged rural districts and created unanticipated collisions. These claims flowed from two of NCLB's funding formulas that Congress had created to distribute money to school districts across the country.

Two of these formulas, which were designed to direct more money to the neediest communities, included mechanisms that gave greater funding weight as either the percentage or raw number of students from low-income families in a district increased.[92] The choice of using percentages or raw numbers to compute a district's aid was determined by which approach made the funding allocation the most generous to a given district. In other words, if counting low-income students as a percentage of all students provided the highest allocation, then the percentage was used. In contrast, the raw number of low-income students would be used if that created the largest allocation. As a result, rural advocates said, urban and larger suburban districts received, on average, more money per low-income student than rural districts because the formula calculation based on the number of students would always be more generous for these larger districts than for rural ones. One study of Pennsylvania, for example, found that in 2008–2009 the Philadelphia public schools, which have thousands of low-income students, received an average of $2,356 per Title I (i.e., low-income) student, while several smaller districts with greater percentages of low-income students but fewer overall numbers than Philadelphia received an average of $1,967.[93]

To their credit, federal system leaders attempted to create added financial flexibility for rural communities in NCLB by including the Rural Education Achievement Program (REAP) in the law.[94] That provision allowed rural districts to transfer funds from several other NCLB programs into particular areas where they perceived important needs. Thus, even though rural schools may have received federal funds as part of antidrug education efforts (a small program contained in NCLB), rural communities could shift that money into programs that trained teachers or provided schools with resources for corrective action and restructuring. This was particularly valuable for rural schools given that federal allocations for any one of NCLB's many programs tended to be quite small and spread so thinly that the funds had a minimal impact. By pooling that money, however, rural communities realized a greater bang for the buck.

Overall, rural advocates and observers praised the REAP program, although no systematic studies of its impact on student achievement exist. More than half of eligible districts participated or indicated they planned to participate in the program. Those failing to take advantage of REAP were mainly districts that lacked knowledge of the program's existence. Fund transfers under the program were used primarily to address the needs of particular student groups by upgrading school technology and hiring and training highly qualified teachers.[95]

Despite general praise for REAP, the evidence on balance suggests that NCLB fostered at best tepid collisions with local practices in rural America. A perceived federal preference for addressing the problems of urban and suburban districts, without substantively impactful adaptations for rural contexts, led many rural school officials to offer little praise for NCLB. While they may have embraced its overall goals, they believed its mechanisms were less suited to fostering needed improvements in rural schools. President Obama and his education secretary, Arne Duncan, did little to ameliorate those views, at least during their first year in power. Federal provisions for increased education aid, as part of the economic stimulus package passed in early 2009, struck some rural advocates as continuing to ignore the particular needs of their communities. While Secretary Duncan and his assistants attempted to reassure rural districts and school officials that the department heard their concerns, many rural officials remained unconvinced. For example, just as the 2009–2010 school year was commencing, one Democratic state legislator and education committee member in South Dakota, Sandy Jerstad, argued that the president and secretary had been "narrowly focused on inner-city solutions for education challenges."[96]

* * *

The fragmented nature of American educational governance and the diverse communities that make up the country influenced NCLB's collisions in local districts and schools. Variation in state expectations meant that the application of the AYP system would produce different results across state lines. Schools that might have performed equally, when measured against some absolute standard, might have made AYP in some states but missed it in others. Such differences in judgment were inevitable once NCLB's authors settled on a theory of administration that empowered state officials to make the crucial substantive choices that would determine how AYP would be applied. Even within individual states, the law's theory of administration also meant that local conditions would greatly influence the collisions. The results on the ground, many steps removed from the federal Education Department, revealed that local capacities, judgments, and political conditions blunted some of the law's potential collisions. In other communities the law's requirements also provided valuable political cover to local policy entrepreneurs who used NCLB to push for more aggressive changes.

It is important to remember that after NCLB became law, it created new administrative responsibilities for local school and district officials, without necessarily eliminating old ones. To their traditional work of managing the daily life of public schools were added new expectations that pushed them to attend more closely to the performance of student subgroups, especially in reading and math. School districts with schools repeatedly missing AYP faced the additional requirement of working with their schools, state education department officials, and potentially organizations beyond the school district that might provide supplemental services or assist in corrective action and restructuring. All of these activities occurred in state and local political environments that contained passionate NCLB loyalists and equally committed opponents.

In the middle of it all were America's teachers. They represented the last important link in NCLB's implementation chain. Through laws, regulations, and lines of communication they were connected to federal, state, and local administrators, school principals, and other school-level administrative staff. In the political science and public administration literature, teachers represent classic examples of frontline administrators who through their actions can define the substantive meaning of the laws they are charged with implementing.[97] The next chapter considers NCLB through the lens of the interests, aspirations, and tasks of the nation's teachers.

5

Teachers and Their Tasks

ANTHONY MULLEN'S TEACHING CAREER began two decades late. Growing up in New York City, he, along with his family, dreamed that someday he would attend college and become a teacher. His working-class parents lacked formal college educations themselves, but they were far from uneducated. During World War II, Mullen's mother was growing up in Europe and had watched as bombs from Hitler's Germany fell from the sky and killed her parents. Several time zones away, Mullen's father left high school early to fight for the United States in the Pacific theater. Sadly, Mullen lost his mother and father when he was a boy, and their dreams of Anthony becoming the first in the family to graduate from college were interrupted. Instead, he worked an assembly line job in a factory before joining the New York City Police Department (NYPD). He served on the NYPD for twenty years, rising to the rank of captain. Still, his ambition to finish college and teach never waned.

Saving his money and attending evening classes in New York, Mullen completed his teaching degree, a master's in elementary education and special education, in 2001. He eventually became a special education teacher in the Arch School, an alternative restrictive educational setting operated by the Greenwich, Connecticut, public school district. Mullen's students at Arch all have severe behavioral and emotional disabilities. He teaches these students because "they are the most complex population to educate" [1] and thus provide him the greatest challenges. His experience as a police officer also has drawn him to these young people. The cold, hard, statistical facts of life motivate Mullen to "mentor students with behavioral and emotional disabilities because more than half of them will go to jail within three years of leaving school," a reality that he believes is nothing short of a national crisis.

What values drive his teaching? Mullen's philosophy embraces a passion for his work and his students; the commitment to persevere, which for Mullen means developing "the ability to teach any student"; and finally, the need to demonstrate a sort of professionalism that "exceeds the sum of acquiring knowledge, pedagogical skills, and earning a state teaching certificate." Professionalism also includes an aspiration to become an artist in the classroom by creating opportunities for students to make something of themselves. It involves cultivating an ability to read young people in ways that few adults can. All children are stories, Mullen believes.[2] Helping them fill their pages with hope, evidence of hard work, and satisfying accomplishments is what great teachers do.

Without a doubt Anthony Mullen is a great teacher. His students, colleagues, and friends in Greenwich all have recognized this. And so has the nation as a whole. In 2009, Mullen was named the National Teacher of the Year. President Barack Obama awarded Mullen his prize at a Rose Garden ceremony at the White House. In his remarks the president praised Mullen for "striving to engage every student, connecting with those no one else can reach, spending hours counseling students individually, listening compassionately, giving them his fullest attention."[3]

No person can question Anthony Mullen's desire to leave no child behind. He has recognized, though, that the No Child Left Behind Act (NCLB) itself raises as many questions as it answers. That federal attempt to improve the nation's schools was comparable to "new dishes set on wobbly tables," he has argued, because its requirements and implicit incentives were fraught with uncertainty for the classroom teachers charged with making it work. "The copious mandates of No Child Left Behind," reasoned Mullen, have prompted "fierce emotional debate from parents and educators" and simultaneously have had significant impacts on "the manner and quality of educational services provided in the classroom."

Put differently, and using the metaphor that drives this book, NCLB collided with classroom practices and affected the ability of teachers to perform the artistry that Mullen and others believe is required. How did those collisions play out in the thousands of classrooms across the United States? Did NCLB's collisions energize teachers, helping them to see persistent challenges in new, productive ways? Did NCLB alter classroom incentives in ways that would narrow persistent gaps in achievement and opportunity that have divided the nation's students for way too long? Those classroom, or "street-level," questions, as political scientist Michael Lipsky once described them,[4] go to the heart of what NCLB's authors aimed to accomplish.

HIGHLY QUALIFIED TEACHERS

If all teachers were as inspiring and skilled as Anthony Mullen, then NCLB's authors probably would have seen little need for the law's teacher quality requirements. Yet in the nation's fragmented system of elementary and secondary education, America's three million teachers vary tremendously in their levels of motivation, knowledge of their subjects, ability to connect with students, and the support they receive from their schools.[5] Several persistent factors complicate efforts to staff schools with quality teachers. Although Americans from colonial times to the present frequently have agreed that education is a noble profession, the evidence shows that the vast majority of the nation's top and even above-average students enter professions other than teaching. Further, the quality of the training that prospective teachers receive at teachers colleges and in certification programs varies widely.[6]

At the local level, staffing schools with excellent teachers is a perennial challenge.[7] Although teacher education programs and alternative routes to teaching in some states produce thousands of potential teachers each year, schools still face shortages in key areas, including special education, math, and science. Further, unlike other countries with more centralized education systems, neither states nor the federal government in the United States controls the job placements of teachers each year. As a result, teacher talent is distributed based primarily on where teachers are willing to live and make their careers, which frequently excludes the nation's most needy communities. Some districts also undoubtedly lose access to the best teacher candidates because their personnel systems are slow, making them unable to interview candidates and make job offers in a timely manner.

Even after the hiring process several factors influence how teachers perform their daily work. Teacher contracts, which are sometimes collectively bargained between district officials and local teacher unions, play a hugely important role.[8] Those documents, which can run several hundreds of pages, commonly include detailed provisions regarding teacher compensation, use of time during the school day, access to professional development, potential rewards, the role of seniority in personnel decisions, the granting of tenure, and teacher dismissal. Contracts constrain how school and district leaders are able to use, reward, and discipline their teaching workforces in the classroom each year.

For example, teacher contracts typically include a standard salary schedule, which governs how the vast majority of teachers in a school district are paid. Some exceptions to the standard schedule exist for certain specialists, including special education teachers such as Anthony Mullen. The key variables usually determining salaries are the amount of education a teacher possesses along with the number of years the teacher has taught in a district. Thus, an English teacher with a master's degree and five years of experience would typically earn the same salary as a teacher with the same degree and experience who teaches in a more-difficult-to-staff area, such as math or science.

Concerns about the quality of American teachers and the distribution of teacher talent moved advocates in Congress, led by Representative George Miller, to develop NCLB's teacher quality provisions. Despite that legislative success of Miller and his allies, the Department of Education essentially ignored NCLB's highly qualified teacher (HQT) provisions as it began implementing the law. The department's primary initial focus was on NCLB's testing and school accountability elements.

As Chapter 3 discussed, the federal Education Department extended deadlines so states had more time to meet the law's teacher requirements, as long as state leaders could demonstrate progress. According to NCLB, states were to have met these requirements by the end of the 2005–2006 school year; however, no state did. Despite that track record, evidence exists to assess the law's progress toward improving classroom teachers and teaching. Did NCLB increase the nation's stock of highly qualified teachers? Did it guarantee that all students, especially low-income students and those who are racial minorities, would have access to them? And did changes in teacher quality, as NCLB demanded, improve the quality of instruction and student learning in the nation's classrooms?

Before examining those questions, here is a recap and brief elaboration of the key definitions and requirements of NCLB's HQT provisions. According to the law, highly qualified teachers possessed three attributes: at least a bachelor's degree, full state certification, and competency in their assigned subjects.[9] The law required states to guarantee that all teachers in core academic subjects were highly qualified. Those core subjects were English (including reading or language arts), math, science, foreign language, civics and government, economics, arts, history, and geography. Individuals who were certified as special education or language specialist teachers and who also taught these subjects to students with disabilities or students who were English-language learners were also required to be highly qualified.

The law also tried to address imbalances in teacher distribution. The problem was that advantaged students typically had better teachers than students who were economically disadvantaged or racial minorities. NCLB required states to ensure that the latter groups were not taught disproportionately by teachers who were not highly qualified. Among other things, states needed to demonstrate where imbalances in teacher distribution existed. Along with local school districts that received Title I funds, the states also were supposed to devise plans to eliminate any imbalances so that access to quality teachers would be unrelated to a student's ethnic, economic, or other characteristics.

How teachers would demonstrate subject matter competency depended on their status in the profession. The law required states to develop exams for new elementary and secondary teachers to gauge whether they possessed the relevant content knowledge. New secondary teachers also needed to show knowledge in their subjects as demonstrated through completing college courses (including majoring in or having the equivalent of a college major) or possessing an advanced degree beyond a bachelor's or advanced certification.

States were allowed to develop other procedures, called a High Objective Uniform State Standard of Evaluation (HOUSSE), to determine whether veteran teachers were competent in their subjects. HOUSSE procedures could involve many activities, including state testing, evaluation of teacher portfolios, and having teachers demonstrate their participation in professional development activities. The HOUSSE method of assessing teachers' content knowledge was meant to be a short-term measure that states were to eliminate after all veteran teachers met the law's requirements. After that occurred, the law's aforementioned requirements for new teachers would be enough. During the legislative process teacher union members were vocal supporters of HOUSSE and pressured Democratic lawmakers, especially Senator Edward Kennedy, to include such provisions in NCLB. Critics decried the policy as a way for veteran teachers to avoid being held to high standards. Given the tremendous variation in quality of teacher professional development activities and the challenge of rigorously evaluating teacher portfolios, the critics saw HOUSSE as mainly designed to protect current teachers, many of whom were union members.[10]

So what progress did the nation make toward accomplishing NCLB's goals for HQTs? The answer to that question comes in two parts: the degree to which teachers became highly qualified and the degree to which all students, including disadvantaged ones, gained access to HQTs. As late as the fall semester of the 2006–2007 school year, 22 percent of states and 6 percent of school districts in a national survey said that they would likely never fully meet NCLB's highly qualified teacher (HQT) requirements.[11] Still, state progress had occurred. For the 2006–2007 school year, on average, states reported that 94 percent of elementary and secondary classes had HQTs, as defined by NCLB. That marked an increase from 87 percent in 2003–2004. Among individual states, forty-two said that over 90 percent of their classes had HQTs in place during 2006–2007.[12] The numbers were similar into 2007–2008, the most recent data available at this time. During that school year, on average, states reported slightly more than 94 percent of classes with HQTs, and forty-three states reported at least 90 percent highly qualified.[13]

The data for the 2007–2008 school year revealed interesting variation in classrooms across the country. States and local districts were more successful in staffing elementary school classrooms with highly qualified teachers than in staffing secondary school classrooms. For example, forty-five states had over 90 percent of elementary classes taught by HQTs, but only thirty-nine had that percentage or better in secondary schools. Across all years for which states and the federal government tracked data, special education teachers had the most difficulty attaining highly qualified status, although progress did occur. Based on teacher surveys, not state reports, 52 percent of special education teachers said they were highly qualified in 2004–2005, and that number increased to 72 percent for 2006–2007. Interestingly, teachers of students with limited English proficiency did not have that difficulty; they reported being highly qualified at rates similar to traditional classroom teachers.[14]

Despite many states reporting a majority of classes with highly qualified teachers, teacher distribution still tended to favor more advantaged students. In 2009, for example, a Department of Education report on teacher quality raised concerns about the "enduring inequity in the distribution of teacher qualifications" before noting, "[I]t is essential that more policy efforts be devoted to redressing the pervasive inequities in teacher quality."[15] Figures 5.1 and 5.2 summarize those inequities. Figure 5.1 shows two comparisons. First, it compares the percentage of all elementary school classrooms that lacked HQTs with the percentage of elementary school classrooms in high-poverty schools that lacked them (part A). Second, it compares the distribution of HQTs in low-poverty and high-poverty schools (part B). The diagonal line in each part represents the line of equity. In other words, if a state were to fall on the diagonal line in part A, it would mean that high-poverty elementary schools would be just as likely to lack HQTs as would all elementary schools. Part B in Figure 5.1 follows a similar logic. Figure 5.2 shows a parallel comparison for secondary schools, first comparing high-poverty schools with all schools (part A) before comparing high-poverty schools with low-poverty schools (part B).

The fact that nearly all states fall below the lines of equity means that students in high-poverty elementary schools were consistently less likely to have highly qualified teachers than were their peers in other schools. Further, the pictures show that many states sink toward the horizontal axis as one moves from part A to part B in Figure 5.1. That means that inequity was much greater when one considers differences between high-poverty and low-poverty elementary schools versus comparing high-poverty schools with all schools. Louisiana, the rightmost state in both part A and part B (but see the table notes for additional important information), reveals this pattern. In that state the horizontal axis in both pictures shows that 17.7 percent of elementary classrooms in high-poverty schools lacked highly qualified teachers. Notice, though, how the state drops on the vertical axis from a value of 11.6 to 5.8 as one moves from part A to part B. That shift illustrates the greater disparities that existed between Louisiana's high-poverty and low-poverty elementary classrooms. The patterns of inequity for secondary schools, which Figure 5.2 shows, are similar to those appearing in Figure 5.1. One main difference is that the number of states with more than 10 percent of classrooms without highly qualified teachers in high-poverty schools was much larger for impoverished secondary schools (eighteen states) as compared with impoverished elementary schools (five states).

Inequities across schools persisted even when teachers met NCLB's formal definition of highly qualified. Highly qualified teachers in schools with large numbers of minorities or impoverished students still tended to have less experience and less course preparation for their teaching fields compared with HQTs in other schools. For example, during the 2006–2007 school year, 40 percent of highly qualified math or English teachers in high-poverty schools had college

Figure 5.1 Elementary School Classes Lacking NCLB Highly Qualified Teachers, 2007–2008

A. Percentage of all elementary school classes without HQTs versus that of high-poverty elementary school classes without HQTs

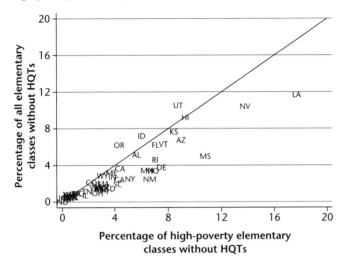

B. Percentage of low-poverty elementary school classes without HQTs versus that of high-poverty elementary school classes without HQTs

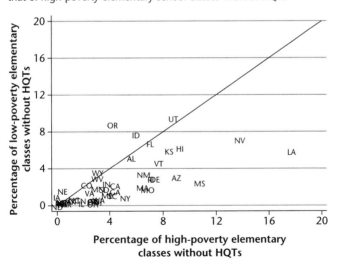

Note: In part A outliers of Maryland (36.0% for high-poverty; 16.1% for all) and Alaska (22.2% for high-poverty; 20.4% for all) have been omitted. In part B, outliers of Maryland (36.0% for high-poverty; 5.8% for low-poverty) and Alaska (22.2% for high-poverty; 29.6% for low-poverty) have been omitted. Data are from Part I of the Consolidated State Performance Reports, 2007–2008 school year. Available from www.ed.gov/admins/lead/account/consolidated/index.html.

Figure 5.2 Secondary School Classes Lacking NCLB Highly Qualified Teachers, 2007–2008

A. Percentage of all secondary school classes without HQTs versus that of high-poverty secondary school classes without HQTs

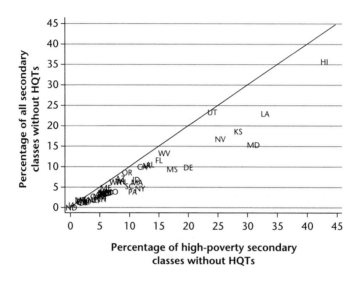

B. Percentage of low-poverty secondary school classes without HQTs versus that of high-poverty secondary school classes without HQTs

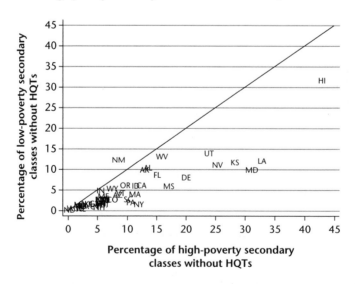

Note: Data are from Part I of the Consolidated State Performance Reports, 2007–2008 school year. Available from www.ed.gov/admins/lead/account/consolidated/index.html.

degrees in their fields, while 59 percent of HQTs in low-poverty schools did. In high-minority schools 15 percent of HQTs had fewer than three years of experience, compared with only 7 percent of similarly qualified teachers in low-minority schools.[16]

Despite these differences, the data show a bright spot that implies some inequities were addressed. Teachers in elementary schools with large numbers of disadvantaged students reported receiving more content-focused professional development in reading and math instruction than did elementary teachers in other schools.[17] Still, an important conclusion that the overall patterns of inequity suggested, according to a Department of Education analysis, was that "the designation of being highly qualified is not a guarantee that students will be taught by teachers with similar skills and knowledge, and the differences among teachers continued to disadvantage the students who were most in need."[18]

Interestingly, although federal officials never clarified the consequences for individual teachers who failed to become highly qualified, the requirement seemed to have detectable effects on teacher and principal behavior. Teachers reported taking action to meet the law's requirements. Based on teacher surveys from 2006–2007, among those who were not highly qualified, 94 percent of general classroom teachers and 93 percent of special education teachers reported taking steps to meet the requirements. These included obtaining full certification, earning graduate degrees, or taking state tests to document their subject matter expertise.[19]

When NCLB became law, some critics argued that its highly qualified teacher provisions would create unnecessary bureaucratic burdens and hurdles. One fear was that meeting those burdens would frustrate teachers and possibly deter them from continuing in the profession.[20] Teachers may have questioned the requirements, but the need to become highly qualified did not seem to foster widespread desires to leave the classroom. Those same teacher surveys from 2006–2007 also found, for example, that among teachers who were not highly qualified, fewer than 10 percent were considering quitting teaching.[21]

Principals and school districts also responded to NCLB's teacher requirements.[22] Over time the evidence showed that they became more likely to consider whether teachers met the law's standard. The response of principals and district leaders was particularly noticeable in schools serving disadvantaged students. Whereas in 2004–2005, 12 percent of principals reported transferring or firing teachers who were not highly qualified, by 2006–2007 that figure was around 20 percent and was even higher in schools that were high-minority or high-poverty or in schools consistently missing adequate yearly progress (AYP). In such schools more than 30 percent of principals reported taking those same actions in 2006–2007. Those personnel decisions occurred despite districts also reporting that it was difficult to recruit new staff who had met NCLB's highly qualified teacher provisions, especially in fields such as math, science, and special education.

Evidence of efforts to implement NCLB's highly qualified teacher requirements notwithstanding, it is unclear whether the collisions that NCLB prompted with state and local practices had improved students' educational experiences. Studies have not examined the specific effects of implementing NCLB's teacher quality requirements on student achievement. A large and growing research literature on teacher quality does exist, and it has produced mixed conclusions about which teacher characteristics are most important for student achievement and other valued outcomes.[23] The evidence suggests that a teacher's subject-matter knowledge is sometimes important, especially in high school math courses. Certification may be less crucial, at least when considering the effects on student test scores. Those two overall findings are valuable to know given that NCLB's definition of *highly qualified* included demonstration of subject-matter knowledge and possession of full state certification.

Despite some overall progress toward meeting NCLB's teacher requirements, wide variation in how states implemented them meant that major differences still existed across the country. Just as in the law's school accountability provisions—in which states identified content standards, wrote student exams, and set cut scores for proficiency—NCLB left states to determine the content of their own teaching certificates and how teachers would demonstrate whether they knew their subjects. Some states, for example, required new teachers to take a standardized exam known as the Praxis II to illustrate their content knowledge. As of November 2007, among the thirty-six states that used the Praxis II for new math teachers, only three states set the passing score above the 50th percentile (that is, the national median score). Further, nine states set the passing score below the 25th percentile. The remaining states fell somewhere between.[24] Such relatively low cutoff scores raised concerns that states' expectations were too low.

To cite another example, states also varied in how much college course work they considered equal to a college major in a subject. For 2006–2007, thirty-three states set such explicit standards. Among those, three states required between fifteen and twenty-one course hours, eleven states required twenty-four, seventeen states required thirty, and three states required between thirty-one and forty-two.[25] Such differences led one federal report to conclude that "the wide variations in state standards raise serious questions about whether all states set high enough standards for teacher quality and whether state standards for highly qualified teachers are all well grounded in what makes for high-quality teaching."[26]

CRITICAL TASKS IN THE CLASSROOM

Considering how states implemented NCLB's highly qualified teacher requirements and how teachers and schools tried to fulfill them provides insights about the law's effect on teaching and learning, but those insights are limited. NCLB's authors crafted accountability mechanisms and teacher requirements to alter the incentives for schools and, as a consequence, to foster transformative collisions so that no child would be left behind. Thus, knowing whether NCLB succeeded in achieving its objectives requires one to analyze how NCLB collided with classroom practices to see if the law affected teacher behaviors in ways that would promote academic gains. Studying those internal classroom dynamics—the crucial points at which teachers attempt to connect with their students—provides some of the most valuable evidence to evaluate whether NCLB's effects matched its authors' ambitions.

A useful way to gauge a law's effects is to see how it alters what political scientist James Q. Wilson calls the "critical tasks" of public administrators.[27] In Wilson's view critical tasks are those activities that an organization's frontline employees do each day to address the challenges before them. He believes that by defining and executing critical tasks, public administrators reveal an agency's true principles and core missions. Therefore, Wilson advises, one should study critical tasks very closely, regardless of whether the organization is a small public school, a large urban police department, a state department of environmental protection, or even the Central Intelligence Agency. In a classroom, how teachers define and carry out their critical tasks is important because in those actions—teacher-to-teacher, teacher-to-student, and so on—teachers give meaning to the federal, state, and school district policies that they must implement. In essence, teachers, through their actions, are making and remaking policy throughout each day.

Several factors influence how teachers, or public administrators in any government agency, define their critical tasks.[28] External constraints are one major factor. A teacher's ability to exercise autonomy in the classroom depends in part on how much freedom the school principal and other school overseers have granted. If lesson plans are quite specific and handed down from above, then teachers will have less freedom to shape their tasks as they see fit. External constraints can become quite complicated, especially when teachers must operate under several that may even conflict.

Teachers' own beliefs about what it means to do their jobs, informed by professional training and experience, are a second major factor that defines their critical tasks. Training and prior experiences provide teachers with lenses through which they can interpret the complicated array of signals that their classroom and school environments transmit every minute of every day. Having seen a situation before, such as a student consistently misspelling the same word or making the same long-division error, teachers can use their training and experience to respond. Similarly, recall that thousands of teachers belong to either the National Education Association or the American Federation of Teachers. Thus, it is no wonder that national union advocacy regarding effective classroom practices, such as concerns over excessive preparation for standardized tests and the need for well-rounded classroom experiences, can influence how local teachers engage principals or district leaders in discussions over these topics.

External constraints and beliefs are important, but some days they are no match for circumstances, the third key factor that affects how teachers define their critical tasks. To take an extreme example, the principal may favor a certain set of classroom critical tasks by ordering teachers to begin each day with a period of guided reading. But that external constraint will be no match for circumstances, such as a student becoming ill or a malfunctioning heater in the middle of January, in helping a teacher to identify critical tasks. The need to put out such fires that unexpectedly yet inevitably break out will lead teachers to adapt their tasks each day. As a result teachers may alter lesson plans on the fly or skip particular concepts from the curriculum that the teacher deems less central.

It is challenging to design educational accountability systems with a proper mix of constraints and incentives that encourage teachers to define critical tasks to help students succeed academically. Put differently, accountability systems in education or other policy areas are supposed to collide with present practices, altering critical tasks where needed and reinforcing existing ones that are promising. In the context of NCLB, for example, a school's need to make AYP was supposed to focus classroom critical tasks on increasing student achievement among all student subgroups. But as prior work on organizational report cards and performance management has shown, this may be difficult in practice.[29] Sometimes the need to demonstrate performance leads frontline administrators to alter critical tasks to serve the accountability system's craving for evidence of success, while simultaneously undermining the substantive goals that the system's designers hoped to achieve in the first place. Thus, evidence of progress proliferates even as larger goals go unrealized. Further, in the process of prioritizing tasks, accountability systems may encourage teachers or other school officials to neglect activities that while clearly important in the long run may have no immediate bearing on whether a school is deemed effective, or, in NCLB's terms, has made adequate yearly progress (AYP).

Although no educational accountability system is perfect, the more effective ones are better at maximizing the chance that school officials and teachers will define critical tasks to accomplish substantive goals that benefit students. In the years after NCLB became law, principals and teachers adjusted to the law's expectations, producing evidence that revealed how they had defined classroom critical tasks to meet its requirements. The next two sections examine that evidence in detail. The first considers NCLB's impact on the critical tasks associated with testing and test preparation. The second focuses more specifically on how NCLB influenced tasks that determine the curriculum of individual classes and entire schools or districts.

TESTING AND DATA

The use of performance management and standards-based accountability to judge schools existed before NCLB became law. Although expectations were still somewhat low, during the 1980s and 1990s, states began demanding higher academic performance from schools and students. Efforts to prepare students for state exams intensified after 2001, when NCLB's requirements began to take effect. Thus, schools faced the twin challenges of determining how to help schools make AYP and ascertaining how to ensure that students succeeded on state exams. In addressing those two issues, school officials and district leaders became increasingly focused on exam preparation. In turn, an array of classroom critical tasks emerged to support that effort.

Examples of school and district strategies were easy to find as NCLB's implementation unfolded. Several activities emerged that altered how teachers organized their lesson plans and teaching methods. First, simply communicating to students and their families the increasing role of tests in school evaluation led local officials to adopt several strategies. These included regular school announcements that would count down the number of days until state tests. Some schools also ran pep rallies that stressed why students needed to perform well for their own good and for the good of the entire school. These rallies or spirit-building exercises sometimes even involved principals or teachers making entertaining wagers with their students. One Maryland principal, for example, promised to sit atop the school building for an entire day, under the blazing sun, if students' scores hit a certain level.[30]

Second, districts instructed classroom teachers to help students become familiar with the style and likely content of state tests. That involved having students work on practice questions, which mimicked state test formats. In some places such teaching occurred each day across all classrooms. For example, students might take part of their first class period to work a math problem (even if their first period was in social studies), which teachers would then discuss. A common approach was for students to regularly complete entire practice exams. John Perry, an elementary schoolteacher from Tampa, Florida, noted that in his school the assistant principal required teachers to administer a practice test each week, alternating weeks between reading and math. In all, the process would consume "a couple of days every two weeks," Perry said.[31]

In short, as the consequences of testing increased, individual teachers and entire schools focused more of their critical tasks on test preparation. The notion that teachers might be "teaching to the test" usually carries negative connotations, but this need not be true.[32] Under certain conditions preparing students to succeed on exams can have important educational benefits. First, consider test format. When many people think about standardized tests or state exams, typically they envision multiple-choice questions with low-level questions and forms where students fill in the bubbles. But even bubble-form tests, with careful design, can assess high levels of critical thinking. Further, standardized tests can contain more than multiple-choice questions. For a test to be "standardized," it simply means that large numbers of students are taking a test with common questions and question formats. The test's design can include many things, including short-answer questions where students write a brief paragraph or show their work on a math problem in addition to choosing the right answer. They may also involve longer essays or even performances. It would make sense, for example, for a standardized exam in speech or music to involve students actually speaking, singing, or playing an instrument. Most standardized tests that students encounter do involve some multiple-choice questions, even though other formats are possible. When tests do involve different question types, they can force students to demonstrate their abilities using high-level thinking and problem-solving skills across several areas.[33]

Second, consider the content of standardized tests. Although millions of people may enjoy the television show *Jeopardy* or the board game Trivial Pursuit, many students (and adults, even) cringe at the thought of taking a standardized test that requires them to recall large bodies of factual information or concept definitions stripped of any real-life context. Certainly, the ability to recall at least some basic facts is valuable if a person is to be culturally literate,[34] but when entire standardized tests focus on factual recall, teaching to the test can become an exercise in filling up students' heads with facts—and oftentimes tips and tricks for remembering them—but not helping students to think critically. Again, standardized tests, even those that contain primarily multiple-choice questions, can be crafted to push students to interpret and evaluate information, not just report back what happened on a particular day in history or identify textbook definitions of concepts from their math or English classes. Teaching to a test that required higher-level thinking skills would force students to master content knowledge because one must know some facts before evaluating or interpreting them, but it would also push students to develop deeper understandings. In preparing for those tests, they would be learning important factual content and exploring it in a rigorous way.

Unfortunately, the evidence shows that many of the reading and math tests that states adopted in response to NCLB expected students to possess few high-level skills and fairly thin levels of knowledge about their subjects. According to one analysis in 2005–2006, for example, fifteen states used reading and math tests with only multiple-choice questions to meet NCLB's requirements. When combined, those fifteen states accounted for 42 percent of the nation's students.[35] As a result analysts inside and outside the standardized testing industry generally concluded, in the words of one comprehensive study of test development, "that many of the tests that states are introducing under NCLB contain many questions that require students to merely recall and restate facts rather than do more demanding tasks like applying or evaluating information."[36] Long-time education observers, former federal officials, and proponents of educational accountability Chester Finn and Diane Ravitch agreed. They lamented, "We're already at risk of turning U.S. schools into test-prepping skill factories where nothing matters except exam scores on basic subjects. That's not what America needs, nor is it a sufficient conception of educational accountability."[37]

Anecdotes from classroom teachers supported these conclusions about the content and rigor of standardized tests. Samantha Cleaver, a former special education teacher in a District of Columbia elementary school, provides one example. While noting that she found "standards to be helpful," she also expressed concern at their influence on the school's critical tasks. "Because the focus is on testing and test prep, the purpose of my school was not comprehension or full understanding and expanding students' minds, but how they performed during one week of the year."[38]

Two factors seem most relevant for explaining why NCLB-inspired tests tended to aim low. The first is that, in general, constructing challenging exams is quite difficult, and the testing industry lacks the capacity to generate the number of tests that states needed after NCLB became law. Even though this book and most other sources discuss "state exams," in reality, state education agency staff typically do not write exam questions. Rather, states contract out that work (in addition to test scoring) to large companies such as CTB/McGraw-Hill, Harcourt Assessment, and Pearson Education. In fact, fewer than ten companies dominate the state test market in the United States.[39] To comply with NCLB, states demanded much from these companies, and the test developers themselves were overwhelmed, unable to develop more challenging exams in time to meet the law's deadlines. The lack of capacity in the testing industry sapped some of the energy from the collisions that NCLB's authors hoped to create, because it moved states to use simpler exams that were easier to construct and cheaper to produce.[40]

A second factor further compounded the tendency toward lower-level questions and multiple-choice formats. The Department of Education's guidance to states about implementing NCLB tended to discourage them from developing innovative and complex test forms that could have provided students with more challenging questions. Federal regulations discouraged the use of adaptive tests, for example, which students take on a computer. With those tests the computer technology pulls up increasingly difficult questions as students answer easier questions correctly. Because NCLB required students to take tests on grade-level material only, states could not develop an adaptive test for 5th-grade reading that challenged students with 6th-grade material, even if the students' answers demonstrated that they already had mastered the 5th-grade expectations.[41]

Despite the tendency for low-level tests to foster classroom critical tasks that discouraged critical thinking, some schools showed that preparing for state exams could involve challenging and interesting classroom instruction. One study of fifteen highly successful schools that served primarily economically disadvantaged students and racial minorities concluded unequivocally that these schools succeeded, in part, because their teachers' critical tasks did not simply focus on preparing students to take state exams. What made these schools successful, the study's author, Karin Chenoweth, noted, was that "they teach a rich, coherent curriculum tied to state standards."[42] In her travels to these schools, which served urban and rural communities with large and small student bodies, Chenoweth noticed that some schools did emphasize tests via the pep rallies noted earlier, and all helped their students become familiar with state test formats and question types. "But none of them," she concluded, "spends a huge amount of time teaching their students what will be on the state tests or teaching them how to 'bubble in' a scoring sheet. . . . They don't teach to the test, particularly in those states where the tests are low-level reading and math tests."[43]

Atlanta's Capitol View Elementary School, introduced in Chapter 4, was one such school that Chenoweth examined. She also studied Port Chester Middle School in Port Chester, New York. When a colleague in another school district suggested to Port Chester's assistant principal, Patrick Smith, that given Port Chester's strong results, the teachers must "teach to the test," Smith replied by saying, "No." At Port Chester, he explained, "we build the curriculum so that the students learn what they need to know to meet state standards."[44] The science department chair, Maria Recchia, went even further in stressing that at their school a teacher's critical tasks involved not just preparing students to take tests. "You want them to know how to interpret, compare, analyze—not for the test but to be productive members of society."[45]

One byproduct of the increasing classroom focus on reading and math achievement since the 1980s, culminating with NCLB, has been the proliferation (some would say needless proliferation) of data about student achievement. In fact, district and school leaders and teachers across the country have increasingly embraced "data-driven instruction," which has further affected classroom critical tasks.[46] Using data to guide critical tasks can involve examining several indicators, including measures of school processes, parent and student satisfaction, and student achievement. The latter has become particularly important, and officials in some schools have often emphasized how careful analysis of student progress drives their teachers' classroom choices about instruction.

For example, Richard Coleman, director of a school serving low-income students in Newport News, Virginia, explained, "It is critical that we teach our teachers how to look at data." That approach, Coleman reasoned, is crucial so teachers can identify students' weaknesses and then adjust their teaching to prevent students from falling farther behind.[47] In the collection of high-performing schools that Chenoweth analyzed, school staff and teachers wanted data but not simply data for their own sake. Rather, according to Susan Swanson, director of urban education in Hamilton County, Tennessee, the "data represent a kid's face or a group of kids' faces. That's a life. That's a future." [48]

When data drive classroom instructional decisions, teachers' critical tasks can change dramatically from prior practices. Rather than relying solely on anecdotal observations, hunches, intuition, or even prior training, teachers using data can scrutinize how their students perform against well-defined academic objectives. Somewhat paradoxically, the annual state exams that students take and that NCLB requires are often the least useful sources of data for teachers. One reason for that is state testing usually occurs as a school year is ending. The results come in too late for teachers or entire schools to act on them before summer, although they can help planning for future years. Further, state test results frequently arrive to teachers and students as overall scores, or scores within broad categories, but do not contain item-by-item or concept-by-concept analyses, which would help teachers use the results to adjust their instruction. In other words, knowing that a student answered 80 percent of a test's questions correctly does not give a teacher any information about which concepts the student found most difficult.

Because state testing under NCLB provided limited information for teachers, many schools began gathering their own standardized achievement data at regular intervals during a semester, sometimes every one to three weeks. That process involved administering what are sometimes called "formative assessments," typically low-stakes tests, quizzes, or performances that enable teachers to gauge how well students are learning the material. One example is an assessment called the Dynamic Indicators of Basic Early Literacy Skills, or DIBELS. Developed at the University of Oregon, DIBELS is a standardized assessment that asks elementary school students to read aloud a brief passage for a minute or two and then retell the story in their own words. Although critics claim that DIBELS leads to some of the same low-level expectations noted earlier, the assessment is widely used across the country. In places where it has been successful, DIBELS has helped teachers to gauge students' word recognition, reading comprehension, and ability to convey ideas in their own words. The results have also helped predict how students will perform later on longer tests.[49]

Formative assessments such as DIBELS are in contrast to state exams, often called "summative assessments," which evaluate students at the end of a course or school year. As NCLB implementation moved forward, formative assessments became so popular that companies producing them saw their businesses grow rapidly.[50] Some districts, though, have developed and use their own formative assessments. In fact, one study of school officials in California, Georgia, and Pennsylvania found that over 80 percent of superintendents said they preferred using local assessments rather than state ones for helping them to make decisions about students.[51] When compared with state exams, results from local instruments could deliver more timely results that principals and teachers could use during a school year.

Examples abound that illustrate the diverse ways schools and classroom teachers have used data to alter classroom critical tasks. When data reveal that entire classes have struggled with key concepts, teachers can develop additional lessons so students understand. Sometimes data from formative or summative assessments indicate that smaller groups of students, but not the whole class, need more help. That can encourage teachers to develop lessons that split students into smaller groups, with each focusing on the most needed areas, and even having advanced students helping their classmates who are behind. Although it takes much work and time to prepare, with the right set of formative assessments, classroom management skills, and support from their administrators, teachers can use data to tailor their instruction to individual students. Some schools have even involved students themselves in analyzing data by investing time in teaching them how to systematically assess their score reports, so they can identify their own strengths and weaknesses.

All of these data-driven activities require teachers and principals to become more adept at quantitative analysis, presentation, and interpretation, which are more demanding tasks than the common practice of maintaining a grade book and calculating interim and then final marks each semester. Schools that have invested in data-driven instruction have often structured the school day so that teachers can work together to analyze student information. Those regular meetings often occur with a lead teacher or district staff member who may be the data coach for a particular subject or class. Where those arrangements are effective, they have helped teachers to work together to develop new lessons or share especially successful ones. Those choices about classroom strategies are based on what data suggest, combined with the teachers' professional judgments, not just intuition or a tendency simply to recycle last year's lessons.[52]

As with any seemingly valuable practice such as data-driven instruction, one should proceed with caution and recognize potential pitfalls. If not used with care, formative assessments can reinforce all of the poor tendencies of teaching to the test. Interim assessments that gauge how well students understand key concepts can be helpful, while those designed primarily to predict how well a student will do on state-mandated exams may be less so. In the latter case the tests themselves, rather than rich content, essentially become the curriculum.[53]

Further, a common saying among statisticians is "garbage in, garbage out." In other words, if one's data-gathering instruments or techniques are poorly designed, then the conclusions they produce will be faulty. In worst-case scenarios they will even generate harmful inferences about students that lead teachers to adopt counterproductive strategies.[54] Avoiding these problems requires that teachers possess at least basic training in statistics and assessment design. They also need follow-up assistance to ensure that they are properly applying that knowledge in the classroom. The aforementioned data coaches have often served this role and in so doing have helped to alter the critical tasks of the teachers they assist.

CHANGES IN THE CURRICULUM

A perceived need to prepare students for state exams has altered the critical tasks of thousands of teachers across the United States. Those changes have also influenced how teachers identify the content of the courses they offer. One dynamic that any accountability system unleashes, and is in fact designed to unleash, is the prioritization of tasks. Some become critical and others secondary. Working under the umbrella of an accountability system, public administrators have incentives to focus on areas that the system identifies as most important while limiting efforts elsewhere. When NCLB passed, reading and math performance drove AYP ratings. Observers across the political spectrum, including leaders in the national teacher unions and conservatives eager to preserve local control of the curriculum, predicted that the law would inevitably push school leaders and classroom teachers to emphasize these subjects at the expense of others. This issue of a narrowed curriculum is one area of NCLB's implementation that researchers have studied in depth.

Like debates over teaching to the test, a push to prioritize topics in the school curriculum may alter teachers' critical tasks in positive or negative ways. On the positive side, an accountability system that prioritizes certain topics could provide a valuable focus for schools whose curriculum is in disarray.[55] For example, in analyzing how they use time, schools may discover that they are shortchanging their students in key subjects, such as reading and math, so pressures to boost achievement in these areas could provide a needed focus. That focus may be quite valuable for new teachers, in particular new elementary school teachers, who must teach their students all subjects, unlike their secondary school colleagues, who often specialize. Choosing from among hundreds of potential topics, readings, and suggested discussion questions and then packaging that content into interesting classroom learning activities can be a cognitively overwhelming task for even the most experienced teacher. Accountability systems can help to create guideposts for teachers trying to set priorities and define critical tasks.

On the negative side, narrowing the curriculum can lead classroom teachers to omit important learning experiences if they or their principals believe certain activities would fail to help a school meet accountability requirements. The substantive consequences of such choices can be severe. In the short run students may lose interest in their studies without exposure to a rich array of topics and activities. In the long run too much narrowing of the curriculum to serve short-term accountability objectives can undermine the broader missions that people expect schools to serve. Those broad missions include preparing students to be well-rounded citizens and community members, not just content experts in a narrow range of subjects.

Anecdotal reports suggest that NCLB led schools and classroom teachers to alter their critical tasks in ways that narrowed the curriculum. While some teachers found this focusing useful, others thought it went too far. Generally speaking, these reports from teachers did suggest that in colliding with local practices, NCLB accomplished one of its principal goals: to help students and schools focus on math and reading, two essential areas that, when learned well, can produce success in other subjects. Providing a focus can be valuable, agreed Anita Yarbrough, a middle school math teacher in Kansas City, Kansas.[56] After NCLB was adopted, Yarbrough began teaching a special math class for students who performed poorly on state exams. She described it as "an extra math class in addition to their regular math class." Students in this class missed out on others, such as art, physical education, or other electives. But, she said, "It's beneficial; the only thing that is going to make them better at math is practicing more math, just as athletes practice to get better at their skills." Jim Sando, a 5th-grade teacher from suburban Philadelphia agreed that "the extent that this [focus on math or language arts] has shined a light on where students are, on a year-to-year basis, that is not a bad thing." But he added that the reading and math focus has distorted teachers' tasks in unproductive ways because it "is not being applied in a way that is going to really help kids. It's much more of a focus on the test, not a focus on the child." [57]

Other observers and teachers attested that the narrowed curriculum unnecessarily limited the learning experiences students need to gain a well-rounded education that prepares them for life beyond school. Award-winning historian David McCullough, for example, has concluded, "Because of No Child Left Behind, sadly, history is being put on the back burner or taken off the stove altogether in many or most schools, in favor of math or reading." [58] Sandra Day O'Connor, former associate justice of the U.S. Supreme Court, and retired congressman Lee Hamilton, who cochair the Campaign for the Civic Mission of Schools, agreed. They have argued that "civic education has been in steady decline over the past generation, as high-stakes testing and an emphasis on literacy and math dominate school reforms." [59] During his campaign for president, then-senator Barack Obama explained that owing to the focus on standardized testing in reading and math, "subjects like history and social studies have gotten pushed aside. Arts and music time is no longer there. So the child is not having the well-rounded educational experience I benefited from and most of my generation benefited from." [60]

Teachers' specific experiences often reflected those more general concerns. In Phoenix, 3rd-grade teacher Casey Bilger noted that his school never explicitly said, "Don't do science or social studies," but still, the school's priorities seemed to undervalue these topics. "There are strict blocks of time for reading, 90 minutes, each day. Then 60 minutes of writing and 60 minutes of math. In reality, there is not time left over for anything else." [61] Hands-on activities also suffered in some classrooms as teachers' critical tasks shifted. One Colorado teacher identified several lessons no longer in his curriculum, including the hatching of baby chicks, dissections, field trips, and community outreach, which included service in local city parks.[62]

With a few exceptions worth noting, quantitative data tend to support the notion that teachers shifted their critical tasks to emphasize reading and math over other subjects. Between 2001 and 2005, the number of states testing students in social studies declined from twenty-seven to nineteen, but for science the numbers rose from thirty-four to forty states. Those results suggested that concerns over civics may have been accurate but that states had not abandoned science, as some anecdotal reports implied.[63] It is also important to remember that NCLB did require annual science testing, but, as Chapter 2 explained, only math and reading results factored into AYP calculations.

At the local level a nationally representative survey of 349 school districts explored how elementary schools used instructional time from 2001–2002 to 2006–2007.[64] It reported that 58 percent of districts increased instructional time in English-language arts by an average of 141 minutes per week and that 45 percent increased time in math by 89 minutes per week. No districts reported increasing time for social studies, science, and art or music, but districts did report decreasing time in those subjects. Specifically, 36 percent decreased time on social studies (average decrease of 76 minutes per week), 28 percent cut back on science (75 minutes), and 16 percent had reduced art and music (57 minutes). In 20 percent of districts, recess was also cut, by an average of 50 minutes per week.

Surveys of individual teachers also uncovered increasing effort in reading and math and decreases in other subjects. The nationally representative Schools and Staffing Survey, administered by the Department of Education every five years or so, found this pattern in 1st- through 4th-grade classrooms when considering the period 1987–1988 to 2003–2004.[65] Interestingly, between 1999–2000 and 2003–2004, teachers reported increasing instructional time in reading by an average of 42 minutes per week. And while they reported declines in science (18 minutes) and social studies (24 minutes)—findings all consistent with NCLB's critics' claims—they also indicated they spent 18 fewer minutes per week on math. This last result is contrary to other findings that suggest math and reading both received more attention. Finally, district-level surveys of teachers in Richmond, Virginia, and Fresno, California, conducted in May and June 2004 also found shifts in teacher time toward tested subjects and away from nontested ones.[66]

While the evidence indicates that many schools narrowed teachers' critical tasks to favor reading and math, other schools showed how to offer a rich curriculum while simultaneously preparing students for state exams in these subjects.[67] Students attending the Osmond A. Church elementary and middle school in New York City, for example, studied diverse subjects including units on Shakespeare; historical and cultural treatments of Africa, Latin America, and Asia; and current events.[68] As a general strategy the school adopted an approach based on the Core Knowledge curriculum, which emphasizes cultural literacy and knowledge in fundamental subjects, while simultaneously encouraging connections between topics. The Core Knowledge program assumes that students must master key content from history, literature, math, science, and the arts in order to be capable citizens. Steeped in that information, students can then produce work requiring higher-order thinking skills, such as analysis, synthesis, and application.

Despite offering a rich curriculum, which does not solely emphasize reading and math or focus primarily on test preparation, Osmond Church has been a top elementary school in New York state, demonstrating high growth and high levels of achievement. The school's success is perhaps even more impressive given its student body. Primarily, the school has served traditionally disadvantaged groups, with blacks, Latinos, and Asians (especially new immigrants from India and Pakistan) composing more than 90 percent of the student body. More than 90 percent have also consistently qualified for the federal free and reduced price meals program, which means that most have come from economically impoverished backgrounds.

The success of Osmond Church is especially notable given evidence that shows disadvantaged students are more likely to experience a narrowed curriculum in their schools. Concerns over making AYP led many leaders and overseers of such schools to adopt a risk-averse approach to the curriculum and teaching. The result was to focus classroom critical tasks intensely on math, reading, and test preparation. In contrast, students in wealthier districts tended to continue enjoying a richer, more diverse curriculum.[69] If allowed to persist, such a bifurcated system would undermine the ambitions of NCLB's authors, who believed that schools should provide all children with challenging and interesting academic experiences. Such divisions would also further widen the chasm between rich and poor in the United States. As Finn and Ravitch have concluded about the likely outcomes of persistent narrowing: "Rich kids will study philosophy and art, music and history, while their poor peers fill in bubbles on test sheets. The lucky few will spawn the next generation of tycoons, political leaders, inventors, authors, artists and entrepreneurs. The less lucky masses will see narrower opportunities."[70]

* * *

When President Bush signed NCLB into law, administrators in the federal Education Department and state capitals were the first people to feel its collisions. The energy from those collisions reverberated across the nation's system of elementary and secondary education, into districts and individual schools, eventually reaching the classrooms and workrooms where teachers instruct students and plan their lessons. Implementation of NCLB's highly qualified teacher provisions resembled federal and state efforts to ensure that schools made AYP. Standards differed across the states, which meant that teachers continued to enter classrooms with varying levels of preparation and skill, even among the ranks of those who were highly qualified. Those results revealed how state and local conditions influenced the collisions that NCLB produced.

NCLB also affected teachers' critical tasks, influencing their classroom practices and the subjects they taught each day. Administering NCLB at the street level was a complex task for teachers, who became increasingly forced to attend to the test-score performances of their students. Those external constraints required many teachers to learn new tasks, alter old ones, and defend practices that for years they and their school administrations had assumed were effective, or at least effective enough to be considered acceptable. The results of these local conversations were not always positive. At the district and school levels, bureaucratic tendencies that focused on producing successes based on standards defined by the AYP system pushed many teachers to organize their tasks primarily around preparing students for tests in a narrow range of subjects. Some schools avoided such tendencies and in the process adopted a rich curriculum that simultaneously produced successful scores on state exams.

As this chapter and those before it have shown, the No Child Left Behind Act collided with state and local policies as well as classroom practices. The law's strongest advocates predicted that its theory of accountability and administration would help produce effective schools and knowledgeable students. The next chapter examines that prediction by considering how students themselves fared after NCLB became law. The examination of NCLB from students' perspectives extends the present discussion about teachers and their tasks by focusing specifically on the learning experiences of two particularly vulnerable student subgroups: those with disabilities and those still learning English. It then assesses the larger picture to see if the law has achieved the goals of boosting achievement and eliminating gaps between student subgroups.

6

Subgroup Accountability and Student Achievement

When Angelica enrolled at Principal Wood's school, he remarked how she had arrived "in an unusual way."[1] As far as school officials could determine, Angelica had moved into the high school's attendance zone and was living with her father's friend. Her dad remained involved in her life but lived at an undetermined address, presumably in another Ohio school district. After enrolling in school, Angelica was described as a pleasant student, although she was failing every class and never appeared to complete her homework. Whether that was consistent with her past academic performance was impossible to determine because her prior school refused to release her records. Her family still owed school fees, which put all record transfer requests on hold. Despite not having a paper trail of Angelica's academic experiences, based on their observations, Principal Wood's staff hypothesized that Angelica might have never passed a high school class.

Recognizing Angelica's high risk of dropping out of school (or worse), Principal Wood, Angelica, her father, and other school officials, as well as staff from the local child protective services office, met to determine how best to meet Angelica's needs. A plan emerged from that conference. But during the discussion a fleeting thought shot across Principal Wood's mind that shook him to the core: "If we just sent her back to her home school, she wouldn't count on our records." That step would have eliminated the chance that Angelica's poor performance, assuming it continued, would count against the school through the state's accountability system. Principal Wood never seriously considered abandoning Angelica, but that the idea even crossed his mind made him take pause. "While we did not send Angelica away, that the thought of such an action would occur to me as my role as principal," he remembered, "is a logical, though unfortunate, consequence of the standards and testing movement in this country and of the No Child Left Behind Act in particular." [2]

Many miles from Angelica's school in Ohio is South Eugene High School in Eugene, Oregon. During 2009, Eric Larson was a student at South Eugene and had a challenging academic year.[3] Like Angelica, who was always described as pleasant, Eric was considered a personable young man with a great sense of humor by his classmates. The challenges Eric confronted during his senior year were unlike Angelica's in so many ways. Eric was a member of his school's math, chemistry, and computer programming clubs. He was also an award-winning pianist (both his parents are music professors). Although he was a straight-A student overall, Eric's passion was mathematics. In high school he remarked that he would often spend ten hours a day or more trying to solve difficult math problems. "I'm interested in math and do it because I love it," he said.[4]

That commitment led him to pursue summer learning experiences that stoked his interest in what math researchers call "fusion categories." Those complicated algebraic structures have abstract applications to theoretical physics and more concrete relevance in computer programming. Eric's passion for math and his stamina for working long hours on a single problem earned him a surprise during his senior year that he described as "the biggest thing that's happened to me so far." [5] In 2009, Eric's work on fusion categories earned him the grand prize in the Intel Science Talent Search. Winning the prize, which is the nation's oldest and most prestigious science award for young people and includes a $100,000 college scholarship, meant that Eric had defeated more than 1,600 other nationwide contestants, including the competition's 40 other finalists. The Intel award is often a useful predictor of future success. Previous winners have included 6 people awarded the Nobel Prize and 10 subsequent winners of distinguished MacArthur "genius" grants.

The cases of Angelica and Eric suggest that schools possess no easy solution when confronting the challenge of serving all children well. Thinking more deeply about the phrase *no child left behind* and specific provisions of the No Child Left Behind Act (NCLB) suggests implicit tensions and paradoxes, which Angelica and Eric's different situations reveal in sharp detail. For example, a key ambition of NCLB's authors was to ensure that all students met challenging academic standards, including students across a diverse set of subgroups defined by race, ethnicity, income, disability, and language status. To realize such a noble goal would be complicated because it encouraged school leaders and teachers to see students as an undifferentiated mass (high standards "for all"), as members of distinct parts of overall school populations ("subgroup accountability"), and as unique individuals (leave "no child" behind). But with students as diverse as Angelica and Eric, how would schools accomplish these three things, which seemed to pull in different directions? The answer to that question was not obvious, but NCLB's system of accountability left local districts and schools to resolve it.

A specific goal that NCLB's authors established was for schools to decrease measurable gaps in achievement between disadvantaged and advantaged students. The subgroup accountability provisions of NCLB focused on that very issue and attempted to foster collisions with school practices that did not serve students well. NCLB's authors saw themselves as advocates for disadvantaged students, who for many years had moved through school without learning rigorous academic content and skills. There was a systematic need, the law's advocates reasoned, to alter school-wide and classroom critical tasks so that all students, and especially disadvantaged ones who often had been shuffled through the system, would enjoy opportunities to excel. This chapter assesses the progress of disadvantaged and other students under NCLB. It first examines two subgroups with particularly challenging needs: students with disabilities and English-language learners. It then considers evidence across many years and subgroups, including those based on race and economic status, to assess NCLB's potential impact on student achievement.

STUDENTS WITH DISABILITIES

Among NCLB's subgroups, students with disabilities represented some of the most diverse and challenging to teach. As of 2007, more than 6 million students with disabilities received services under the Individuals with Disabilities Education Act (IDEA), a law designed to guarantee that these students have equal access to educational opportunities. In all, students with disabilities represent approximately 9 percent of the total student population in the United States.[6] These students are a diverse lot with conditions ranging from relatively mild learning disabilities that need minimal educational interventions, to those with speech, vision, or language problems, to those with more severe conditions such as emotional disturbances, autism, and other physical impairments that sometimes require full-time help from medical personnel during the school day.

One primary goal of IDEA has been to include students with disabilities in the regular daily life of school. Specifically, schools are to educate these students in the "least restrictive environment," alongside their nondisabled peers when possible. In many ways IDEA has made great progress toward fulfilling that objective. Based on data from 2007 the Department of Education estimated that nearly 60 percent of students with disabilities spent over 80 percent of their school day in traditional classroom settings.[7]

Like other NCLB student subgroups, the law required test scores of students with disabilities to factor into adequate yearly progress (AYP) calculations of schools and school districts. Even though the 1997 reauthorization of IDEA required states to include students with disabilities in their assessment systems, most states did not until NCLB's requirements became law.[8] NCLB's supporting regulations, developed by the federal Education Department, did create certain exceptions and allowances for how these students would participate in state assessments and how their scores would enter the calculations.

To account for varying needs among students with disabilities, NCLB identified four categories of test takers. First, there were students with minor disabilities who would take regular assessments, just like their nondisabled peers. Second, there were students with disabilities who also were to take regular assessments, but with some accommodation that addressed their disability without providing an unfair advantage. A third group of students would take alternative assessments based on different achievement standards, still linked to grade-level material. In other words those students would take tests on the same material as their peers, but their work would be evaluated against achievement standards that defined acceptable performance differently. Only 1 percent of all students who took such alternative assessments could have their scores count for AYP purposes; in practice, this category was designed to include students with the most severe cognitive disabilities. Finally, federal regulations issued in 2007 created a fourth category of students who could take alternative assessments with modified academic achievement standards. Up to 2 percent of all students could participate in these assessments and have their scores contribute to AYP calculations. The purpose of creating that group was to better serve students falling somewhere between those needing the most dramatic adaptation from state expectations and those needing little or no adjustments.[9]

The students with disabilities subgroup created at least two tensions for special education and traditional teachers. Those tensions affected these students' experiences and how teachers defined and executed their classroom critical tasks. The first tension involved the degree to which students with disabilities should have their own accountability system, versus including them under the NCLB umbrella. Some classroom teachers and disability advocates argued that while it was fine for students with relatively mild learning or behavioral disabilities, NCLB-style accountability was inappropriate for others. A major concern was the emotional effect that testing could have. One advocate, for example, had "heard numerous stories from legislators that students with disabilities are being humiliated by having to take tests that they know they can't do. Special education teachers say, 'We didn't become special education teachers to humiliate these students, to remind them they can't do the work.' The testing makes students with disabilities feel like failures."[10]

Others suggested that the intense focus on reading and math, especially when other subjects suffered, may have been especially inappropriate for certain students. One school administrator explained that incorporating "employability and life skills in an accountability system" could really benefit many students with disabilities. Unfortunately, this administrator continued, "The academic focus on NCLB has pushed out some career and technical education classes, which is what some students with disabilities really need. So it's hard for us in special education to provide students with disabilities with appropriate classes in occupational training." [11] Another disabilities advocate echoed that point by asking, "Why require students [especially those with the most severe cognitive disabilities] to take an 11th-grade math test, for example, when they really need to learn skills for a job?" [12]

Focusing on relatively traditional academic testing, other teachers, administrators, and advocates argued, could also fundamentally clash with a student's Individualized Education Program (IEP), which is a tailored plan of instruction and support that IDEA guarantees to all students identified for special education services. A perceived need to meet accountability requirements for NCLB directed some special education and regular classroom teachers to alter their instruction for students with disabilities, which sometimes resulted in teaching that was inappropriate given a student's IEP. As the previous quotes just suggested, some IEPs contain goals designed to help students live and work independently after leaving school. Several of those goals or other life skills are not "academic" in the traditional sense, especially as measured by math or reading exams. The pressure to perform in more traditional academic environments meant that some students with disabilities received less instruction in the sorts of time or personal management skills, for example, that their IEPs had identified as important goals. [13]

Others challenged the notion that any student, regardless of disability, should be excluded from systems designed to promote educational accountability, NCLB included. Chief among these concerns was that exempting certain students entirely would take the pressure off schools and districts to challenge them academically, or worse, that these students might receive little or no attention at all. In practice, disabilities advocates feared that dropping some students from required testing could return schools to practices of the 1970s and earlier, before IDEA became law. During that era, according to one witness who testified before Congress, school officials would commonly call parents and say, "[Y]our retarded child is uneducable and untrainable; come take him home." [14]

One special education teacher, Julie Grant, who supported NCLB's approach to accountability, worried that removing special education students from the AYP equation would cause students to suffer. "If the expectation is not there for special education students," she asked, "then what are their teachers teaching them? Are we just writing them off?" [15] In Maryland one parent of a child with Down's syndrome explained her support for NCLB this way: "Those of us who know the potential of the law are trying to cling to it" because of the attention and opportunities it was designed to offer students like her child. [16]

Of particular concern to such parent advocates were the exceptions that NCLB and its regulations allowed for students with more than mild disabilities. By some estimates, exempting certain students from regular testing and standards (students in the third and fourth categories described earlier) had the potential to exclude up to 20 percent of students with disabilities from regular state testing experiences. In debating the merits of those exceptions, that number seemed way too high to many disabilities experts, advocates, and teachers. A fear existed that such exemptions created incentives that would encourage schools to push students with relatively mild disabilities away from rigorous academic opportunities they were well equipped to handle.[17]

While disagreements raged on over the appropriateness of including the disabled subgroup in AYP calculations, a second tension existed as NCLB's accountability requirements placed new classroom pressures on special education teachers. These teachers saw their core tasks altered as they tried to serve these students' needs while simultaneously meeting NCLB's requirements. NCLB now competed for their attention with the complicated work already involved in designing and implementing IEPs, as IDEA required. Certainly, some of the new tasks that NCLB prompted did improve how special education teachers worked with their students. For example, NCLB's focus on reading and math achievement led many special education teachers to collaborate more closely with teachers in traditional classrooms who were content area experts. Such collaborations helped both kinds of teachers to better understand each other's challenges. In the process, that teamwork provided special education teachers with more opportunities to expose their students to the school's general curriculum.[18] Having traditional classroom teachers and special education teachers working together served the IDEA goal of educating students to their fullest potential in the least restrictive environment.

Teachers of students with the most significant disabilities, even those who took modified state exams using modified standards, faced numerous new challenges. Those included determining how best to accommodate these students and modify expectations in light of their disabilities but also how to actually administer the tests. One school administrator suggested, for example, that it "takes 30 days to administer one test to a severely disabled student," in particular, "one who has cerebral palsy and is in a wheelchair." [19] Further, special education teachers and other members of student IEP teams had to develop new expertise in assessment so they could make difficult judgment calls about appropriate accommodations that did not modify the content or expectations of exams taken for accountability purposes. Determining which accommodation was appropriate depended partly on the student's disability but also on the actual exam itself. Some appropriate accommodations on one test for one particular student's disability could be inappropriate modifications for another student taking a test developed by another test company. Without proper guidance from the state on how to proceed, IEP teams faced complex situations, in addition to their already challenging work of simply teaching their students, their primary purpose in the classroom.[20]

The core dilemma that created competing critical tasks for special education teachers can be simply stated. Teachers of students with disabilities were instructed, via IDEA and a student's IEP, to customize instruction to best meet a student's needs. But simultaneously, the accountability requirements of NCLB pushed a sort of standardization that made it difficult to customize instruction and assessment without undercutting the very benefits of standardization, namely, that results would be comparable across individual subgroups within schools and also across schools within a state. If accommodations and adjustments to expectations were not incorporated into the accountability system, then the goals and requirements of IDEA would be undercut and students with disabilities would be unable to fully participate. If, however, large numbers of students with disabilities benefited from tailored adjustments to standards and tests, then NCLB's goal of holding all students to the same high standards and producing comparable results across subgroups and schools would be compromised.[21]

ENGLISH-LANGUAGE LEARNERS

In addition to their peers with disabilities, students who were still acquiring English, known as English-language learners (ELLs), posed additional challenges. By way of background one should note the massive expansion of this subgroup as immigration during the past three decades has changed the demographics of the nation, certain states, and individual communities. Estimates have suggested that more than 5 million ELLs attend school in the United States, amounting to roughly 10 percent of the nation's total student population. Approximately 80 percent of these students speak Spanish as their first language, but as a group they speak more than 400 different languages.[22] Although overall school enrollments increased by only 3 percent nationwide between 1996 and 2006, enrollment of ELLs increased by more than 60 percent during this same period.[23]

Recent growth in the ELL population occurred mostly in places unaccustomed to much language diversity. During the 2005–2006 school year, almost 60 percent of ELLs lived in just five states (California, Florida, Illinois, New York, and Texas), but other regions experienced tremendous growth, including the Southeast, the wider Midwest (beyond Illinois), and the mountain West.[24] In Tennessee, during any given year over 100 different native languages are now represented in the schools, and in North Carolina the number of ELLs doubled, from 60,000 to 112,500 between the years 2002 and 2007 (coinciding with NCLB's launch, incidentally).[25] Reports from Georgia and Utah have shown school districts recruiting teachers from Mexico to meet the needs of their growing populations of Spanish-speaking students.[26]

Some local communities have seen a huge influx of ELLs during the past twenty years. The Springdale Public Schools in Arkansas, for example, had essentially no ELLs among its 8,000 students in 1990. By 2008 approximately 40 percent of the district's 17,400 students, around 7,000 total, were ELLs.[27] The explosive growth in the number of ELLs and their tendency to achieve at lower levels than their peers were two reasons why NCLB's authors included this subgroup into school AYP calculations. Just as NCLB implementation was beginning, in 2003–2004, the evidence from reading and math exams showed that ELLs scored consistently below state performance goals in two-thirds of the states.[28]

Like the rules governing NCLB's subgroup of students with disabilities, which allowed for some modifications to assessments and standards, the law permitted some flexibility in how ELLs participated in state testing. A few points especially are important. First, students new to the United States and classified as ELLs did not have to take their state's reading test. Although they needed to take their state's math test, the results did not have to count for AYP purposes for one year. Second, after that initial year NCLB required such students to participate in state testing and have those scores count for AYP purposes, but exceptions could be made. Those exceptions, if their state allowed them, enabled ELLs to take state tests in their native language for up to three years, and states were allowed to extend that time period for two additional years on a case-by-case basis. Third, these students were allowed to receive accommodations on state tests. Paralleling accommodations for students with disabilities, those exceptions were supposed to enable students to overcome their limited English abilities and to show their content knowledge but not give them an unfair advantage. Many states provided such accommodations, including, for example, offering students extra time to take the tests, allowing teachers to read aloud or explain directions in English and the students' native language, and letting students use English or bilingual dictionaries during the test.

Adjustments to NCLB's regulations in 2004 also made an important change in how AYP calculations reflected ELL students' scores. These changes emerged given that the ELL subgroup, as created, was a highly fluid category unlike others based on race or ethnicity. In other words students would leave the ELL subgroup once they gained enough competency speaking and understanding English so they could meaningfully participate in traditional classrooms with native English speakers. By definition, then, that meant ELLs taking state reading tests in English would have been very unlikely to pass state tests and that schools with large numbers of ELL students would never have made AYP for that reason. To remedy this problem, the federal Education Department changed regulations to allow schools to count student scores in the ELL subgroup for up to two years after students gained competency in English. That change was intended to better account for the fluidity of the subgroup and to avoid unfairly penalizing schools that effectively helped their students become capable English speakers.

Considering students' needs and teachers' critical tasks, parallels existed between teachers who worked with ELLs and those who educated students with disabilities. Both sets of teachers experienced new tensions and had to manage unfamiliar critical tasks after NCLB became law. Like special education teachers,

ELL teachers enjoyed the attention that NCLB brought to their students. For example, two major immigrant advocacy groups, while criticizing NCLB's implementation, defended the law's spirit and overall approach. The Mexican American Legal Defense and Educational Fund called NCLB "among our nation's most critical federal civil rights measures," and the National Council of La Raza argued that "English-language learners must be included in the No Child Left Behind Act's system of assessment and accountability." [29]

One virtue of NCLB, ELL advocates and teachers argued, was that it brought added attention, resources, and focus on these students, who for many years were underserved and not challenged academically. H. Gary Cook of the Wisconsin Center for Education Research, located at the University of Wisconsin, noted, "Before NCLB, very few states had their own ELL assessments. Now the assessments are associated with state standards. That's a good thing." [30] That change also spurred teachers to collaborate in new ways. Eva Rogozinski, an English-as-a-second-language (ESL) resource teacher in Clifton, Ohio, explained that owing to NCLB, "there's more communication between ESL teachers and mainstream teachers, and the English-language learners aren't thought of as a separate entity." Further, she expressed confidence that the new and extensive training that teachers received to help middle and high school ELLs succeed in mainstream classes would not have occurred absent the push that NCLB provided. Joseph Telles, a program coordinator for ELL students in the Los Angeles public schools, added that because of the presence of the subgroup in AYP calculations, NCLB "shone the light on our group," which produced "a lot more focused in-service training" for teachers who had ELLs.[31] Training involved both ELL teachers and traditional classroom teachers, so both groups gained a greater understanding of how to help their students succeed.

Not surprisingly, teachers and ELL advocates were not uniformly positive about NCLB's effect on classroom and school tasks. Even ELL teachers who liked the added attention, training, and opportunities to work closely with traditional classroom teachers still chafed at some of the law's effects. Jania Kusielewicz, an ELL district supervisor in New Jersey, stated approvingly, "I don't like to give the No Child Left Behind Act any credit, but it has given [English-as-a-second-language] teachers clout in the mainstream." But she also believed that the law's accountability mechanisms were "unconscionable" because, in her words, they were "punishing schools for having a high number of English-language learners." [32] Rogozinski, the teacher quoted earlier, also agreed that although the added attention was great, she disapproved of her school entering improvement status because its ELL achievement was too low.

Others were more uniformly negative and feared that the added attention ELL students received came at an unacceptable cost to these students. Specifically, they worried that the testing and accountability requirements undercut these students' educational experiences and distorted their teachers' critical tasks. One ELL teacher reported that the demands of standardized testing meant that his students missed almost one-fifth of their instructional days that formerly had been devoted to helping them acquire English. These students also had two nontested subjects, science and social studies, dropped from their schedules.[33] Others reported shifting their daily teaching away from strategies to help their ELLs practice and develop English and toward strategies to help them pass standardized tests.

Teachers and district leaders in the Fairfax County schools, in the Virginia suburbs of Washington, D.C., were so concerned about having their students take state exams for NCLB that they resisted the requirements and clashed directly with the federal Education Department for several months. One teacher was concerned, for example, that her 8th graders who were learning from a 4th-grade text would be baffled by questions on the state's reading test. "They'd shut down. They'll just put their heads down," she predicted.[34] Fairfax officials eventually relented and obeyed the NCLB requirements, but, still, they questioned the value of having all their ELLs participate in state testing. School board member Phillip Niedzielski-Eichner noted that "once we go through this exercise to accommodate the Department of Education, the system is still going to have 5,000 kids who have a test in front of them, and perhaps 10 percent can take it." As a result, the district reassured its ELL test takers that they could stop the exam at any time, something that the district's superintendent, Jack Dale, called "the humane thing" to do.[35]

One specific tension ELL teachers faced was that of the sometimes competing requirements that NCLB demanded they fulfill for their students. The bulk of the discussion of ELL students in this section has focused on Title I of NCLB, which included the law's testing and AYP requirements. But NCLB contained other parts, too, including Title III, which contained many provisions centered on the goal of helping students become fluent English speakers.[36] Depending on state and local implementation choices, these two parts of the law created a dilemma for some ELL teachers that complicated their critical tasks. One author explained the tension by noting that "while Title I puts pressure on schools to keep students classified as ELL to improve that subgroup's performance, Title III generates incentives to reclassify [them as competent in English] as soon as possible."[37] The dilemma was particularly acute in states that allowed ELLs to take state proficiency tests in their native languages.

One study found that as of January 2009 thirteen states—including California, New York, and Texas, all with large ELL populations—allowed students to take assessments in their native languages in at least some grades and subjects.[38] In some states with that option, which ironically was an attempt by the federal government to offer states and local districts added flexibility, districts instructed ELL teachers to gear their instruction toward the language of the test. For tests offered in the student's native language, that approach may have helped the school meet AYP and thus achieve Title I's objectives for school accountability, but at the same time it may have undercut the teachers' ability to achieve the Title III objective of helping students to gain competency in English.

One professor of special education and bilingual education at the University of Texas, Alba Ortiz, explained the potential classroom effects of the native-language exams. Her state offered Spanish-language exams for reading and math to ELL students in 3rd through 6th grade. As a result, Ortiz said, "The early-grade teachers want to teach only in Spanish so the students will pass the test." That practice altered classroom tasks and morale of other teachers because "the 4th- and 5th-grade teachers are frustrated they don't get students who can be proficient in English before they reach middle school." [39] Because making AYP each year was a short-term objective, while having students develop language skills was a more long-term one, NCLB appeared to create incentives for schools to react to the more immediate circumstances and consequences, which pushed teachers to define their critical tasks accordingly.

For schools that tested all ELLs in English, teachers and school administrators faced the added critical task of choosing appropriate test accommodations. Making those choices was difficult because little solid research exists on which accommodations are most appropriate for which circumstances.[40] One comprehensive study of state assessments for ELLs found that state policies guiding local school officials and teachers were unclear and too often treated accommodations for students with disabilities as equivalent in effectiveness for ELLs, although research has not supported this practice. The result in some cases, as local officials and teachers tried to choose appropriate accommodations, was to distort the test results from ELL students and unknowingly invalidate the results.[41]

STUDENT ACHIEVEMENT PATTERNS

When NCLB became law, its authors' grandest ambitions were that all students would be proficient in reading and math by 2014 and that gaps between student groups would vanish. During the law's implementation, how far has the nation progressed toward achieving those goals? This is a complicated question to answer for several reasons, chief among them being the fragmented and decentralized environment in which American education policy operates each day. Recall that NCLB's theory of administration relies heavily on state and local judgments, policies, and decisions to achieve the law's objectives. Still, several studies have attempted to address whether NCLB has improved overall reading and math achievement while narrowing achievement gaps. Different cuts at the data reveal some positive signs, but other reasons exist to remain cautious or even worried.

A first way to assess NCLB's potential impact on student achievement is to examine state test results. One should read this evidence carefully, though. Attributing causal impacts to NCLB is difficult because other policies and reforms could have influenced achievement. Although NCLB represents an important force influencing educational practices, it is but one initiative among many affecting critical tasks in the nation's schools and classrooms. States and localities did not cease to adjust their own policies that might have affected student achievement, such as altering teacher training and principal recruitment or adjusting penalties and rewards associated with their own state-level accountability systems. Determining the independent impact of NCLB when other initiatives are operating simultaneously is a tall task.

Analyzing state test scores also necessarily limits one's analysis to changes within individual states. As previous chapters have discussed, NCLB allows states to set their own standards and write their own tests. Differences in standards and test content means it is impossible to directly compare results across state lines. Further, because state testing policies and expectations themselves changed during NCLB's implementation, within-state comparisons are possible only when state systems remained constant. With those limits in mind, what has the evidence from state tests shown?

In general, student performance on state tests has improved since NCLB became law, although gains were inconsistent across grade levels and subjects. One comprehensive set of studies, which examined states only where testing systems remained constant, showed large majorities of states making progress across multiple student subgroups. Analyzing state trends from 2001–2002 to 2007–2008, the Center on Education Policy found that among 4th graders, students made gains in reading and math, although the results varied by subject and subgroup.[42] Math gains were stronger than reading gains, with at least 80 percent or more of the states examined seeing growth across all subgroups in math. These gains occurred across the achievement spectrum for students who were previously low, middle, or high achievers. For reading, gains existed but tended to be for students in the middle of the distribution, rather than for those at the highest or lowest. Up to a third of the states in some cases actually saw the percentage of students achieving at advanced levels decline in reading.[43]

Earlier reports, which examined trends through 2005–2006, found related gains for reading and math in elementary, middle, and high schools. But those reports indicated that gains were more consistently present and stronger for elementary schools and that declines in some states were more prevalent for high school students. Overall, though, state trends across grades and subjects showed improvement much more frequently than they showed decline. For example, gains in students scoring proficient in reading occurred in elementary, middle, and high schools, in 88, 85, and 76 percent of states where comparisons were possible, while math gains, at these same three levels of schooling occurred in 95, 95, and 80 percent of states, respectively.[44] A different analysis of state assessment trends for 4th and 8th graders, conducted by the federal Education Department for 2004–2005 to 2006–2007, also found states generally gaining across all of NCLB's subgroups. "On average," the report's authors explained, "79 percent of the states showed achievement gains from 2004–05 to 2006–07 for each group."[45]

Achievement gaps between student subgroups also narrowed on state tests as NCLB's implementation deepened. Analyzing state trends across achievement gaps, subjects, and elementary, middle, and high school grade levels from 2001–2002 to 2007–2008, the Center on Education Policy found improvements occurring more than 70 percent of the time. For example, differences between black and white students decreased in 77 percent of the gaps analyzed; for Hispanics and whites gaps closed 79 percent of the time; and gaps between students from low-income families and those not from low-income families declined 70 percent of the time. Importantly, when gaps narrowed, typically it was because lower groups improved at accelerated rates, not because the achievement of higher groups declined.[46]

While the dominant pattern was for gaps to narrow, in some instances they widened. That occurred most frequently for gaps based on income. Among 4th graders, for example, low-income students in 28 percent of states fell farther behind those who were not low income on reading, and in 25 percent of states they fell farther behind in math. For middle school students, these reading and math gaps widened in 19 and 23 percent of states, respectively; and for high school they widened in 29 and 33 percent of states.[47] The same Education Department study just cited also found generally narrowing achievement gaps when comparing state results from 2004–2005 with those from 2006–2007.[48] Alongside these generally positive results, both of these studies emphasized that remaining gaps across grade levels still were quite large. In other words, based on state test results, the evidence showed that even with narrowing gaps, much work remained to guarantee that all students achieved at high levels.

Unfortunately, the data on ELL students and students with disabilities are much harder to interpret. Several reasons complicate analyses of these data and render any conclusions about overall performance across the states speculative at best. For one thing state policies governing testing of these students have been inconsistent across the years. This was partly due to adjustments in federal regulations and guidance, which changed how states were allowed to incorporate students into their testing systems. Also, local application of state rules and guidance could mean that accommodations for particular disabilities might vary from one year to the next or even across communities.

One published study from the Center on Education Policy did consider a limited set of trends in the disabled subgroup, while affirming all of the caveats mentioned in the previous paragraph and noting that the results provide at best a "rough indicator of achievement trends for this group."[49] The study considered trends for 4th graders from 2006 to 2008, as well as a more in-depth snapshot from 2008 of 4th graders, middle school students (typically 8th graders), and high school students. Two primary findings emerged. First, although students with disabilities gained ground in some states and lost ground in others, overall gains were more common. Across 2006 to 2008, there were results for 4th graders only. The results showed that between 58 to 69 percent of states reported gains in 4th-grade reading and math achievement, which included gains for students achieving at low, middle, and high levels. Between 26 and 33 percent of states reported declines in one or more of these levels, while approximately 10 percent of states reported no difference across those same achievement levels.[50]

Second, large achievement gaps existed between students with disabilities and their nondisabled peers. The findings on gaps were speculative, however, and based on snapshot results from 2008 only. Given that students with disabilities are sometimes taking tests based on alternative standards and forms, or may have accommodations, strict comparisons between that group's proficiency percentages and the percentages of other subgroups should be read with caution. Still, the reported gaps were large. Representative examples include 4th-grade reading, where across states the median percentage of students with disabilities scoring proficient or better was 41 percent, compared with 79 percent of nondisabled students scoring at those levels. In high school math the medians were 22 percent and 69 percent, respectively. The report's authors concluded that "disparities of 30 or 40 percentage points are common."[51] Whether those gaps represented improvements over previous achievement gaps was impossible to tell because the data were from a single test year.

Despite some reported improvements in state test results, some observers and analysts questioned their utility in measuring changes in student achievement. A better measure, they argued, is the National Assessment of Educational Progress (NAEP) tests because only the NAEP allows one to compare states directly. Taken by samples of students and administered by the federal government, the NAEP is also immune to state policies or practices that may artificially inflate achievement levels, an argument explored momentarily in more detail. Another virtue of NAEP is that it has been tracking achievement for several years, allowing one to explore changes over time, including trends before and after NCLB became law.

In fact, two sets of NAEP results exist. The "long-term NAEP," which is administered every few years or so to nine- and thirteen-year-olds, has existed since the 1970s and allows one to draw inferences about the nation as a whole. The "main NAEP," which 4th-, 8th-, and 12th-grade students have taken since the early 1990s, provides an additional national snapshot but also snapshots of individual states' performances. Given the state-level information in the main NAEP, the ensuing discussion focuses primarily on that set of results.

Even with its advantages, NAEP tests are by no means perfect indicators of student progress. A provision in NCLB did require all states to participate in the main NAEP, but participation was optional prior to 2002. Even in requiring participation, NCLB did not demand that states incorporate NAEP-specific expectations into state standards and testing systems, nor did it create any formal consequences for states or students based on NAEP performance. Further, the NAEP has a deserved reputation for containing very difficult material, which would challenge even students in some of the world's highest-performing countries. Thus, low results on the NAEP tests do not necessarily mean that students are failing to learn important content. Finally, the NAEP is no better positioned than state tests to examine the explicit effects of NCLB on student achievement. The best that these results typically can show is potential or suggestive relationships.

Examining trends on the main NAEP reveals a mixed picture of student achievement, with overall results less than encouraging. Two figures present these trends visually. Figure 6.1 shows results for student subgroups in 4th-grade reading and math, while Figure 6.2 presents analogous results for 8th graders. These figures and other analyses of the data reveal several important results.[52] On the up side, students across NCLB's racial and ethnic subgroups have gained ground in recent years. Between 2002 and 2009, black, Hispanic, and white 4th graders all improved in reading, although not by large amounts. For math the period of 2000 to 2009 (prior to 2002, reading and math tests were not always administered in the same year) also showed gains for all three of these groups. For 8th graders, black, Hispanic, and white students all gained in math from 2000 to 2009 as well.

It is difficult to attribute these changes in NAEP scores to NCLB, though. As Figures 6.1 and 6.2 show, scores have held steady or increased across most years since the early 1990s, suggesting that the more general state standards movement, which emerged before NCLB became law, is likely having an impact as well. Still, one study from researchers with the National Bureau of Economic Research analyzed state-level NAEP results and controlled for prior state policies, which helped them to isolate potential effects of NCLB.[53] Those authors reported some gains but not uniform ones across subjects or subgroups. Specifically, the authors found that NCLB seemed to produce detectable increases in 4th-grade math achievement, in particular among white and Hispanic students, and for students across subgroups who were low and high achievers.

In addition to subgroup improvements, trends after NCLB became law showed that some achievement gaps between white students and their black and Hispanic peers narrowed, although the improvements were not always large or uniform across groups. From 2002 (just after NCLB was adopted) to 2009, results from the main NAEP in 4th-grade reading showed a 4.3 point drop in the white-black gap and a 2.6 point drop in the gap between whites and Hispanics. In 8th-grade reading for those same years, the gap between blacks and whites remained essentially the same, while Hispanics gained on whites by 2.6 points. Declines in the math gaps were more consistently large from 2000 (the last main NAEP in math administered before NCLB became law) to 2009. Among 4th graders, blacks caught up to whites by 4.5 points and Hispanics gained on whites by 5.6 points; for 8th graders gaps narrowed by 8.0 and 5.1 points, respectively.[54]

Figure 6.1 4th-Grade Reading and Math Trends on the Main NAEP, by Student Subgroups

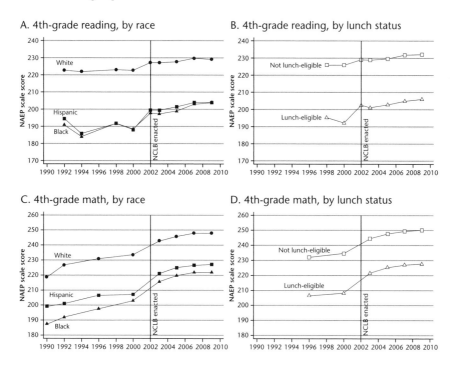

Note: "Lunch-eligible" and "not lunch-eligible" refer to student eligibility for the federal reduced-price breakfast and lunch program. Students eligible for this program come from families with low incomes. Data available from the National Assessment of Educational Progress, using the NAEP Data Explorer at http://nces.ed.gov/nationsreportcard/naepdata/.

Other evidence suggests that gains in student achievement were limited. While achievement has not fallen on NAEP since NCLB became law, the just-cited National Bureau of Economic Research study, which used the main NAEP and controlled for prior state policies, found that achievement gains were limited to 4th-grade math. NCLB appeared to have no noticeable impact on 4th-grade reading, nor was there evidence that the law had positive effects on 8th-grade NAEP scores in reading or math.[55] Figure 6.1 shows that scores in 4th-grade reading across whites, blacks, and Hispanics also appeared to flatten out between 2007 and 2009; a similar result in those years appears for math. Finally, Figure 6.2 shows essentially a flat trend line for whites and blacks in reading, with Hispanics doing only slightly better from 2002 to 2009.

The evidence regarding achievement gaps is not entirely positive either. In addition to the results based on racial subgroups, Figures 6.1 and 6.2 compare

Figure 6.2 8th-Grade Reading and Math Trends on the Main NAEP, by Student Subgroups

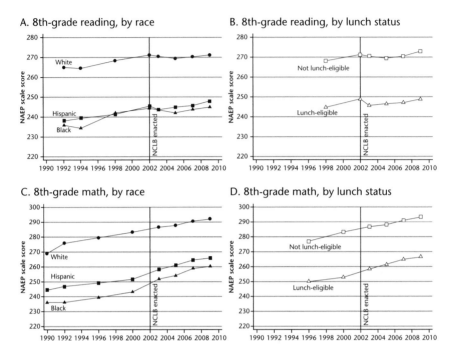

Note: "Lunch-eligible" and "not lunch-eligible" refer to student eligibility for the federal reduced-price breakfast and lunch program. Students eligible for this program come from families with low incomes. Data available from the National Assessment of Educational Progress, using the NAEP Data Explorer at http://nces.ed.gov/nationsreportcard/naepdata/.

students who were eligible for federally subsidized school meals (a proxy for poverty) and those who were not. Across subjects and grade levels, achievement gaps between these two groups barely budged after NCLB became law, showing students from economically disadvantaged families lagging far behind their non–economically disadvantaged peers. Across all of the subgroup comparisons in Figures 6.1 and 6.2, the results also show that the achievement gaps remaining in 2009 were still quite large. Despite some narrowing of gaps between students of different races, the distance between whites and others remained between 20.7 and 31.7 points, depending on the subject and grade level under consideration. Gaps based on lunch eligibility also were large, ranging from 22.5 to 26.9 points.[56]

Simultaneously comparing state-level results on the main NAEP with results from state-developed tests raises additional questions about the substantive information that state tests can convey. Specifically, critics identified discrepancies between state results on the main NAEP and state-developed tests. The data showed that many states with relatively high or growing levels of proficiency on state tests were the very states that had lower percentages of students scoring proficient or better on the NAEP.[57] Those findings prompted questions about whether state test results should be taken seriously. If student performance in reading and math were actually improving, then results from state tests and the main NAEP should have moved in concert, it seemed. But this did not always occur. Critics inferred that states likely played statistical games with their own testing and accountability systems to show higher levels of achievement than were warranted. Observers also worried that these discrepancies meant that state expectations simply were too low when compared with the more demanding standards for NAEP.

State defenders and some impartial observers responded that discrepancies between state test results and NAEP results did not provide ironclad evidence that state tests should be discounted. In part, citizens often tend to trust results from sources closer to home, such as state-developed exams, and remain somewhat skeptical of measures seeming to come from the outside. In addition to those perceptions about which results are more trustworthy or accurate, because content standards differ between the NAEP and state tests, it is possible that the samples of students who took the NAEP may have been answering questions about topics they had not yet studied. Because NCLB created no formal consequences for states doing poorly on the NAEP, states had little incentive—other than to avoid the public embarrassment and political problems that relatively lower NAEP scores can produce—to focus systematically on improving NAEP results. Finally, debates have long existed over whether NAEP cut points that define basic, proficient, and advanced levels of achievement have been set appropriately. It may be true that states expect too little of their students, but simultaneously, the NAEP may expect too much, some have argued.[58]

REGRESS OR PROGRESS?

Leaving aside the discrepancies that have existed between the NAEP and state test results, and assuming for a moment that state test gains were real, some analysts wondered if the cost of making these gains was too high and if it undermined the law's overall objective to leave no child behind. Their fear was that meeting short-term objectives for achievement, which could have produced gains, may have encouraged states to develop accountability systems that distorted teachers' critical tasks. On that point it is interesting to consider the so-called bubble kids—those students scoring just below proficient levels on state tests. Given NCLB's requirements, moving as many students as possible past the proficiency line in reading and math was an important goal to achieve in order for schools to make AYP. With yearly state targets defining required proficiency levels (see the example in Figure 4.1), analysts noted that schools possessed incentives to emphasize instruction of the bubble kids, which, counter to NCLB's stated goals, would likely leave many children behind.

Focusing on nearly proficient students would allow schools to strategically use their resources to fulfill AYP requirements, given that students near proficiency were likely the easiest to move to the next level. As a result, students in the tails of the achievement distribution—those way behind or those already way ahead— were likely to receive less attention. That focus may have helped schools to meet short-term AYP objectives, but it effectively would have undermined schools from assuring that 100 percent of students were proficient by 2014, NCLB's long-term goal. In worst-case scenarios critics worried that students the farthest behind would simply give up and perhaps even drop out of school, while the highest performers would become bored and not strive to reach even higher.

Reports from teachers suggested that in responding to NCLB's requirements, many schools focused on the bubble students at the expense of others.[59] Quantitative survey evidence from a nationally representative sample of teachers suggested that schools seemed to be in danger of losing focus on the highest achieving students. When asked whether "getting underachieving students to reach 'proficiency' has become so important that the needs of advanced students take a back seat," 44 percent somewhat agreed and 34 percent strongly agreed, while only 15 percent somewhat disagreed and 6 percent strongly disagreed (1 percent was not sure).[60]

In focus groups with the surveyed teachers, discussion about bubble students repeatedly surfaced, indicating that students at both ends of the achievement spectrum may have received less attention. As one focus group participant said, "At our school, we really broke it all down and we looked at all the gainers and sliders, the kids who have gone up over the last year or have gone down. All the kids that are what we called 'on the bubble.'" According to this teacher, during the previous two years, "all of our focus has gone to those kids." [61] A different study across three states and several school districts noted that in many schools the push for data-driven instruction led schools to refocus a school's critical tasks on the bubble students. More than 75 percent of principals surveyed said that "their school or district encourages teachers to focus on these [bubble] students"; and between 25 and 33 percent of teachers, depending on the district and state, agreed that they adjusted their classroom practices to meet this objective.[62]

If classroom critical tasks shifted to focus on the bubble kids, what impact did this have on student achievement? Researchers disagreed on this matter, as reviews of the growing literature have shown.[63] Additional work has failed to settle the issue. For example, in an analysis of NAEP performance for the highest- and lowest-achieving students from 2000 to 2007, Brookings Institution researcher

Tom Loveless found that students near the bottom gained ground while achievement at the top stagnated. That suggested that schools may have been meeting the needs of their lowest achievers but not their highest ones. Another study of 5th-grade student achievement in Chicago, conducted by two University of Chicago economists, found detectable and noteworthy gains in reading and math among students in the middle of the achievement distribution but stagnating performance for students at the low end and mixed performances for the highest achievers.[64] A final analysis of state test scores found gains across the achievement spectrum, which suggested a focus on the bubble may not have undermined performance of the highest and lowest achievers. Although that was the general pattern, the study noted that some states saw declining percentages of students scoring at advanced levels in elementary and high school reading. The authors concluded that even if teachers were targeting those on the bubble, "the effect is not so extreme as to thwart growth at the advanced level."[65]

After NCLB became law, the growing numbers of studies examining student achievement sparked more debates than they settled. Observers still disagreed about whether the nation should celebrate or question the achievement gains that some studies reported. Jack Jennings, president of the Center on Education Policy, suggested that NCLB and the states deserved some credit for progress. "By no means are we saying that we're in nirvana; there's a long way to go," he said. "But as a nation, if we ask schools to narrow the achievement gap and that's what the schools are doing, we should give them credit for it."[66] Harvard education professor Daniel Koretz disagreed. "We know that we are creating, in many cases, with our test-based accountability system, illusions of progress." A key reason, he said, is "If you tell people that performance on that tested sample is what matters, that's what they worry about, so you can get inappropriate responses in the classroom and inflated test scores. . . . There is nobody involved in this system who has an incentive to look for good instruction anymore."[67]

Even with disagreements persisting, a few points seem clear given the patterns of student achievement that researchers discovered. A few findings possess near unanimous, if not unanimous, support from those who have examined NCLB and its potential effects on student achievement. First, despite some suggestive evidence that student achievement increased, it is doubtful that students were uniformly learning rich and interesting content that pushed them to think deeply about important topics and issues, as the discussion in Chapter 5 suggested. Second, even if one agrees that achievement gaps narrowed, the remaining gaps were large and still worrisome, as Figures 6.1 and 6.2 showed. Third, nearly all achievement gains tended to be concentrated in the elementary school grades. High achievement at those levels did not necessarily translate into similar performance as students progressed through middle school and into high school. Finally, even if student achievement continued to increase on state tests at rates discovered as of 2009, only a very small number of states would meet NCLB's goal of having 100 percent of students proficient in reading and math by 2014. Among the twenty-seven states with consistent tests and accountability expectations in 2009, continued growth in 4th-grade achievement at typical rates would mean that only three states would meet the 100 percent goal by NCLB's deadline.[68] Overall, while some observers celebrated gains and agreed that NCLB's incentives altered classroom practices (sometimes for good and sometimes for ill), nearly everyone agreed that much work remained for the nation to have educational equity and excellence for all students.

7

Federal Leadership and the Future of Educational Accountability

Presidents Barack Obama's inauguration on January 20, 2009, may have been a historic day for the United States, but it was also a workday on Capitol Hill. After the inaugural events, the Senate convened for business at 3:00 P.M. and in moving through the day's agenda confirmed Arne Duncan as the nation's ninth secretary of education. Like Rod Paige, President George W. Bush's first education secretary, who formerly had been superintendent in Houston, Duncan came to Washington after having led another large urban school system, that of Chicago, from 2001 to 2008. In contrast, whereas Paige began his work with the Elementary and Secondary Education Act (ESEA) reauthorization bursting from the starting blocks—on President Bush's second day in office, he announced his plan to leave no child behind—reauthorizing the overdue ESEA was neither Duncan's nor the Obama administration's first priority. Rather, during 2009 and into early 2010, the new president focused on advancing an economic stimulus package, developing a revised strategy for American military efforts in Iraq and Afghanistan, and reforming the nation's health care system.

Despite the president's packed agenda, one fact about education policy was clear as Obama began his term. The success of future federal education reforms would depend on learning smart lessons from the implementation of the No Child Left Behind Act (NCLB) and incorporating that knowledge into policy. True learning, though, would require more than simply scrutinizing facts, figures, and compelling stories that NCLB's implementation had generated. In addition to knowing those details, Obama and his team also would have to study carefully the theories of action that motivated NCLB's authors in the first place. Tweaking a requirement on teacher quality, funding school restructuring at higher levels, or making other changes could perhaps improve implementation in some measurable sense. But if the problems were more fundamentally rooted in the law's basic assumptions, then improvements might require something different altogether.

Prior chapters have considered NCLB from several perspectives. Those include the vantage points of system leaders in federal and state government bureaucracies and of local decision makers, especially principals and classroom teachers. Such views provide diverse angles for assessing NCLB's theories of accountability and administration, its specific mechanisms, and the collisions it initiated across the American federal system. The law's track record also provides insights into possible roles the federal government might play in future efforts to hold schools accountable for educational results. After briefly discussing how the Obama administration attempted to pivot from NCLB with its own proposals, this concluding chapter examines in detail some of the broader lessons and principles that NCLB's implementation suggests about accountability and the future of the federal role in American schools.

OBAMA REVEALS HIS EDUCATION PRIORITIES

Although matters other than education occupied most of Obama's attention during 2009 and early 2010, Secretary Duncan's rhetoric and actions did begin to reveal the administration's education priorities. Most of the secretary's initial work was devoted to distributing nearly $100 billion in federal aid for education. Congress approved those funds on February 13, 2009, as part of Obama's $787 billion stimulus package, formally known as the American Recovery and Reinvestment Act (ARRA), designed to jumpstart the struggling American economy. The size of the education portion of the stimulus was unprecedented. It was nearly double the entire federal education budget during the previous two years combined.

Early implementation of the education stimulus suggested to some reform-minded advocates that the federal government was unwilling to aggressively push needed changes. The complaints flowed primarily from analyses of the state and local activities that the bulk of the education stimulus money, approximately $60 billion, supported.[1] Critics asserted that the funding, which started flowing in the spring of 2009, was merely saving current jobs and plugging holes in state and local budgets, rather than leveraging urgent reform initiatives.[2] With the federal Education Department holding several billions of dollars of potential influence, critics wondered why it failed to demand more for its money.

Despite the critics' frustrations, the inability of the early rounds of the stimulus package to prompt deeper reforms also made sense for at least two reasons. First, competing goals within the package itself challenged state and local administrators to meet the reformers' demands for substantive changes while simultaneously using the money swiftly to prompt economic recovery. As one state official put it, a tension existed between "getting the money out quickly and spend[ing] it effectively on long-term efforts." [3] Few concrete ideas existed for how to administer those activities equally well, especially given the fiscal turbulence and low morale that state and local education leaders were trying to manage during the economic downturn.

Second, criticizing Duncan and his team for sidestepping needed reforms was partially unfair because it blamed Education Department bureaucrats for problems that Congress helped to create. The law that governed distribution of the $60 billion noted earlier limited the secretary's ability to influence state and local actions, given that formulas dictated where most of the stimulus money would go.[4] Further, although states were required to use stimulus dollars to support action in several broad reform areas, arguably, state and local actions to meet NCLB's continuing requirements and activities already on their agendas were designed to serve many of these goals.[5] Supporting ongoing actions that were generally consistent with the stimulus' requirements may have frustrated those who disliked prevailing approaches, but Duncan had limited power to force more dramatic efforts.

Still, the secretary did possess important discretion to assert federal priorities using a smaller but still consequential part of the stimulus package known as the Race to the Top (RTTT) fund.[6] While most education dollars in the stimulus package were allocated through congressionally determined procedures, the $4.35 billion in this fund were different. Those dollars were not simply a large pie that formulas would divide equally among the fifty states.[7] Rather, states competed for a slice, and Duncan wielded ultimate authority in selecting the winners. Thus, while small in comparison with the overall stimulus, RTTT represented the largest-ever federal education grant that an education secretary had discretionary power to distribute.

The rules governing RTTT were published on November 18, 2009, and advanced four specific priorities. States competing for the money were to show how they would support (1) efforts in the development of internationally benchmarked academic standards and student assessments; (2) teacher and principal recruitment, development, and retention; (3) construction of state systems that would link data on student success to information about teachers and school practices; and (4) efforts to turn around the nation's lowest-performing schools. Interested states were offered two phases to apply for RTTT grants. One deadline came on January 19, 2010. The second was for states that either chose not to apply or failed to win a grant in phase one; the phase two application deadline was June 1, 2010.

For both phases the federal Education Department recruited panels of experts to evaluate the states' applications. Those reviewers used thirty specific criteria and a defined point system to score the state proposals. A total of 500 points was possible, and state scores were ranked from best to worst. The top applicants, based on a cutoff score that Duncan and his staff identified, were invited to Washington to make formal presentations to the expert reviewers and federal education officials. Based on the scoring process and the presentations, Duncan decided the winners and the grant amount each winner received.

Up until the phase one deadline, Duncan emphasized that the competition would be difficult and the losers would outnumber the winners. "Just watch," he noted in explaining the high bar that successful proposals would have to clear, "people will be stunned by what we do."[8] Among the forty-one applicants for phase one awards, sixteen were identified as finalists in March and invited to present their proposals in Washington. Of those sixteen only Delaware and Tennessee eventually won phase one grants. Phase two had thirty-five applicants and nineteen finalists. The following ten winners were named in late August: the District of Columbia, Florida, Georgia, Hawaii, Maryland, Massachusetts, New York, North Carolina, Ohio, and Rhode Island. In both phases, Duncan named winners based on the reviewers' scores, choosing not to use his discretion to award grants to other lower-scoring applicants.

Although technically RTTT was separate from the ESEA, observers across the country used RTTT scoring criteria to infer the direction Obama and his team would take in the next ESEA reauthorization, which was still stalled through the summer of 2010. Federal education officials agreed that was the proper way to see the fund. For example, Duncan called RTTT "a huge start" but still "just an opening act." Others affirmed that the reauthorization would build on the key areas emphasized in the overall education stimulus package, and the RTTT criteria, in particular.[9]

In Secretary Duncan's first major speech on the ESEA reauthorization, which he delivered on September 24, 2009, he assessed NCLB and the nation's overall educational progress since the ESEA had become law, in 1965.[10] Duncan began by restating the common view that Americans believe education to be "the one true path out of poverty—the great equalizer that overcomes differences in background, culture and privilege" and "the only way to secure our common future in a competitive global economy." In that brief passage the secretary reaffirmed the need to promote educational equity and excellence. Among Duncan's criticisms of NCLB, he highlighted one as most important. "The biggest problem with NCLB," he said, "is that it doesn't encourage high learning standards. In fact, it inadvertently encourages states to lower them. The net effect is that we are lying to children and parents by telling kids they are succeeding when, in fact, they are not. We have to tell the truth, and we have to raise the bar."

Six months later, on March 13, 2010, the Obama administration released its ESEA reauthorization proposal. Titled "A Blueprint for Reform," the plan was similar to President Bush's NCLB proposal in that it was a narrative explanation of priorities, goals, and proposals, rather than a specific bill ready for introduction in Congress.[11] The blueprint kept the administration's promise that it would build on the expectations and assumptions of the RTTT competition. Specifically, the blueprint identified five priorities, which Table 7.1 summarizes.

First, the proposal aimed to support the development of common college- and career-ready standards across the states. Those standards would drive the development of improved assessments. In turn, the revised state assessments would measure whether students were learning rigorous material, chart growth in achievement, and encourage the use of research-based instruction. This first priority built on the RTTT's goal of nudging states to identify a common package of rigorous expectations that they could use to evaluate their schools. It also represented a major break with NCLB, which simply required each state to develop its own standards but did not demand consistency across the states.

The push for consistency attempted to leverage work that the states themselves had begun in 2008. Known as the Common Core State Standards Initiative, this effort was led by the National Governors' Association and the Council of Chief State School Officers, which represents state education agency leaders. All but two states (Texas and Alaska) joined the initiative. The initiative aimed to make state academic standards more consistent and ambitious by working with state leaders and other organizations.[12] In implicitly linking the ESEA proposal to the work of the Common Core, the Obama administration hoped to encourage more uniformity and rigor, yet inoculate itself from political criticism that the administration was advancing "federal standards" and therefore threatening state and local control of education.

The second priority in Obama's blueprint was to guarantee that all schools would have great teachers and principals. This priority contained elements similar to NCLB by supporting the equitable distribution of these key school members and aiming to improve teacher and principal recruitment, especially in the neediest schools. On the other hand, the second priority broke with NCLB by pledging to support the development of "highly effective" rather than simply "highly qualified" teachers. Highly effective teachers would be defined and rewarded by states and districts, in part, by their ability to improve student achievement, not only by their accumulation of credentials and demonstrated expertise in their subjects.

The focus on performance was also consistent with expectations in the RTTT competition. In that contest, state applicants needed to show how they would design data systems and performance expectations that would facilitate analyses of how teachers and principals had contributed to growth in student achievement. Duncan foreshadowed this preference in remarks during 2009 by arguing, "Teacher evaluation in this country is fundamentally broken. In a country where teacher evaluation is divorced largely from student progress, student success, how do you defend that?"[13]

Third, the blueprint aimed to ensure educational equity and opportunity. Paralleling NCLB's provisions regarding student subgroups, the goal was to ensure that all students were included in state accountability systems and were

Table 7.1. President Obama's ESEA Reauthorization Blueprint

1. College- and career-ready students
   - Develop and adopt common state standards in English-language arts and math that guarantee all students will be prepared for college and a career.
   - Develop better assessment systems to promote academic rigor, measurement of student growth, and improved classroom instruction.
   - Ensure that students receive a well-rounded education, with models of instruction supported by evidence of effectiveness.

2. Great teachers and leaders in every school
   - Design systems to identify and reward effective principals and teachers based on student growth and other factors.
   - Guarantee equitable distribution of effective teachers and leaders across all schools.
   - Improve pathways for preparing and recruiting new teachers, especially for high-need schools.

3. Equity and opportunity for all students
   - Include all students in accountability systems, reward progress and success, and offer flexibility while requiring dramatic interventions in the poorest-performing schools.
   - Provide all of the nation's diverse learners with appropriate instruction and challenging curriculum.
   - Ensure that high- and low-poverty schools have comparable resources to guarantee equity.

4. Raise the bar and reward excellence
   - Continue Race to the Top initiative for states and expand the program to involve individual school districts.
   - Support effective public school choice.
   - Promote a culture of college readiness by expanding access to college-level, dual-credit, and other accelerated high school courses.

5. Promote innovation and continuous improvement
   - Use the Investing in Innovation (i3) fund to scale up successful programs.
   - Support, recognize, and reward local innovations by creating fewer, more flexible federal funding streams, including more competitive programs.
   - Tackle persistent achievement gaps by engaging communities and families to ensure that students are safe, supported, and healthy.

Note: Summarized from U.S. Department of Education (2010a).

provided access to appropriate, challenging instruction. States would have some flexibility to meet the equity and opportunity goals, but more specific and dramatic interventions would be required in the worst-performing schools. The latter requirement paralleled NCLB's language for schools in corrective action and restructuring (see Table 2.2). It also extended elements of the RTTT fund, which had required states to show how they would implement one of four reform models—turnaround, restart, school closure, or transformation—for these most challenged schools. Ensuring equity and opportunity also meant, the proposal declared, that high- and low-poverty schools should have comparable resources.

The fourth priority was to raise expectations and reward excellence. This priority made explicit reference to RTTT, explaining that the fund would be continued for states and also enlarged to allow school districts to apply directly for a share of the money. Also paralleling RTTT was the discussion of expanding public school choice. Among other forms of choice, the proposal noted support for the development of more public charter schools, a reform model that, given the high variability in charter school performance, had prompted some discussion and controversy when similar language was included in RTTT. Interestingly, the administration's proposal abandoned the public school choice provisions as well as supplemental educational services that NCLB required for schools in improvement.

The fifth and final priority focused on promoting innovation and continuous school improvement. To advance that effort, the administration promised to invest in successful programs and expand them so more students could benefit. One way to finance such efforts, the blueprint stated, was to consolidate several individual federal education programs into fewer, larger, and more flexible funding streams. Although not specifically identified, some of those streams would be distributed through grant competitions that would likely parallel the RTTT contest. A last element of this priority recognized that eliminating persistent achievement gaps would require engaging communities and families to guarantee the nation's students were safe, supported, and healthy. The assumption was that students lacking those basic needs would have much difficulty achieving in school.

Initial reactions to the administration's blueprint ranged from supportive to cautiously optimistic to openly hostile, including major criticism from the nation's two largest teacher unions, the National Education Association (NEA) and the American Federation of Teachers (AFT).[14] Some union members felt betrayed, after having worked hard to help Obama win the White House. They wondered whether the president was simply taking their support for granted without attending to their concerns, especially about linking teacher evaluations to student performance. How much students learn, they argued, is affected by many factors beyond a teacher's control.

Secretary Duncan defended the administration's ESEA proposal in a congressional hearing on March 17, 2010. He anticipated future success with the Obama administration's approach, given that adopting the proposed comprehensive reforms would be "one of the most dramatic changes in the law's history. It will fundamentally change the federal role in education. We will move from being a compliance monitor to being an engine for innovation."[15] Students of recent history were likely not surprised by those sentiments, given that nearly every ESEA reauthorization proposal had been advanced with similar optimism. A decade earlier, as Chapter 2 described, President Bush had promised that NCLB would put the nation's schools on a new path of reform that would ensure better outcomes. In another parallel, the blueprint's promise to have all American students ready for college or careers by 2020 looked just as ambitious as NCLB's requirement that all students be proficient in reading and math by 2014.

Initial reactions to Obama's ESEA blueprint were one thing, but how the proposal would fare in the legislative process was quite another. During 2009 and 2010, the rambunctious debates over health care reform suggested that building a political coalition on Capitol Hill to pass the ESEA reauthorization would be challenging. Throughout 2009 and into 2010, the Republican leaders in Congress, who were the minority party in the House and Senate, worked to keep their members in line in opposing Obama's initiatives. Measured in terms of the dollars involved, the ESEA was less significant than the economic stimulus or health care reform, yet the issue was still a top concern for millions of voters. Those included teachers, members of the business community who had been stalwarts in the standards movement, and parents who expressed concerns over the increasing focus on standardized tests.

As Obama released his blueprint and Duncan defended it on Capitol Hill, several new variables also compounded the administration's political challenges. Although Representative George Miller, a major architect of NCLB and chair of the House education committee, would lead Democratic efforts in the House, the 2009 death of Senator Edward Kennedy, who had been a major broker of all federal education policy dating to the 1960s, meant that the Democrats had lost one of the most skilled and tenacious members of their legislative team. In addition, Republican leadership and membership of the House and Senate education committees had also shifted, bringing in many new members since 2001. Major shifts also existed within the ranks of the all-important committee staff on both sides of the political aisle. Nearly all staff assigned to work on the ESEA reauthorization were new to that task, having had other positions when staff and members developed NCLB. Finally, looming not too far in the distance were the 2010 midterm elections. The time needed for campaigning and fund-raising, not to mention the new political calculations that election seasons bring, would all intersect to influence the ability of Obama, Duncan, party leaders, and rank-and-file Democrats and Republicans to develop an ESEA reauthorization bill with enough support to pass.

TAKING STOCK

As a value guiding public policy and administration, accountability has gained an almost cultlike following in governments around the world. NCLB, RTTT, and the Obama administration's ESEA blueprint all embraced approaches intended to promote collisions with prevailing practices by ensuring accountability for educational results. Driving such support have been perceptions that government bureaucracies will underperform without measurable objectives and consequences for poor performance. Accountability systems are supposed to create desired results through their potential to disrupt, reorient, and refocus unimportant agency priorities and improper tasks while preserving effective practices.

In the years after NCLB became law, this latest ESEA reauthorization created collisions that reverberated across the country. Elected officials in Washington crafted the law to promote accountability for increasing achievement and eliminating gaps between student groups. Lacking a robust administrative capability to remake schools on their own, federal leaders borrowed the capacity of state and local government bureaucracies to do the heavy lifting required to realize those grand ambitions. In exchange for federal education aid, state and local implementers needed to design accountability systems consistent with NCLB's mandates. But because these implementers were not blank slates, and because they defined critical tasks using their own values and professional judgments, it was no wonder that federal ambitions would sometimes collide with the prerogatives driving people working in state and local institutions.

Federal leaders intended those collisions to occur, in fact. After decades of federal assistance through the original ESEA and its various reauthorizations, the law's main objectives remained unfulfilled. In demanding substantive results, not just procedural ones, federal leaders reasoned that if NCLB delivered a major disorienting jolt to state and local institutions, then so be it. The point of accountability under the law was not to guarantee that adults remained comfortable, but to ensure that children were learning.

As previous chapters have shown, NCLB's collisions sparked many reactions in states and local communities. The law's overall objectives enjoyed near unanimity. It is hard to imagine an argument challenging the belief that all students should achieve at high levels and that success in school should be unrelated to one's ethnic background, family income, language spoken at home, or disability status. NCLB's methods and mix of incentives, flowing from its theories of accountability and administration, were another story altogether. While opinion polls and anecdotes suggested that criticisms were more common than praise, reactions were not uniformly negative. Overall, as the following discussion explains, NCLB prompted both transformative and potentially destructive collisions.

In broad terms NCLB's collisions with state and local institutions produced at least three positive results. First, the law pushed state and local education officials, principals, and teachers to focus more intensely on the achievement of disadvantaged students and gaps between student groups. Simply supporting programs to serve disadvantaged students' needs was no longer enough. As Secretary Duncan argued in praising the law, "I will always give NCLB credit for exposing achievement gaps, and that we measure our efforts to improve education by looking at outcomes, rather than inputs." [16] Similarly, as Chapter 6 showed, teachers of English-language learners, even while sometimes complaining about the law's requirements, admitted that their students received more attention than ever before because of NCLB. Parents and advocates for students with disabilities could use NCLB's requirements as a powerful lever to demand that these students receive rigorous academic experiences, as would their nondisabled peers, not simply access to public schools that failed to challenge them. Summing up these views, Adam Gamoran, an educational sociologist at the University of Wisconsin, has argued that "the big success of No Child Left Behind so far is to galvanize attention to the challenges we face, particularly the challenges of inequity." [17]

A second positive result from NCLB's implementation was that it forced state and local education bureaucracies to improve their technical capabilities. That was true for staff in state education agencies, school districts, and individual schools. Certainly, such technical progress varied, yet improvements did exist and have the potential, if used wisely in the future, to help improve students' academic experiences.

Chief among the technical improvements were advances in the collection and use of data. NCLB's numerous reporting requirements for adequate yearly progress (AYP) and teacher quality revealed that many states possessed antiquated and disconnected systems, which prevented them from tracking and integrating sometimes even basic information about their students and teachers. Although progress was slow in some states, most acknowledged that their systems had improved since 2001. Even in the area of teacher quality, where Chapter 3 showed that NCLB implementation was generally anemic, a Department of Education survey in 2006–2007 found that thirty-nine states reported possessing better data systems because of NCLB's influence. Those improvements included developing the capabilities to track teachers and their qualifications and to ensure that data were accurate and sufficiently detailed. Such changes can serve many purposes, among them measuring the spread of teaching talent across a state, crucial information that provides a basis for addressing inequities in teacher distribution.[18]

Improved capabilities also manifested themselves at local levels. Teachers received more training in using data to identify their students' academic weak spots and to develop lesson plans that addressed these weaknesses. Interestingly, as Chapter 5 explained, local data use typically relied less on state test results and much more on intermediate or formative assessments. Although the quality of those formative assessments varied, they provided teachers and other school staff with launching pads for discussing such important matters as the progress of individual students and the design of lesson plans.

Beyond using data, the AYP requirement to assess all students and track achievement in reading and math also pushed schools and districts to help teachers collaborate more to meet their students' academic needs. Complaints about

AYP notwithstanding, the evidence does suggest it was a catalyst in several schools for constructing systems to bridge gaps between regular classroom teachers and their peers who teach special education or who instruct English-language learners. Collaborating with their colleagues helped teachers in traditional classrooms develop a keener sense of how to reach these unique student populations, while the latter two groups of teachers became more adept at using their specialized training to help students learn substantive course content.

Third, in states and communities that embraced NCLB, the law provided policy entrepreneurs with valuable political cover. In short, NCLB served as a ready excuse to push through sometimes difficult, but necessary, policy and administrative changes. Perhaps these changes would have occurred anyway, without NCLB, because a defining characteristic of policy entrepreneurs is that they work doggedly to advance the causes that inspire them.[19] Still, these advocates for change, working inside and outside government, found NCLB to be quite helpful for providing a needed push or sometimes even a "fall guy" to blame when they advanced difficult decisions that upset prevailing interests. For example, Chapter 4 profiled the case of Kalamazoo, Michigan, principal Kevin Campbell, who urged his local superintendent to wield the powers that NCLB provided so that he could remedy his school's broken culture.

Reenergizing a struggling cause was one way that some advocates for students with disabilities interpreted NCLB's influence in their field. Even though reforms to the Individuals with Disabilities Education Act (IDEA) had required states to consider academic outcomes for students with disabilities, those requirements languished until NCLB came along and incorporated the disabled subgroup into AYP calculations for schools and districts. That policy decision and the ensuing changes it sparked even led some disabilities advocates to conjecture that NCLB may have done more than IDEA to advance these students' academic fortunes.[20] Although IDEA was instrumental in helping students with disabilities gain access to traditional public schools, many still suffered from stereotypes that claimed they could not learn rigorous material. In forcing schools to monitor the achievement of students with disabilities, NCLB enabled many such students to prove the stereotypes wrong.

Local school advocates also found cover with NCLB's ambitious objectives, in particular its demand for universal student proficiency in reading and math. The law's critics and even some of its supporters believed that demand was unrealistic. Admittedly, it would be difficult for a politician to justify supporting less-than-universal proficiency, because such a view would implicitly suggest it would be all right to leave some children behind. Objectively speaking, however, it was unrealistic to expect that the goal of universal proficiency could have been realized for the entire nation.

But locally some schools proved the skeptics wrong by coming close or actually meeting the universal proficiency goal. When those success stories occurred in seemingly unlikely places, such as Capitol View Elementary in Atlanta (see Chapter 4), it helped to bolster the claims that advocates for disadvantaged students had made for years—namely, that the evidence proved how students can overcome seemingly impossible barriers of poverty and other disadvantages when they encounter high academic expectations and work with energized teachers, principals, and staff. That does not mean the work is easy, nor does it suggest that NCLB generated these results widely in disadvantaged schools across the nation. Nevertheless, some schools working in otherwise desperate circumstances did rise to the academic challenges that NCLB created. In so doing, the results they produced collided with prevailing assumptions about which students were poised to excel.

Alongside the positives, NCLB collided with state and local institutions in unproductive and even destructive ways. Those impacts undermined the law's principal objectives and other worthy homegrown goals of state and local education officials. They also sowed frustration among politicians, advocates, parents, and public administrators at all levels. The evidence suggests two broad and significant problems arising from the implementation of NCLB.

First, NCLB's specific requirements created incentives for states and local districts to alter practices in ways that decreased academic quality. That does not mean that state policymakers, local officials, and school staffs consistently embraced academic rigor for all students before NCLB became law; there was much room to improve based on the state of American education in early 2001. Nevertheless, ample evidence shows that after that year, NCLB's levers and incentives seemed to push expectations down rather than up. Individual communities and schools that maintained high expectations did so by acting against numerous incentives that led others in the opposite direction. Although devoting serious attention to the academic prospects of disadvantaged students was long overdue, and NCLB rightly deserves credit in this area, the law seemed to direct state and local education officials to make explicit trade-offs between equity and academic excellence for all students.

Meeting NCLB's universal proficiency requirement in reading and math posed a dilemma for states. On one hand, the demands of adulthood and citizenship in the shrinking twenty-first-century world required students to learn rigorous content and valuable habits of mind during their elementary and secondary school years. Meeting such expectations would enable the nation's learners to enjoy future success in college, their communities, and the workplace. If states designed standards and exams with that level of performance in mind, then schools would face huge challenges in getting all students to achieve at proficient levels or better by NCLB's 2014 deadline. As a result, states would likely see only a small number of schools consistently meet AYP. In turn, states and school districts would have to manage the remedies and offer the potentially costly assistance that NCLB required for schools in improvement status.

On the other hand, one way to avoid having large numbers of schools miss AYP was to water down state expectations so that more students would achieve proficiency.[21] Thus, large numbers of schools would avoid entering improvement status, which would alleviate the implementation burdens confronting states and districts. It would also allow states and districts to concentrate resources on the schools in most dire need of assistance. With lighter academic demands, states could certify that students were proficient in reading and math, but substantively that would mean little if expectations were low. By and large states chose relatively lower expectations, which blunted the collisions that NCLB's authors had hoped to create.

The law's focus on meeting proficiency targets to satisfy AYP created other incentives that collided with practices designed to push all students to the highest levels of achievement. Such a focus on getting students over the proficiency bar had negative effects at both ends of the achievement spectrum. Consider the case of students who were so advanced that they could have earned a proficient score even before the school year began. Ironically, students with strong mastery of reading and math could actually perform less well as they moved from 3rd through 8th grade, and schools would still get credit for a job well done if the students' scores nevertheless remained above the proficiency line. In the process, encouraging students to strive for excellence was undermined.

Making most of a school's AYP calculation contingent on whether a specified percentage of students across subgroups scored at proficient levels each year also created bad incentives for schools where many students were far behind. In such a school, although students might have made fantastic progress, the school still could miss AYP if that progress did not get enough students over the proficiency bar. For example, in a school where all students were reading three years below grade level, rigorous instruction that enabled them to catch up two years' worth of material in a single year would not be rewarded, because the students still would have been below proficiency expectations.

Further, as Chapter 4 discussed, schools could demonstrate major gains among all subgroups but one, and that would be enough to miss AYP. There was no intermediate ranking or designation for such schools. A high-poverty school that missed AYP because one subgroup performed below expectations in either reading or math received the same label and faced the same consequences as another high-poverty school in which all subgroups performed too low in both subjects.[22] The law contained no provisions to differentiate between schools missing AYP by a lot and those missing it by only a little.

The failure to distinguish between such schools had important consequences on the ground. Schools missing AYP were commonly called "failing," even though NCLB's advocates and the law itself rejected the term in favor of "needing improvement." That labeling and the required changes in schools consistently missing AYP made it difficult for districts and principals to recruit excellent teachers. When schools missed AYP, it also challenged these leaders to keep morale high among current staff, especially in schools that may have worked wonders to produce dramatic achievement gains—sometimes having students leap multiple grade levels of achievement in a single year—that nevertheless still showed disadvantaged youngsters falling below the state's grade-level expectations. According to many such teachers and principals, NCLB's authors seemed to devalue that sort of legitimate academic progress.

A second harmful collision that NCLB created was that the law caused concerns over procedural bureaucratic requirements to mushroom, despite promises from the law's advocates that it would stress substantive outcomes, such as increasing student achievement and decreasing achievement gaps. As a result state and local education officials spent much time showing how they had complied with those procedural expectations. That was a safe strategy, for, as James Q. Wilson has observed, high performance does not always generate praise for government agencies, but public administrators typically can avoid formal reprimands or controversy when they do one thing well: follow the rules.[23] Despite the stated intent of NCLB's authors to emphasize substantive outcomes rather than administrative processes, compliance-oriented behavior persisted.

In state education agencies across the country, the process of designing accountability plans to meet NCLB's requirements consumed literally thousands of hours. As state plans took shape, federal Education Department officials and their assistants considered the state proposals to determine where plans were strong and weak. Almost as soon as the Department of Education approved these plans, and concrete implementation started unfolding, states began proposing changes. Those adjustments—which some observers interpreted as evidence of legitimate policy learning and others viewed as states' attempts to blunt the law's collisions from forcing real changes—required additional submissions and approvals from federal overseers. When approved, the changes cascaded down the delegation chain as state agencies communicated revised roles, responsibilities, and expectations to local districts and schools. Ironically, sometimes the increased flexibility that materialized after federal officials approved state changes or adjusted regulations actually complicated the work of school district officials. Every change from above, which did not always come with helpful explanations or technical assistance, demanded new local efforts to understand the substance of the changes and then to revise bureaucratic routines accordingly.

State and local agents sometimes calibrated their responses to NCLB's requirements by taking cues from the signals of their federal principals. Investing more in implementation of those areas where federal overseers paid the most attention bolstered claims that NCLB had not prompted a national movement to leave no child behind, but rather a bureaucratic shuffle to comply with some aspects of the law while sidestepping others, if possible. As Chapter 4 showed, for example, when it became clear that state fulfillment of all the law's highly qualified teacher provisions was a low priority for federal Education Department leaders, states essentially failed to develop rigorous equity plans to guarantee that disadvantaged students would have access to excellent teachers. Even when states could report that teachers in a high percentage of classes met NCLB's teacher quality standards, some teacher quality advocates lamented that state expectations were so low that compliance, per se, did not necessarily mean that excellent teachers staffed all the nation's classrooms.

At the local level, a drive to comply with NCLB's AYP requirements led schools to focus on increasing test scores in reading and math. In some places, that prompted what NCLB's advocates had hoped to see: school principals, teachers, and staff searching for creative ways to offer challenging academic programs, while simultaneously ensuring that students were prepared to succeed on state reading and math tests. Yet in many places, especially the nation's most disadvantaged communities, NCLB's advocates were disappointed. The need to raise students to proficiency led schools to adopt other strategies that focused on meeting bureaucratic requirements and undermined the law's broader objectives.

State testing requirements and AYP expectations spawned negative aspects of teaching to the test that taught students to memorize trivial facts and learn narrowly applicable test-taking strategies, rather than pushing them toward broader understanding and deep critical thinking. Those instructional strategies often struck school officials as a safer approach for complying with the law's requirement to increase the percentage of students scoring at proficient levels or better each year. Amid all of the bureaucratic busyness that NCLB's collisions sparked, evidence from the National Assessment of Educational Progress (NAEP), specifically results from the main NAEP for 4th and 8th grades (presented in Chapter 6), showed that achievement gains remained at best on their pre-NCLB trajectory. And further, those NAEP results and state tests themselves also showed that gaps in achievement between student subgroups remained large.

NCLB'S POLICY THEORIES IN PRACTICE

Revisiting the policy theories that motivated NCLB's authors is one way to begin considering how the federal government might promote accountability for educational results in the future. As Chapter 2 explained, NCLB embraced two theories of action. The law's theory of accountability was grounded in the view that schools would improve if governments measured their performance, made the results transparent, and confronted poorly performing schools and districts with tough consequences. Its theory of administration recognized Washington's limited ability to engineer such an approach in the American federal system. Therefore, the theory favored giving state governments the lead administrative role in organizing and managing accountability systems. A crucial point regarding administration was that NCLB's authors left states to decide what students needed to know and be able to do and how well they needed to demonstrate their knowledge and skills.

Federal leaders and NCLB's supporters believed that the law's theories of action and its principal levers would help students accomplish two goals. Students would learn more valuable content in reading and math, and achievement gaps between student groups would narrow. In short, supporters believed that based on NCLB's theories of action, the law would promote educational excellence and equity.

Policy theories ultimately succeed or fail not based on the elegance of their presentation but on how well they perform in the real world. In NCLB's case, the bulk of the evidence shows that there were major gaps between what the law's theories proposed would happen and how implementation unfolded at federal, state, and local levels. Although NCLB created positive momentum and inspiring results in some states and local communities, overall its theories of action were fundamentally in conflict with the institutional landscape on which American schooling operates. That conflict prevented NCLB from realizing the grandest ambitions of its authors and from avoiding problems that plagued prior ESEA reauthorizations.

The general tendency of states to lower academic expectations and rigor was a devastating blow to NCLB's prospects for success. In responding to NCLB's mandates, state accountability systems produced results that struck many observers, elected officials, and public administrators as invalid measures of school performance. As Secretary Duncan noted in the opening passage of this chapter, given the level of expectations, it was a lie to assert that children were truly learning. Despite some examples from earlier chapters that proved exceptions to Duncan's overall conclusion, the balance of opinion and evidence supported his view.

According to public administration scholars, such a lack of confidence in results will prevent accountability systems based on performance from accomplishing their substantive goals. These scholars have shown that such systems ultimately will fail when interested individuals, especially those subject to the system's requirements, lack confidence in the information, metrics, and results used to assess performance. As William Gormley and David Weimer have argued in their comprehensive analysis of organizational report cards, "Although we have emphasized the importance of six criteria in evaluating report cards, we believe that validity is of special importance. An invalid report card may have an impact on organizational behavior, but that impact may very well be dysfunctional." [24] Donald Moynihan has echoed and extended that sentiment. While arguing that several factors influence the effectiveness of performance management systems, "the key challenge," he notes, "is fostering performance information use" and, in particular, use by administrators in government agencies. [25]

If agency administrators lack faith in performance measures, then they will be unlikely to use them to inform their actions. Instead, they will rely on other information.[26] During NCLB's implementation, state agency officials and local school personnel who criticized AYP results while praising the metrics from their homegrown state accountability systems illustrated this tendency. Those arguments were perhaps not surprising in light of Beryl Radin's observation that "it is not easy to craft a strategy for performance measurement activity that addresses the tensions surrounding the intergovernmental system." When multiple layers of government are involved, she explained, "[o]ne of the most vexing problems in the performance area involves the availability of 'good' data—data that have been verified and can be believed to be valid by all parties to the relationship." [27]

The problem of invalid measures in systems promoting accountability for performance is by no means unique to elementary and secondary education. The scholars quoted above have offered general principles that can inform the design of intergovernmental accountability systems in numerous other policy areas. The particular case of NCLB is informative for those larger efforts because it reveals what can happen when theories of action clash with real-world realities and ensuing concerns over the validity of accountability measures become paramount. In education some knowledgeable observers believe that those concerns and the nation's experience with NCLB risk undermining the entire educational standards movement.[28] Shifting away from accountability-based approaches would certainly bring joy to some people, who believe that the effort to define standards and measure performance is anathema to the larger purposes that schools are supposed to serve. But those who reject standards entirely are a small minority. Even many of the most vocal critics of NCLB are not necessarily anti-standards but simply believe the law was an inappropriate attempt to use standards to drive results.[29]

In addition to the question of whether test results were valid measures to guide improvement, also consider problems that emerged based on NCLB's assumptions regarding federal, state, and local administrative capacity. The policymakers who drafted NCLB believed that with support from the federal Education Department, state and local administrative capacities would be sufficient to implement the law and, as a result, promote educational equity and excellence. In practice, states and local school districts encountered great difficulties managing NCLB's myriad requirements given their own capabilities and the assistance they received from the Education Department.

In this context "support" includes many things beyond simply providing adequate financial resources. Indeed, as prior chapters have shown, implementers and some members of Congress complained that federal budgets for NCLB fell way below what was required. Even if one leaves aside the debate over whether NCLB was adequately funded, other dimensions of support were noticeably weak. When considering the day-to-day activities of public administrators in state education agencies, local school districts, and individual schools, perhaps even more valuable than additional funds would have been greater clarity and better federal guidance about how to implement the law.

Shifting expectations, lengthy delays in offering states feedback, and sometimes conflicting advice depending on which federal administrator a state official happened to encounter compounded the complex environment in which state and local education officials worked. In such settings, as political scientist Bryan Jones has argued, public administrators will seek solutions that make their cognitively challenging workloads more comprehensible, manageable, and politically defensible, which can prevent innovative or needed policies from seeing the light of day.[30] NCLB's focus on negative incentives for public bureaucracies that failed to achieve even limited goals—remember that schools would miss AYP unless students were "proficient," not "advanced"—accentuated the tendencies that Jones has described. If the negative consequences vastly outnumber the positive ones, then public administrators likely will be even more risk averse in their behavior. An alternative approach containing penalties for failure but also rewards for success could have altered this administrative equation.

Finally, even robust federal financial support would have been inadequate to bolster the capacity deficits that states encountered when they turned to private testing companies to help them develop and score state assessments. The bureaucratic race toward easily scored tests with low expectations was at least partially a result of financial limits in state budgets, the implementation schedule that NCLB defined, and the fear among state system leaders that standards that were too demanding would cause far too many schools to miss AYP. But equally significant were the limited capabilities of testing companies, which struggled to help states develop the hundreds of tests needed across the country. With state administrative capacities stretched and testing companies overwhelmed, it was no wonder that states shied away from developing rigorous, challenging, and interesting assessments within NCLB's mandated time frames. Again, with federal process requirements commanding that all states offer math and reading tests in prescribed grades, but with no federal expectations about the content or rigor of these tests (except that they be aligned with state standards), it was no wonder, as James Q. Wilson would say, that powerful circumstances drove state education officials toward choices that undercut educational equity and excellence yet still were consistent with the rules.[31]

Notwithstanding the positive effects of NCLB discussed earlier in this chapter, the law's theories of action and its specific levers combined during implementation to produce low expectations and an intense focus on bureaucratic processes over substantively valuable outcomes. By leaving states to define content and performance standards for students, yet simultaneously requiring them to adopt a prescribed accountability framework (i.e., the AYP system), administrators in the federal Education Department could not escape the process-oriented focus that critics believed had undermined previous ESEAs. The same dynamic unfolded in the area of teacher quality. NCLB left states to decide what quality meant but compelled them to meet certain bureaucratic requirements. Administratively, the required capacity to implement NCLB was simply more than federal, state, and local governments, as well as the nation's testing industry, possessed. In short, NCLB's theories of accountability and administration were fundamentally in conflict with the institutional landscape on which American education operates.

Despite NCLB's shortcomings, overall support for reforms based on educational standards remains high, as the Obama administration's RTTT and ESEA reauthorization proposals have shown. More generally, across policy areas the energy behind the performance movement in the public sector reveals no signs of losing steam. Since the early 1990s, states have invested hundreds of millions of dollars and thousands of hours in standards-based accountability systems to try to improve results. Given those trends, it is worth considering how to refashion a federal role in education that could leverage the standards movement while simultaneously simplifying administration, avoiding perverted incentives, and promoting educational equity and excellence. The next section offers some closing thoughts on how one might craft a federal role in education to advance those objectives.

FEDERAL LEADERSHIP AND EDUCATIONAL PERFORMANCE

The disconnect that existed between NCLB's theories of action and the policy world that implemented the law revealed many weaknesses in the federal government's ability to promote accountability for meaningful educational results. Still, the law's track record and the longer historical performance of the ESEA dating back to 1965 do show that the federal government can be a valuable player in advancing the nation's educational goals. The main challenge in moving ahead is to focus federal action in areas where the government is positioned to succeed and to steer clear of the common failure modes that have too often fostered administrative busyness or confusion but not substantively valuable results.

Based on its historical record of involvement in K–12 education and the more recent experience derived from NCLB's implementation, what strengths could the federal government bring to future efforts in education that would improve results for the nation's students? At least five federal strengths seem apparent.[32] First, federal leaders possess a powerful platform to highlight pressing issues and to help the country set broad aspirational goals. The proliferation of traditional and new media outlets and the need to fill airtime on round-the-clock television and radio programs provide leaders in Washington with more opportunities than ever to transmit messages to the nation. Those numerous outlets give them a powerful voice to help citizens recognize the gravity of compelling national problems in education, be they the lack of educational opportunities for students with disabilities that existed prior to IDEA, the persistence of gaps in opportunity and achievement for the nation's most disadvantaged students, or the need to help push the nation's highest performers to new heights.

Second, the federal government is uniquely positioned to redistribute valuable resources to address state and local needs and, in turn, influence the content of policy. The promise of resources in exchange for following federal mandates has been an effective carrot, especially in areas with deep poverty and a lack of equal opportunities. And the evidence shows that money talks. According to political scientist Gerald Rosenberg, for example, a major engine prompting school desegregation in the South was federal grant programs whose dollars exerted a "powerful and attractive force on segregated schools."[33] More recently, despite state and local criticisms of NCLB, no state formally refused federal assistance in order to avoid the law's consequences. States' efforts to refashion certain education policies to position themselves to win RTTT funds also illustrate the influence of federal dollars quite clearly.[34] As Figure 1.1 showed, federal funds cover only a small fraction of national K–12 education expenditures, but that money provides important flexibility on the margins of state and local budgets, especially given that these governments, in contrast with the federal government, typically cannot run budget deficits. Especially when economic times are tough, as they have been for a number of years during NCLB's implementation, states and local communities rely quite heavily on federal education dollars.

Third, the federal government is capable of creating incentives that alter behaviors on the ground. Beyond simply urging action from the bully pulpit or offering money to encourage policy changes, the record shows that federal policies and money can influence courses of action in school districts and classrooms. The trick, of course, is to ensure that federal efforts avoid creating confusing incentives that confound policy implementers or direct them into unproductive behaviors. The creation of perverse incentives proved to be one of NCLB's major problems. As economist Diane Whitmore Schanzenbach put it, in one sense the law did seem to be working because "people are responding to the incentives under NCLB right now." The problem, she suggested, was that "some of the incentives are bad."[35]

Fourth, the federal government is effective at gathering or forcing into the open information about pressing needs, important trends, and useful educational practices. As a collator and publisher of educational data that provide a broad array of indicators about American education, the federal government has no peer. Further, unlike state and local governments, which use education budgets for operational and capital expenses, federal dollars can also seed potentially valuable research studies. Findings from those reports help develop a knowledge base about potentially promising initiatives that others can try to replicate and adapt to their own circumstances.

A related but slightly different contribution federal leadership can make is to force behaviors that promote greater transparency among state and local governments that administer education. The requirement that all states participate in NAEP testing is one concrete illustration that came out of NCLB. Additionally, the law also forced individual schools and districts to be more forthcoming about their students' performances and the resources, especially concerning teaching, that individual schools possessed. Clearly, there were major problems with the AYP metrics, as the prior discussion about validity illustrated. Still, the principle of providing people with more information for evaluating the nation's public schools was, and remains, one that the federal government should continue to affirm.

Finally, taken together, the previous four federal strengths coalesce to produce a fifth one, which is worth identifying explicitly. By using the bully pulpit, offering resources, creating incentives, and making relevant information widely available, the federal government can create conditions that enable state and local reformers to promote needed changes. To reiterate a point made earlier in this chapter, although NCLB produced some destructive collisions, in some places it also emboldened committed educational leaders, teachers, and parents who, with the law's help, pushed for needed changes that improved the lives of thousands of children. Those successes are indeed commendable, and they provide evidence showing that federal policy can help cultivate conditions that propel rather than undermine effective educational changes. But it would be folly to construct federal policy relying on such better angels among us. In choosing between hoping that people do the right thing and offering them incentives that strongly encourage them to do so, policymakers should always favor the latter.

Moving from those five strengths into specific federal policies that create educational accountability systems will depend on several technical and political factors. Different programs of action are possible that could build upon the federal government's comparative advantages. If crafted in light of Washington's strengths and weaknesses, such a federal role could help state and local governments focus their energies on boosting educational achievement and decreasing achievement gaps, instead of being mired in bureaucratic process requirements that undermine rather than enhance the validity of performance measures.

The policy choices that members of Congress, President Obama, and future officeholders make will be conditional on how they and their constituents in states and localities engage several crucial questions. Some questions, such as "What defines a good education?" or "What is educational excellence?" are perhaps unanswerable in any objective sense. Disagreements will always persist, yet they still beg examination because doing so can help to define the ways in which the federal government could contribute. The country may never agree on what precisely defines educational excellence, but through serious discussion and debate a consensus might emerge over what role the federal government should play in helping to ensure excellence in the various ways that people might define it.

In moving forward from NCLB, another set of questions involves the degree to which the country should accept educational differences across the nation's thousands of schools and school districts. How much variation in educational expectations and opportunities for students should the nation tolerate? If citizens agree that more uniformity should exist—for example, all schools should have high expectations and provide students with rich learning opportunities—would they also be willing to make the investments and institutional changes required to limit the current variation that exists across the country? The matter of how much variation is tolerable is perhaps the elephant in the living room that the nation has not seriously attempted to address. Doing so would require people to think deeply about the structure of American federalism and its influence on results.

During NCLB's implementation, a major criticism that emerged was over state variability in educational outcomes and other measures of quality. Some states claimed to have rising student achievement, but the results must have been due to low expectations, critics asserted, because other states with historically more effective educational systems did much worse. Further, states could demonstrate that large numbers of students had high-quality teachers in the classroom, but, as Chapter 5 showed, some states demanded much more than others in fulfilling NCLB's highly qualified teacher provisions. That such cross-state differences would exist was perhaps a foregone conclusion the moment that NCLB's authors decided to let states define the substantive content of key outcomes, such as the level of knowledge required for students to make proficiency in reading and math or the methods by which teachers would demonstrate that they knew their subjects.

Based on the criticisms of NCLB that have surfaced, many people seem to agree that too much variation is unacceptable. In saying that results are too variable, Americans implicitly are suggesting that they have in mind some universal standard leading them to conclude that students in some states are learning too little and teaching talent is more equitably distributed in some states than in others. If Americans and their leaders believe that too much variability in expectations prevents the country from achieving educational equity and excellence, then on its face it would seem that the federal government should play a more aggressive role in promoting educational accountability. But deciding to embark on such a path without recognizing the limits of the federal government's strengths in education would be a recipe for re-creating the same problems that flowed from NCLB.

Perhaps the most direct way to more uniformly keep expectations high across the country would be for the federal government to embrace a uniform set of rigorous academic standards and expectations. It could then rely on states and localities to develop the proper mix of policies and administrative routines to ensure that students achieve at those high levels. Such a strategy would be more consistent with what advocates of liberation management, discussed in Chapter 2, have favored. In that approach leaders at the top set key substantive goals, turn loose policy implementers to design bureaucratic processes to achieve them, and then measure the results and hold implementers accountable for their performance.

Setting tough standards and unleashing states and localities to meet them would be more consistent with liberation management and would reverse the inverted approach that NCLB's authors crafted by letting states define substantive goals while having the federal government specify the required procedures. However, the nation's tradition of state and local control over school curriculum, which Chapter 1 explained, provides a large political barrier preventing that approach. Even Secretary Margaret Spellings recognized as much in admitting, during 2007, "I'm not sure people want me to be the person setting standards for their schools." [36] The Obama administration's RTTT fund and ESEA blueprint implicitly agreed. While both encouraged the states to adopt common, uniform, and rigorous standards, they refrained from having the federal government manage or oversee such an effort.

Regardless of whether the states reach greater agreement over what students should know and be able to do, in the foreseeable future members of Congress, the president, and the federal Education Department will continue to rely heavily on the policies, financial and administrative capabilities, and judgments of states and local school districts to implement federal education policies. Crafting a new role that better recognizes the constraints limiting federal power in education could enable federal policy to make valuable contributions. With such an acknowledgment, the vast majority of influence over the nation's schools would still reside in state and local governments. No doubt, that would prove frustrating to reformers who wish to see Washington play a more aggressive role and who have witnessed states and localities make past choices that seem to undermine equity and excellence.

Still, if educational results, not the administrative details, are most important, then it should not matter if federal leaders or their colleagues at other levels of government wield the most power. The point would be to engineer federal advocacy, funding, incentives, and information to help state and local governments improve opportunities and results for the nation's students. The specific policies that emerged from such a process could take many forms. Federal policymakers working in concert with state and local representatives who would be responsible for administering federal initiatives would need to engage in frank and difficult discussions to work out the details and engineer the required political compromises.

An honest recognition of federal limits and an attempt to strategically leverage state and local strengths would be preferable to a different approach, which has tended to dominate the legislative process since the first ESEA became law. Simply put, such an approach would be to ignore or downplay fundamental questions about federalism, educational governance, or administrative capabilities. Further, it would involve passing new versions of the ESEA with revised requirements, perhaps even generous funding, and continued federal demands that states and local communities guarantee equitable educational opportunities and greater academic excellence. In short, with such an approach federal leaders would continue to demand results and accountability but essentially ignore the crucial institutional or administrative realities that ultimately determine success.

Proceeding down such a path would likely re-create the same frustrations over process and invalid outcome measures that NCLB produced. It would also continue the tradition of requiring the adoption of accountability systems that serve primarily symbolic and political ends but do little to help agency administrators or school officials manage their activities to encourage high performance.[37] Sadly, after that effort ran its course, the country likely would be several billions of dollars poorer but no closer to eliminating educational inequities or guaranteeing academic excellence than when it started.

Systems of accountability can enjoy success when they overcome several technical, administrative, and political hurdles, but success also requires another key ingredient—confidence. Just as a nation's currency is valuable only if people believe it is a trustworthy means of exchange, accountability systems need to inspire confidence to persist and ultimately succeed. People subject to accountability provisions in education (such as school and district personnel) and others who rely on the results of accountability systems to inform their decisions (parents, elected officials, and overseers in state and federal bureaucracies) must believe that the system's judgments are accurate, intellectually honest, reliable, and fair and that they promote valuable outcomes. The judgments must also inform real-world, not hypothetical, choices, which was a major problem with NCLB's school choice provision. That option may have sounded good in theory, but in many communities it did not amount to a real choice for students owing to limited or no transfer options. Properly conceived, federal policy can help support educational equity and excellence.

When federal policy theories become too divorced from administrative realities and the implementation environments in which programs take shape, promoting real accountability that serves positive ends becomes harder to achieve. That potential difficulty is true of all policy areas, not just education, as prior research and classic works have shown. In their important study of Great Society economic development programs, for example, Jeffrey Pressman and Aaron Wildavsky revealed several reasons why noble federal ambitions are often dashed when they collide with difficult realities on the ground.[38] What Pressman and Wildavsky demonstrated was not that federal initiatives are always doomed, but rather there are conditions, often predictable, under which success or failure is likely to emerge. An essential task for federal policymakers in any area, then, is to think carefully about federalism, institutions, politics, and administrative conditions and then design accountability systems that enhance prospects for success. Recognizing the reality that the American system of educational governance and administration is likely to remain fragmented and diverse is crucial for conceiving a federal role that can produce transformative rather than destructive collisions.

Notes

Chapter 1

1. The full text of Obama's inaugural address is available from the White House Web site at www.whitehouse.gov/blog/inaugural-address/.

2. Baumgartner and Jones (1993); Kingdon (1995); Skowronek (1997).

3. Spellings's quotes are available from the U.S. Department of Education's archived Web site at www.ed.gov/news/photos/2007/0917/edlite-0917_1.html.

4. For additional treatments of the importance of administrative capacity in education, see Manna (2006b), Cohen and Moffitt (2009), and Kaagan and Usdan (1993).

5. Rothstein, Jacobsen, and Wilder (2008, Chapter 1); Tyack and Cuban (1995); Perkinson (1991).

6. Kaestle and Smith (1982); Manna (2006b); Davies (2007).

7. National Commission on Excellence in Education (1983).

8. Quoted from Chapter 2 of *A Nation at Risk*. Available from the U.S. Department of Education's archived Web site at www.ed.gov/pubs/NatAtRisk/risk.html.

9. For a summary of the critics' claims, see Berliner (1995).

10. Manna (2006b, pp. 99–104). The national education goals are available on-line at http://govinfo.library.unt.edu/negp/.

11. Educational Testing Service Policy Information Center (1990).

12. Manna (2008, p. 6).

13. Ravitch (2001); Manna (2006b); Graham (1984); Cross (2004).

14. Ravitch (2001). See also Cross (1979).

15. U.S. Department of Education (1993a and 1993b). Readers should recognize that Title I of the original ESEA was renamed "Chapter 1" during the 1980s and early 1990s, until 1993, when it again was called Title I.

16. General Accounting Office (2000); U.S. Department of Education (2001).

17. The Education Trust (2004).

18. U.S. Department of Education (2007c); Magnuson (2008); Manna (2008).

19. U.S. Department of Education (1993a, p. 48).

20. Manna (2008); Jennings (1998); Cross (2004).

21. Reviews of the literature are in Wayne and Youngs (2003), Haycock (2004), Goe and Stickler (2008), and Ravitch (2004).

22. Haycock (1998).

23. Brownstein (2002).

24. The program that the ESEA absorbed was the Eisenhower Professional Development Program, which had been part of the Education for Economic Security Act of 1984. For background on the Eisenhower program, see Manna (2008).

25. U.S. Department of Education (1999b), (1999a), and (1998).

26. Cohen (2002).

27. The remaining 4 percent did not know. Survey by Phi Delta Kappa and the Gallup Organization, June 14–July 3, 2008. iPOLL Databank, Roper Center for Public Opinion Research, University of Connecticut (www.ropercenter.uconn.edu/data_access/ipoll/ipoll.html).

28. The remaining 9 percent either did not know, did not answer, or offered some other answer. Cited in Hochschild and Scott (1998, p. 98).

29. Hanushek and Lindseth (2009); Evans, Murray, and Schwab (1997).

30. National and state-level school and district counts cited in U.S. Department of Education (2008a), downloaded from http://nces.ed.gov/programs/digest/d08/tables/dt08_087.asp.

31. On the concept of policy venues, see Baumgartner and Jones (1993).

32. Many works have examined the politics of education at federal, state, and local levels. Examples include Sundquist (1968), Wirt and Kirst (1997), DeBray (2006), McGuinn (2006), Manna (2006b), Davies (2007), Henig (2004), Henig et al. (1999), and Wong et al. (2007). For the views of practitioners working in the national political arena, see Bell (1988), Jennings (1998), and Cross (2004).

33. Petrocik (1996).

34. For research on teacher unions and their influence, see Hannaway (2006), Koppich (2005), Moe (2006), Loveless (2000), and Radin and Hawley (1988).

35. Timpane and McNeill (1991); Wirt and Kirst (1997); DeBray-Pelot (2007)

36. Haycock (2001); The Education Trust (n.d.).

37. Hess and Finn (2007).

38. Kahlenberg (2008).

39. McKluskey (2007).

40. National Conference of State Legislatures (2010).

41. Meier and Wood (2004).

42. Tyack and Cuban (1995).

43. Light (1997).

Chapter 2

1. Jacobson (2008); McCarty, Poole, and Rosenthal (2006). See also relevant updates from Keith Poole at http://polarizedamerica.com.

2. The quotes are from Gorman (2001b). Excellent discussions of Kress's background and his relationship with Bush, which these passages draw upon, appear in Gorman (2001a) and EdNext (2007).

3. Gorman (2001b).

4. Manna (2006b, Chapter 6).

5. Useful accounts of the congressional political dynamics are available from Rudalevige (2003), McGuinn (2006), Manna (2006b), and Gorman (2001a).

6. Jeffords (2001).

7. EdNext (2007, p. 33).

8. White House Office of the Press Secretary (2002).

9. The entire law is Public Law 107–110. It is available on-line at www.ed.gov/policy/elsec/leg/esea02/index.html.

10. Mathematically: $(10\% \times 40) + 40 = 44$.

11. Percentages were calculated based on data from U.S. Department of Education (2008a, Table 87), which provided the total number of schools and school districts, and U.S. Department of Education (2009d, pp. 17 and 20), which allowed for computation of the number of Title I schools and Title I school districts.

12. Hess and Petrilli (2006, p. 73).

13. The law also included requirements that classroom teacher aides in Title I schools were highly qualified. Requirements for these aides were less rigorous than for classroom teachers but still involved a combination of credentialing (in this case having at least two years of college and at least an associate's degree) and demonstration of subject matter knowledge in reading, writing, or math (depending on the subjects in which the aide assisted) and knowledge of how to teach those subjects as well. All new aides hired in Title I schools were required to meet these standards; veteran aides had until 2005–2006 to meet them.

14. Pressman and Wildavsky (1984); Stone (1989); Weiss (1998).

15. Pressman and Wildavsky (1984).

16. Wilson (1989); Moe (1989).

17. Wilson (1989).

18. Gormley and Weimer (1999, p. 1).

19. Gormley and Weimer (1999, p. 23).

20. Gormley and Weimer (1999, pp. 134–137). Moynihan (2008, p. 36) discusses a slightly different, but related, version of external and internal relationships in his examination of measurement and performance management. He argues that measuring an organization's performance can enhance external accountability, which he considers the relationship between government officials and the public. It can also promote internal accountability, which involves the relationship between bureaucrats (e.g., school and agency officials) and elected officials (e.g., school board members, legislators, and chief executives, such as mayors, governors, or even presidents).

21. Walton (1986); Senge (1990); Moynihan (2008).

22. See Radin (2006, p. 4) for the quote. She notes on pp. 4 and 7 that education is one of the key areas where these ideas have been tried.

23. See Radin (2006, chapter 2).

24. A classic example is Osborne and Gaebler (1992). See also Light (1997), his discussion of "liberation management."

25. The Education Trust (2004).

26. Hess (2003).

27. Miller (1992); Bendor (1988); Bendor, Glazer, and Hammond (2001); Moe (2006).

28. The student might, however, suffer some consequence or earn some reward based on state law. That distinction between the expectations of NCLB and those of the states will emerge in more detail in later chapters.

29. Clotfelter and Ladd (1996). See also Chubb and Moe (1990).

30. For a related distinction between market and governmental approaches to accountability and policy administration, see Strach (2007), which describes the potential for families to be "hidden administrators," implicitly charged with policy implementation. That is in contrast with the formal and explicit role government bureaucracies and civil servants often play.

31. Ravitch (1995).

32. For examples of the NCTM's work on math standards, see www.nctm.org/standards/.

33. Information on the African-centered curriculum in Detroit is available at http://africancentered.detroitk12.org/.

34. Manna (2006b).

35. Wilson (1989).

36. Light (1997).

37. Moynihan (2008); Wilson (1989); Pressman and Wildavsky (1984).

Chapter 3

1. The initial claim from Paige's staff that this was the first meeting of its kind, as well as ensuing quotes from the speech, are from Paige (2002).

2. Zelman quote is from Olson (2002). Other chief quotes are from Danitz (2002).

3. Olson (2002).

4. NCLB implementation occurred in the District of Columbia and Puerto Rico, in addition to the fifty states.

5. General Accounting Office (2002, p. 3).

6. Olson (2002).

7. Ibid.

8. Ibid.

9. General Accounting Office (2003b).

10. Hoff (2004).

11. Olson (2002).

12. Hoff (2004).

13. Goertz (2005).

14. Robelen (2003b).

15. Ibid.

16. Hoff (2004).

17. Goertz (2005, p. 79).

18. For examples of the critics, see Lewin (2007), Wiener (2006), and The Education Trust (2003b).

19. Information on the NAEP, including results and examples of test questions, is available at http://nces.ed.gov/nationsreportcard/.

20. Associated Press (2006).

21. Gordon (2006).

22. National Center for Education Statistics (2007).

23. Center on Education Policy (2007a, 2008b).

24. Cronin et al. (2007).

25. Borsuk (2003).

26. Lusi (1997); Manna (2006b).

27. For a general discussion of state capacity challenges, see Goertz (2005) and National Conference of State Legislatures (2001).

28. Henriques (2003); Dillon (2003a).

29. General Accounting Office (2002).

30. General Accounting Office (2002, pp. 3–4).

31. McNeil (2006); "Test scores released . . ." (2007).

32. Manna (2007, pp. 21–22). See also Government Accountability Office (2004c).

33. Olson (2006).

34. Olson (2002)

35. Government Accountability Office (2006b, p. 5). Additional evidence on supplemental educational services implementation appears in Center on Education Policy (2007d) and U.S. Department of Education (2008b).

36. Hoff (2009).

37. Milbank (2002); Robelen (2002).

38. Schemo (2002).

39. Manna (2006a, p. 480).

40. Associated Press (2003).

41. Manna (2006a, p. 480).

42. The quote is from Robelen (2003a). See also Salzer (2003).

43. White House Office of the Press Secretary (2003).

44. U.S. Department of Education (2003).

45. Manna (2006a, pp. 485–487).

46. A complete list of the thirty-one elements is in Government Accountability Office (2004c, pp. 43–44).

47. Manna (2006a).

48. The Education Trust (2003a, p. 1).

49. The Education Trust (2003b, p. 4).

50. General Accounting Office (2003a, p. 29).

51. Government Accountability Office (2005).

52. Government Accountability Office (2005, p. 44).

53. The two quotations appear in U.S. Department of Education (2009c, pp. 31–2).

54. Jones (2001); Wilson (1989).

55. Manna (2006c).

56. Dillon and Schemo (2004); Paige (2004a).

57. Spellings (2005).
58. Spellings (2007).
59. Business Roundtable (2005).
60. Goldstein (2004). Secretary Spellings eventually issued additional regulatory changes governing alternative assessments and special education students. Those changes are discussed in detail in Chapter 6.
61. Associated Press (2004b).
62. Associated Press (2004a).
63. U.S. Department of Education (2005). See also Hoff (2005).
64. U.S. Department of Education (2005).
65. Gewertz (2005).
66. Hickok (2008).
67. "Sweeping program cuts . . ." (2005). See also Hoff (2007a).
68. Kingdon (1995).
69. Manna (2006b).
70. Center on Education Policy (2004b).
71. Klein (2007).
72. Alpert (2008).
73. See McNeil (2007) on governors, National Conference of State Legislatures (2005) on state legislative positions, and Hoff (2006) on chiefs. On the impacts of the sluggish economy on NCLB implementation, see Dillon (2003b), McNeil (2008), and Government Accountability Office (2009a).
74. Quotations from letter are from Paige (2004b). The quotation before the school boards group is from Center on Education Policy (2004b, p. 8).
75. Government Accountability Office (2004d, p. 4).
76. See Walsh (2009) regarding the court's decision to rehear the case. The appeals court *en banc* decision is U.S. Court of Appeals for the Sixth Circuit. *School District of the City of Pontiac, et al.,* Plaintiffs-Appellants v. *Secretary of the United States Department of Education,* Defendant-Appellee (No. 05–2708). Argued December 10, 2008, decided and filed October 16, 2009.
77. Weisman and Paley (2007).
78. Paley (2007).
79. Fagan (2007).
80. Baker (2007).
81. Ibid.
82. Quotes from Clinton and Devine appear in Dillon (2007).

Chapter 4

1. Background on Capitol View appears in Chenoweth (2007).
2. Test results are from the Georgia Department of Education, located at www .doe.k12.ga.us/. To see the results, follow the link for "Adequate Yearly Progress," which provides school-level results.
3. Chenoweth (2007, p. 166).

4. The case of T. C. Berrien and quotes from McLeod come from Winerip (2003d).

5. The school's improvement was not enough to satisfy NCLB's safe harbor provision for AYP, which Chapter 2 discussed.

6. Pressman and Wildavsky (1984).

7. Tyack and Cuban (1995). See also Lipsky (1980).

8. Government Accountability Office (2004c) contains examples from actual state accountability system plans. This report also explains (p. 18) that NCLB required states to set their starting points—the initial AYP expectation in the first year—based on state test score results from 2001–2002, the year before NCLB took effect.

9. Hoff (2008b).

10. Popham (2003).

11. Olson (2003).

12. Data in this paragraph are from the Center on Education Policy (2004a, pp. 56–57).

13. Although 2002–2003 was the first year that NCLB was in effect, it was still possible at that time for schools to have missed AYP requirements for two years or more. The reason was because NCLB built its requirements on top of the previous requirements from its predecessor law, the Improving America's Schools Act (IASA). That iteration of the Elementary and Secondary Education Act (ESEA) also required states to have schools demonstrate AYP, but it based those calculations on slightly different requirements. Therefore, a school missing AYP under the IASA's rules and then missing it under NCLB's rules would become a school in need of improvement. See Chapter 2 for discussion of the differences between IASA and NCLB.

14. Numbers for 2007–2008 and 2008–2009 are based on reports from forty-seven states and the District of Columbia. They come from Hoff (2009) and EPE Research Center (2008a, 2008b, and 2008c).

15. Hoff (2009).

16. See Kane and Staiger (2001) and Kane, Staiger, and Geppert (2002). A more technical presentation of these ideas appears in Kane and Staiger (2002).

17. Kane, Staiger, and Geppert (2002, p. 58).

18. For examples of state n-sizes and this debate, see Government Accountability Office (2004c) and Klein (2006).

19. Kane, Staiger, and Geppert (2002, p. 58); Meier and Wood (2004); Sunderman, Kim, and Orfield (2005).

20. Mathematically, $0.90^2 = 0.81$, or an 81 percent chance, and $0.90^6 = 0.53$, resulting in a 53 percent chance. These calculations assume that one group's performance on a test is independent of another group's performance.

21. This is a major theme in Meier and Wood (2004).

22. LeTendre (n.d.); Rothstein, Jacobsen, and Wilder (2008); Meier and Wood (2004)

23. The Education Trust (2004, p. 1).

24. Gormley and Weimer (1999); Radin (2006); Moynihan (2008).

25. U.S. Department of Education (2006); Manna (2008).

26. The 7 and 19 percent figures are from U.S. Department of Education (2006); the 17 percent figure is from U.S. Department of Education (2008b); the 20 to 23 percent figure is from Manna (2008) and Borja (2007); under 15 percent comes from Hoff (2008a). Studies have conjectured that the recent decline in participation is likely due to the inability of the number of approved supplemental educational services providers to keep pace with the growing number of schools that have entered improvement status and have been required to offer students these services.

27. Sunderman (2007).

28. See examples cited in RAND (2009), and Government Accountability Office (2004b) and (2006b).

29. Hess and Finn (2007); RAND (2009).

30. Both quotes are from Borja (2007).

31. See examples cited in RAND (2009), Government Accountability Office (2004b) and (2006b).

32. Hoff (2008a).

33. Manna (2007, pp. 24–25).

34. U.S. Department of Education (2006, p. xviii).

35. Hannaway and Cohodes (2007). Another choice program also existed for students with disabilities.

36. Examples of the overcrowding issue in New York City are discussed in Winerip (2003c, 2003b, and 2003a).

37. Manna (2007, p. 27).

38. DeBray (2005, p. 182).

39. One study, U.S. Department of Education (2007b), found no effects of choice but cautioned that small sample sizes were a major factor limiting inferences from the study.

40. U.S. Department of Education (2008b).

41. For a collection of reviewed studies, see Manna (2008, p. 14), Sunderman (2007, p. 6), and the July 2, 2009 entry on Debbie Viadero's education research blog at *Education Week,* http://blogs.edweek.org/edweek/inside-school-research.

42. U.S. Department of Education (2007b).

43. Sunderman (2007, p. 6).

44. The GAO's numbers are from Government Accountability Office (2007, p. 19), and the *Education Week* numbers are based on my calculations from data in EPE Research Center (2008b).

45. Government Accountability Office (2007, pp. 3–4).

46. Center on Education Policy (2008a).

47. Center on Education Policy (2008a, p. 9).

48. Schemo (2007).

49. Government Accountability Office (2007, p. 22); Manna (2007, p. 37).

50. Center on Education Policy (2008a, p. 10).

51. Ibid., p. 23.

52. Kowal and Hassel (2007). In this same study the authors described similar restructuring efforts at Balboa Elementary School in San Diego. Balboa's effort also

"resembles standard school improvement efforts, with its emphasis on professional development and reorganizing instructional time. Leadership, governance, and the school's policy environment have remained largely constant" (p. 277).

53. Ibid., p. 274.

54. Government Accountability Office (2007, p. 23).

55. Ibid., pp. 28–29.

56. Center on Education Policy (2008a, p. 10).

57. See, for example, Turque (2009).

58. Kowal and Hassel (2007, p. 281).

59. Ibid., pp. 280–281.

60. For discussion of the restructuring debate, see Mead (2007) and Center on Education Policy (2008a).

61. Center on Education Policy (2008a, p. 12).

62. Government Accountability Office (2007, pp. 24).

63. Schemo (2007).

64. Both state officials quoted in Manna (2007, pp. 39–40).

65. What NCLB requires is from Government Accountability Office (2007, pp. 9–10); the 42 percent figure appears on p. 5. See also U.S. Department of Education (2006) on schools receiving limited assistance from districts during 2003–2004.

66. Center on Education Policy (2008a, pp. 25–26).

67. Manna (2007, p. 40).

68. Manna (2007, p. 38); Maxwell (2006).

69. Kowal and Hassel (2007, p. 287).

70. Hannaway and Rotherham (2006).

71. Cited in Manna (2006c, p. 167).

72. Kowal and Hassel (2007, p. 280).

73. Many arguments are summarized in Hannaway and Rotherham (2006). The NEA and American Federation of Teachers (AFT) have published numerous articles and studies defending their positions, many of which are available on the unions' Web sites at www.nea.org/home/NoChildLeftBehindAct.html and www.aft.org/issues/schoolreform/nclb/index.cfm, respectively.

74. Center on Education Policy (2008a) and Government Accountability Office (2007) both conclude this.

75. Government Accountability Office (2007, pp. 30).

76. Hoff (2009).

77. Jimerson (2005, p. 4).

78. Data are for the 2006–2007 school year. Percentages were computed by the author using data from the Common Core of Data, http://nces.ed.gov/ccd/bat/.

79. Robelen (2005).

80. McNeil (2009).

81. Tonn (2007).

82. Center on Education Policy (2008d, pp. 9–10). Based on a survey of districts with at least 200 students, this study found that large percentages of rural districts had too few students who were black (78 percent of districts), Asian (87 percent),

Hispanic (69 percent), Native American (82 percent), or English-language learners (69 percent) to have their scores count toward AYP in reading, but 77 percent had enough students with disabilities and 84 percent had enough who were from low income families. The percentages were similar for AYP ratings on math tests.

83. Government Accountability Office (2004a, p. 13).

84. Ibid., p. 18.

85. Tonn (2007). On the profit motive of SES providers as a limit, see also Government Accountability Office (2004a, 2006b).

86. The quote is from Clements (2007, p. 242). Colorado's case is briefly discussed in Medler (2007, p. 243). See also Rural School and Community Trust (2006).

87. Center on Education Policy (2008d, pp. 15–17). The math difference was statistically significant at the p<.01 level. Regarding NCLB's school choice option, rural districts were less likely to rate it as important or very important for reading (3 versus 7 percent) and math (5 versus 7 percent), with both differences being statistically significant at the p<.01 level. The low p-values mean that these differences were likely to have been real, not illusory.

88. McNeil (2009).

89. General issues on recruitment and retention of teachers in rural areas appear in U.S. Department of Education (2007d), Government Accountability Office (2004a), and Center on Education Policy (2008d).

90. Government Accountability Office (2004a, pp. 26–7).

91. Ibid., pp. 18–23.

92. These two formula grants are the Targeted Grants to Local Educational Agencies and the Education Finance Incentive Grant Program, which are described in Section 1125 and Section 1125A of NCLB, respectively.

93. Strange, Johnson, and Finical (2009, p. 9). See also Rural School and Community Trust (2007).

94. See Title VI of NCLB. See also U.S. Department of Education (2007a) for a good description of the program.

95. On support for REAP, see National Rural Education Advocacy Coalition (2009). On general implementation, see U.S. Department of Education (2007a).

96. Quotation is from McNeil (2009). See also Richard (2005) for similar complaints during Bush's time in office.

97. Lipsky (1980); Wilson (1989); Pressman and Wildavsky (1984); Jones (2001). See also Tyack and Cuban (1995).

Chapter 5

1. Unless otherwise noted, this quote and others from Mullen come from his application for National Teacher of the Year, located on-line at http://programs .ccsso.org/proj ects/national_teacher_of_the_year/national_teachers/13292.php.

2. This reference to children as stories comes from Mullen's speech at the White House on April 28, 2009; see White House Office of the Press Secretary (2009).

3. White House Office of the Press Secretary (2009).

4. Lipsky (1980).

5. Data on the number of teachers are in U.S. Department of Education (2008a), available from http://nces.ed.gov/programs/digest/index.asp.

6. Levine (2006).

7. Ravitch (2004).

8. Hannaway and Rotherham (2006). A comprehensive collection of teacher contracts is available from the National Council on Teacher Quality; www.nctq.org/tr3/search.jsp.

9. These requirements and others are nicely summarized in plain language in U.S. Department of Education (2009c).

10. On some of the debates over HOUSSE, see Petrilli (2005) and Feller (2006)

11. Center on Education Policy (2007b, pp. 1–3).

12. U.S. Department of Education (2009d, p. 45).

13. Figures for 2007–2008 based on author's analysis of Part I of the Consolidated State Performance Reports, 2007–2008 school year. See www.ed.gov/admins/lead/account/consolidated/index.html.

14. U.S. Department of Education (2009c, p. xxv). See also Center on Education Policy (2007b) for discussion of difficulties special education teachers have faced.

15. U.S. Department of Education (2009c, p. 140).

16. Ibid., pp. 52–3.

17. Ibid., pp. xxx–xxxi.

18. Ibid., p. 59.

19. Ibid., pp. 48–49.

20. Ibid., pp. 32–33.

21. Ibid., pp. 48–49.

22. Ibid., pp. xxvi–xxviii.

23. For a summary of several dozen studies, see Goe and Stickler (2008) and Wayne and Youngs (2003). See also Government Accountability Office (2009d, p. 4) and U.S. Department of Education (2009d, pp. 43–44) for more concise discussions of the literature.

24. U.S. Department of Education (2009d, p. 44).

25. Commonly, three or four course hours equals one class. U.S. Department of Education (2009c, p. 15).

26. U.S. Department of Education (2009c, pp. 139–140). See also McClure, Piché, and Taylor (2006).

27. Wilson (1989).

28. The main points in this paragraph are summarized from Wilson (1989).

29. Radin (2006); Gormley and Weimer (1999).

30. Hernandez (2009). The students succeeded, and the principal fulfilled her end of the bargain.

31. Rothstein, Jacobsen, and Wilder (2008, p. 195).

32. Mathews (2006).

33. See, for example, Resnick, Stein, and Coon (2008, p. 129).

34. Currently, perhaps the most eloquent proponent of this position is E. D. Hirsch. See, for example, Hirsch (2009).

35. Toch (2006, p. 17).

36. Ibid., p. 15.

37. Finn and Ravitch (2007).

38. Rothstein, Jacobsen, and Wilder (2008, p. 187).

39. Toch (2006, p. 13).

40. Government Accountability Office (2009a); Toch (2006).

41. Merrow (2007); Ash (2008).

42. Chenoweth (2007, p. 217).

43. Ibid.

44. Ibid., p. 185.

45. Ibid.

46. Kanstoroom and Osberg (2008); Marsh, Pane, and Hamilton (2006); Data Quality Campaign (2007).

47. Hoff (2007b).

48. Chenoweth (2007, pp. 217–218).

49. Information on DIBELS is available at https://dibels.uoregon.edu/. Critics of DIBELS, cited in Manzo (2005), suggest that it focuses on speed and repetition but not comprehension, and further that it suffers from important validity problems.

50. Marsh, Pane, and Hamilton (2006, p. 5).

51. Ibid.

52. See, for example, Chenoweth (2007, pp. 92–93).

53. Resnick, Stein, and Coon (2008, pp. 128–129).

54. Marsh, Pane, and Hamilton (2006, pp. 3 and 11).

55. Rothstein, Jacobsen, and Wilder (2008, pp. 46 and 186).

56. Quotations from Yarbrough are from Rothstein, Jacobsen, and Wilder (2008, p. 198).

57. Rothstein, Jacobsen, and Wilder (2008, p. 198).

58. Ibid., p. 46.

59. O'Connor and Hamilton (2008).

60. Rothstein, Jacobsen, and Wilder (2008, p. 47).

61. Ibid., p. 184.

62. Ibid., p. 50.

63. Toch (2006, p. 17).

64. Center on Education Policy (2008c, p. 2), but see U.S. Department of Education (2009d, p. 28) for a cautionary note on these results.

65. U.S. Department of Education (2009d, pp. 27–28).

66. Sunderman, Kim, and Orfield (2005, pp. 91–93).

67. This approach to integrating the curriculum is not always accepted. For instance, John Perry, a 4th-grade reading and writing teacher in Florida explained, "A couple of summers ago, a team member and I worked hard to integrate social

studies into our language arts teaching. But our principal said, 'We won't be focusing on social studies; we will focus only on the FCAT test content.' " Cited in Rothstein, Jacobsen, and Wilder (2008, p. 195).

68. Details in this paragraph about Osmond Church come from Achievement Alliance (2007).

69. Rothstein, Jacobsen, and Wilder (2008); Merrow (2007); Finn and Ravitch (2007).

70. Finn and Ravitch (2007).

Chapter 6

1. Angelica's story, including this quote, comes from Wood (2004, pp. 33–34).

2. The two quotes in this paragraph are from Wood (2004), pp. 33 and 34, respectively.

3. Background on Eric's case comes from Seitz (2009) and Brugger (2009).

4. Seitz (2009).

5. Brugger (2009).

6. Government Accountability Office (2009c, p. 4). Based on data from fall 2007.

7. Government Accountability Office (2009c, p. 5). Others may split their day between traditional classrooms and those with special education teachers. A still-smaller group may attend schools that specialize entirely in serving students with disabilities.

8. Center on Education Policy (2007c).

9. Reder (2007, pp. 2–3) contains a nice summary of these various categories and the rules for how student scores are counted.

10. National Council on Disability (2008, p. 76).

11. Ibid., p. 80.

12. Ibid., p. 82.

13. See National Council on Disability (2008) for an extended discussion of tensions with IEPs and NCLB.

14. Gilhool (1995).

15. Schemo (2004).

16. Ibid.

17. Samuels (2009). See also National Council on Disability (2008, p. 56).

18. Chenoweth (2007); Center on Education Policy (2007c); National Center for Learning Disabilities (2007).

19. National Council on Disability (2008, pp. 81–82).

20. Reder (2007, p. 6).

21. See, for example, National Council on Disability (2008, pp. 78–81), Center on Education Policy (2007c, p. 5), and Reder (2007, pp. 2–3).

22. See Thompson (2009) on overall totals and Government Accountability Office (2009c, p. 6) on claims about 80 percent Spanish and 400 languages spoken.

23. Government Accountability Office (2009c, p. 6).

24. Ibid.

25. Tennessee's case appears in Cech (2009); North Carolina's is in Maxwell (2009).

26. Thompson (2009).

27. Maxwell (2009).

28. Government Accountability Office (2006a).

29. The MALDEF quote appeared on the organization's Web site at http://maldef .org/education/public_policy/no_child_left_behind/. The La Raza position appears in National Council of La Raza (2006).

30. Cech (2009).

31. Both quotes are from Zehr (2006).

32. Zehr (2006).

33. Monroe (n.d.).

34. Glod (2007a).

35. The quotes from Niedzielski-Eichner and Dale come from Glod (2007b).

36. Government Accountability Office (2006a, pp. 9–10) nicely summarizes Title III's requirements.

37. Sunderman (2008, p. 60).

38. Cech (2009). See also Lazarín (2006, p. 10).

39. Zehr (2006).

40. Government Accountability Office (2006a).

41. Willner, Rivera, and Acosta (2008).

42. The Center on Education Policy's (2009a) analysis excluded English-language learners and students with disabilities because of the many federal regulatory changes affecting these subgroups after NCLB became law. Those changes made it impossible to establish consistently measured trends.

43. Center on Education Policy (2009a, pp. 1–2).

44. Center on Education Policy (2007a, Tables 2 and 6).

45. U.S. Department of Education (2009d, p. 8). Like the Center on Education Policy studies, this report examined only states where assessment systems remained constant over the time studied.

46. Center on Education Policy (2009a, p. 16).

47. Ibid., pp. 10–12.

48. U.S. Department of Education (2009d).

49. Center on Education Policy (2009c, p. 1).

50. Ibid., p. 11.

51. Ibid., p. 13.

52. U.S. Department of Education (2009d, pp. 10–14).

53. Dee and Jacob (2009).

54. The long-term NAEP (not shown in Figure 6.1 or 6.2), though more limited in time, shows some improvement, too. Considering prior performance in 1999 and the most recent results available, from 2004, the gap in reading between black and white nine- and thirteen-year-olds has narrowed. See U.S. Department of Education (2009a).

55. Dee and Jacob (2009).

56. Analysis of the long-term NAEP (again, not depicted in the figures) showed that math achievement gaps between black and white thirteen-year-olds did not change between 1999 and 2004, despite narrower gaps among thirteen-year-olds in reading and improvements among nine-year-olds in both subjects. See U.S. Department of Education (2009a); see also Cavanagh (2009) for a summary of the report.

57. Many sources have discussed discrepancies between state tests and the NAEP and whether state expectations are too lenient. See, for example, Carey (2006, 2007); Fuller et al. (2007); U.S. Department of Education (2009d); Resnick, Stein, and Coon (2008, p. 125); Center on Education Policy (2007a); and Cronin et al. (2007).

58. For examples of arguments on both sides, see U.S. Department of Education (2009d, p. 4), King (2007), and Sawchuk (2009).

59. Resnick, Stein, and Coon (2008, p. 129); Rothstein, Jacobsen, and Wilder (2008, pp. 183, 189, and 193).

60. Finn et al. (2008, p. 61). Comparable data from before NCLB's enactment do not exist, so it is impossible to determine if these opinions represent a change from prior years.

61. Finn et al. (2008, p. 62).

62. Marsh, Pane, and Hamilton (2006, pp. 6–7).

63. Center on Education Policy (2009d, pp. 11–12); Finn et al. (2008, p. 15).

64. Neal and Schanzenbach (2009).

65. Center on Education Policy (2009d, p. 14).

66. Sawchuk (2009).

67. Cech (2008).

68. U.S. Department of Education (2009d, pp. 8–9).

Chapter 7

1. Those dollars came from three elements of the stimulus package: the State Fiscal Stabilization Fund, a new program created as part of the stimulus, and additional dollars for two existing federal education programs—Title I of NCLB and IDEA.

2. Government Accountability Office (2009b).

3. Center on Education Policy (2009b, p. 5). See also Gewertz (2009).

4. Smarick (2010); Government Accountability Office (2009b).

5. For example, a Government Accountability Office (2009b) study of local use of stimulus funds estimated that about 80 percent of school districts gave great weight to "improving results for students" and 70 percent stressed "increasing educators' long term capacity" in deciding how to spend the money (p. 54). See also examples of reform cited in Center on Education Policy (2009b).

6. Detailed information about RTTT is available on-line at www2.ed.gov/programs/racetothetop/index.html.

7. U.S. Department of Education (2009b).

8. McNeil (2010a).

9. Duncan's quote comes from McNeil (2010b). See also Klein (2009).

10. Duncan (2009).

11. U.S. Department of Education (2010a).

12. See the Common Core State Standards Initiative, available at www.corestandards.org/. The cited passage comes from the organization's Frequently Asked Questions document.

13. Klein (2009).

14. Klein (2010); National Education Association (2010); American Federation of Teachers (2010).

15. U.S. Department of Education (2010b).

16. Duncan (2009).

17. Hoff and Manzo (2007).

18. U.S. Department of Education (2009c, pp. 25).

19. Examples of the concept of policy entrepreneurship appear in Sheingate (2003), Mintrom (1997, 2000), and Manna (2006b).

20. Center on Education Policy (2007c).

21. Another strategy, discussed in earlier chapters, was to make the minimum size of the NCLB-defined student subgroups quite large. Recall that if subgroups contain a certain number of students, then judgments based on subgroup performance do not factor into AYP calculations. Rather, students' scores are simply included in the overall performance of the school.

22. The example here also assumes that NCLB's safe harbor provision would not benefit the school with only one subgroup missing AYP. See Chapter 4's discussion of safe harbor.

23. Wilson (1989).

24. Gormley and Weimer (1999, p. 233).

25. Moynihan (2008, pp. 194 and 200).

26. Ibid.

27. Radin (2006, p. 179).

28. Kahlenberg (2008).

29. Rothstein, Jacobsen, and Wilder (2008); Accountability Committee (2009).

30. Jones (2001).

31. Wilson (1989).

32. This discussion draws on and elaborates on ideas from Manna (2008).

33. Rosenberg (2008, p. 97)

34. Associated Press (2010).

35. Aarons (2009).

36. Hoff and Olson (2007).

37. Moynihan (2008); Radin (2006).

38. Pressman and Wildavsky (1984).

Works Cited

Aarons, Dakarai I. 2009. Studies weigh NCLB's broad impact. *Education Week,* August 13.

Accountability Committee. 2009. School accountability: A broader, bolder approach. Washington, D.C.: Broader Bolder Approach to Education Campaign.

Achievement Alliance. 2007. It's being done: P.S./M.S. 124 Osmond A. Church School. Washington, D.C.: Author.

Alpert, Bruce. 2008. Obama, McCain differ on education. *Times-Picayune,* October 23.

American Federation of Teachers. 2010. AFT disappointed with administration's ESEA blueprint. March 13. www.aft.org.

Ash, Katie. 2008. Adjusting to test takers. *Education Week,* November 19.

Associated Press. 2003. States voice doubts about federal education law. December 10. www.cnn.com.

———. 2004a. Administration eases testing participation rules. March 29. www.cnn.com.

———. 2004b. 'Highly qualified' rules eased for some teachers. March 15. www.cnn.com.

———. 2006. Huge gaps in state, federal test scores. www.cnn.com. March 3.

———. 2010. States change laws in hopes of Race to Top edge. *Education Week,* January 20.

Baker, Peter. 2007. An unlikely partnership left behind. *Washington Post.* November 5.

Baumgartner, Frank R., and Bryan D. Jones. 1993. *Agendas and instability in American politics.* Chicago: University of Chicago Press.

Bell, Terrel H. 1988. *The thirteenth man: A Reagan cabinet memoir.* New York: The Free Press.

Bendor, Jonathan. 1988. Formal models of bureaucracy. *British Journal of Political Science* 18 (3): 353–395.

Bendor, Jonathan, Amihai Glazer, and Thomas Hammond. 2001. Theories of delegation. *Annual Review of Political Science* 4:235–269.

Berliner, David C., and Bruce J. Biddle. 1995. *The manufactured crisis: Myths, fraud, and the attack on America's public schools.* Reading, Mass.: Addison-Wesley.

Borja, Rhea R. 2007. Companies want changes in NCLB tutoring policies. *Education Week,* January 24.

Borsuk, Alan J. 2003. Reforms in test scoring may make students look better. *Milwaukee Journal Sentinel,* June 11.

Brownstein, Ronald. 2002. Federal funds should educate, not just employ. *Los Angeles Times,* February 4.

Brugger, Joe. 2009. Eugene high school student wins $100,000, a laptop, and a bright future. *Oregonian,* March 10.

Business Roundtable. 2005. Press release: No Child Left Behind receives high marks at Business Roundtable forum. February 9. www.businessroundtable .org.

Carey, Kevin. 2006. Hot air: How states inflate their educational progress under NCLB. Washington, D.C.: Education Sector.

———. 2007. The Pangloss index: How states game the No Child Left Behind Act. Washington, D.C.: Education Sector.

Cavanagh, Sean. 2009. Black-white achievement gap narrows on NAEP. *Education Week,* July 16.

Cech, Scott J. 2008. Testing expert sees 'illusions of progress' under NCLB. *Education Week,* October 1.

———. 2009. Weigh proficiency, assess content. *Education Week,* January 8.

Center on Education Policy. 2004a. From the capital to the classroom: Year 2 of the No Child Left Behind Act. Washington, D.C.: Author.

———. 2004b. Title I funds: Who's gaining, who's losing and why? Washington, D.C.: Author.

———. 2007a. Answering the question that matters most: Has student achievement increased since No Child Left Behind? Washington, D.C.: Author.

———. 2007b. Implementing the No Child Left Behind teacher requirements. Washington, D.C.: Author.

———. 2007c. NCLB's accountability provisions for students with disabilities: Center on Education Policy roundtable discussion. Washington, D.C.: Author.

———. 2007d. State implementation of supplemental educational services under the No Child Left Behind Act. Washington, D.C.: Author.

———. 2008a. A call to restructure restructuring: Lessons from the No Child Left Behind Act in five states. Washington, D.C.: Author.

———. 2008b. Has student achievement increased since 2002? State test score trends through 2006–2007. Washington, D.C.: Author.

———. 2008c. Instructional time in elementary schools: A closer look at changes for specific subjects. Washington, D.C.: Author.

———. 2008d. Some perspectives from rural school districts on the No Child Left Behind Act. Washington, D.C.: Author.

———. 2009a. Are achievement gaps closing and is achievement rising for all? Washington, D.C.: Author.

———. 2009b. An early look at the economic stimulus package and the public schools. Washington, D.C.: Author.

———. 2009c. Has progress been made in raising achievement for students with disabilities? Washington, D.C.: Author.

———. 2009d. Is the emphasis on "proficiency" short-changing higher- and lower-achieving students? Washington, D.C.: Author.

Chenoweth, Karin. 2007. *It's being done: Academic success in unexpected schools.* Cambridge, Mass.: Harvard University Press.

Chubb, John E., and Terry M. Moe. 1990. *Politics, markets, and America's schools.* Washington, D.C.: Brookings Institution.

Clements, Stephen. 2007. Rural Kentucky districts: "do-it-yourself" school improvement. In *No remedy left behind: Lessons from a half-decade of NCLB,* ed. F. M. Hess and C. E. Finn Jr. Washington, D.C.: American Enterprise Institute.

Clotfelter, Charles T., and Helen F. Ladd. 1996. Recognizing and rewarding success in public schools. In *Holding schools accountable: Performance-based reform in education,* ed. H. F. Ladd. Washington, D.C.: Brookings Institution.

Cohen, David K., and Susan L. Moffitt. 2009. *The ordeal of equality: Did federal regulation fix the schools?* Cambridge, Mass.: Harvard University Press.

Cohen, Michael. 2002. Unruly crew. *Education Next* 2 (3): 43–47.

Cronin, John, Michael Dahlin, Deborah Adkins, and G. Gage Kingsbury. 2007. The proficiency illusion. Washington, D.C.: Thomas B. Fordham Institute.

Cross, Christopher T. 1979. Title I evaluation. A case study in congressional frustration. *Educational Evaluation and Policy Analysis* 1 (2):15–21.

———. 2004. *Political education: National policy comes of age.* New York: Teachers College Press.

Danitz, Tiffany. 2002. School chiefs meet on new ed bill. January 15. www.state line .org.

Data Quality Campaign. 2007. Maximizing the power of education data while ensuring compliance with federal student privacy laws. Austin, Texas: Author.

Davies, Gareth. 2007. *See government grow: Education politics from Johnson to Reagan.* Lawrence: University of Kansas Press.

DeBray, Elizabeth H. 2005. NCLB accountability collides with court-ordered desegregation: The case of Pinellas County, Florida. *Peabody Journal of Education* 80 (2):170–188.

———. 2006. *Politics, ideology, and education: Federal policy during the Clinton and Bush administrations.* New York: Teachers College Press.

DeBray-Pelot, Elizabeth. 2007. Dismantling education's 'iron triangle': Institutional relationships in the formation of federal education policy between 1998 and 2001. In *To educate a nation: Federal and national strategies of school reform,* ed. C. F. Kaestle and A. E. Lodewick. Lawrence: University Press of Kansas.

Dee, Thomas S., and Brian A. Jacob. 2009. The impact of No Child Left Behind on student achievement. Typescript. An earlier version was presented on August 12, 2009, at the NCLB: Emerging Findings Research Conference at the Urban Institute, Washington, D.C.

Dillon, Sam. 2003a. Before the answer, the question must be correct. *New York Times,* July 16.

———. 2003b. State cutbacks put schools and federal law to the test. *New York Times,* August 31.

———. 2007. Democrats make Bush school act an election issue. *New York Times,* December 23.

Dillon, Sam, and Diana Jean Schemo. 2004. Union urges Bush to replace education chief over remark. *New York Times,* February 25.

Duncan, Arne. 2009. Reauthorization of ESEA: Why we can't wait. September 24. www.ed.gov/print/news/speeches/2009/09/09242009.html.

EdNext. 2007. Confessions of a "No Child Left Behind" supporter. *Education Next* 7 (2):30–37.

Educational Testing Service Policy Information Center. 1990. The education reform decade. Princeton, N.J.: Educational Testing Service.

EPE Research Center. 2008a. School districts: Adequate yearly progress and improvement status under NCLB. Washington, D.C.: Editorial Projects in Education.

———. 2008b. Schools and districts: Stages of improvement under NCLB. Washington, D.C.: Editorial Projects in Education.

———. 2008c. Schools: Adequate yearly progress and improvement status under NCLB. Washington, D.C.: Editorial Projects in Education.

Evans, William N., Shelia E. Murray, and Robert M. Schwab. 1997. Schoolhouses, courthouses, and statehouses after Serrano. *Journal of Policy Analysis and Management* 16 (1):10–31.

Fagan, Amy. 2007. Bush-Democrat alliance on education law feared. *Washington Times,* January 12.

Feller, Ben. 2006. Ed. dept. eases teacher quality rule. *Associated Press,* September 7.

Finn, Chester E., Jr., Michael J. Petrilli, Tom Loveless, Steve Farkas, and Ann Duffett. 2008. High-achieving students in the era of NCLB. Washington, D.C.: Thomas B. Fordham Institute.

Finn, Chester E., Jr., and Diane Ravitch. 2007. Not by geeks alone. *Wall Street Journal,* August 8.

Fuller, Bruce, Joseph Wright, Kathryn Gesicki, and Erin Kang. 2007. Gauging growth: How to judge No Child Left Behind. *Educational Researcher* 36 (5): 268–278.

General Accounting Office. 2000. Title I program: Stronger accountability needed for performance of disadvantaged students. Washington, D.C.: Author.

———. 2002. Title I: Education needs to monitor states' scoring of assessments. Washington, D.C.: Author.

———. 2003a. No Child Left Behind Act: More information would help states determine which teachers are highly qualified. Washington, D.C.: Author.

———. 2003b. Title I: Characteristics of tests will influence expenses; information sharing may help states realize efficiencies. Washington, D.C.: Author.

Gewertz, Catherine. 2005. Ed. dept. grants N.Y.C., Boston waivers on NCLB tutoring. *Education Week,* November 16.

———. 2009. States stung by criticism on use of federal aid. *Education Week,* October 12.

Gilhool, Thomas K. 1995. Testimony on the 20th anniversary of the Individuals with Disabilities Education Act (Part B) before the Subcommittee on Disability Policy of the Senate Committee on Labor and Human Resources and the Subcommittee on Early Childhood, Youth, and Families of the Committee on Economic and Educational Opportunities. 104th Cong., 1st sess.

Glod, Maria. 2007a. Fairfax vs. 'No Child' standoff heats up. *Washington Post,* January 11.

———. 2007b. Va. schools yield, yet may shape 'No Child.' *Washington Post,* April 23.

Goe, Laura, and Leslie M. Stickler. 2008. Teacher quality and student achievement: Making the most of recent research. Washington, D.C.: National Comprehensive Center for Teacher Quality.

Goertz, Margaret E. 2005. Implementing the No Child Left Behind Act: Challenges for the states. *Peabody Journal of Education* 80 (2):73–89.

Goldstein, Lisa. 2004. Long-awaited spec. ed. Testing rules issued. *Education Week,* January 7.

Gordon, Robert. 2006. The federalism debate: Why the idea of national education standards is crossing party lines. *Education Week,* March 15.

Gorman, Siobhan. 2001a. Behind bipartisanship. *National Journal,* July 14, 2228–2233.

———. 2001b. The making of a Bush loyalist. *National Journal,* April 28, 1246–1248.

Gormley, William T., and David L. Weimer. 1999. *Organizational report cards.* Cambridge, Mass.: Harvard University Press.

Government Accountability Office. 2004a. No Child Left Behind Act: Additional assistance and research on effective strategies would help small rural districts. Washington, D.C.: Author.

———. 2004b. No Child Left Behind Act: Education needs to provide additional technical assistance and conduct implementation studies for school choice provision. Washington, D.C.: Author.

———. 2004c. No Child Left Behind Act: Improvements needed for education's process for tracking states' implementation of key provisions. Washington, D.C.: Author.

———. 2004d. Unfunded mandates: Analysis of reform act coverage. Washington, D.C.: Author.

———. 2005. No Child Left Behind Act: Improved accessibility to education's information could help states further implement teacher qualification requirements. Washington, D.C.: Author.

———. 2006a. No Child Left Behind Act: Assistance from Education could help states better measure progress of students with limited English proficiency. Washington, D.C.: Author.

————. 2006b. No Child Left Behind Act: Education actions needed to improve local implementation and state evaluation of supplemental educational services. Washington, D.C.: Author.

————. 2007. No Child Left Behind Act: Education should clarify guidance and address potential compliance issues for schools in corrective action and restructuring status. Washington, D.C.: Author.

————. 2009a. No Child Left Behind Act: Enhancements in the Department of Education's review process could improve state academic assessments. Washington, D.C.: Author.

————. 2009b. Recovery Act: Status of states' and localities' use of funds and efforts to ensure accountability. Washington, D.C.: Author.

————. 2009c. Teacher preparation: Multiple federal education offices support teacher preparation for instructing students with disabilities and English language learners, but systematic departmentwide coordination could enhance this assistance. Washington, D.C.: Author.

————. 2009d. Teacher quality: Sustained coordination among key federal education programs could enhance state efforts to improve teacher quality. Washington, D.C.: Author.

Graham, Hugh Davis. 1984. *The uncertain triumph: Federal education policy in the Kennedy and Johnson years.* Chapel Hill: University of North Carolina Press.

Hannaway, Jane, and Sarah Cohodes. 2007. Miami-Dade county: Trouble in choice paradise. In *No remedy left behind: Lessons from a half-decade of NCLB,* ed. F. M. Hess and C. E. Finn Jr. Washington, D.C.: American Enterprise Institute.

Hannaway, Jane, and Andrew J. Rotherham, eds. 2006. *Collective bargaining in education: Negotiating change in today's schools.* Cambridge, Mass.: Harvard Education Press.

Hanushek, Eric A., and Alfred A. Lindseth. 2009. *Schoolhouses, courthouses, and statehouses: Solving the funding-achievement puzzle in America's public schools.* Princeton, N.J.: Princeton University Press.

Haycock, Kati. 1998. Good teaching matters: How well-qualified teachers can close the gap. *The Education Trust, Thinking K–16,* Summer.

————. 2001. How to bring a campaign slogan to life: An open letter to President Bush. *Harvard Education Letter* 17, no. 2.

————. 2004. The elephant in the living room. In *Brookings papers on education policy,* ed. by D. Ravitch. Washington, D.C.: Brookings Institution.

Henig, Jeffrey. 2004. *Mayors in the middle: Politics, race, and mayoral control of urban schools.* Princeton, N.J.: Princeton University Press.

Henig, Jeffrey R., Richard C. Hula, Marion Orr, and Desiree S. Pedescleaux, eds. 1999. *The color of school reform: Race, politics, and the challenge of urban education.* Princeton, N.J.: Princeton University Press.

Henriques, Diana B. 2003. Rising demands for testing push limits of its accuracy. *New York Times,* September 2.

Hernandez, Nelson. 2009. Students' strong scores give principal a lift, too. *Washington Post,* September 15.

Hess, Frederick M. 2003. Refining or retreating? High-stakes accountability in the states. In *No child left behind? The politics and practice of school accountability,* ed. P. E. Peterson and M. R. West. Washington, D.C.: Brookings Institution.

Hess, Frederick M., and Chester E. Finn, Jr., eds. 2007. *No remedy left behind: Lessons from a half-decade of NCLB.* Washington, D.C.: American Enterprise Institute.

Hess, Frederick M., and Michael J. Petrilli. 2006. *No Child Left Behind primer.* New York: Peter Lang.

Hickok, Eugene W. 2008. Secretary Spellings' unintended legacy. *Education Week,* December 10.

Hirsch, E. D. 2009. *The making of Americans: Democracy and our schools.* New Haven, Conn.: Yale University Press.

Hochschild, Jennifer, and Bridget Scott. 1998. The polls—trends: Governance and reform of public education in the United States. *Public Opinion Quarterly* 62:79–120.

Hoff, David J. 2004. Accountability conflicts vex schools. *Education Week,* March 10.

———. 2005. States to get new options on NCLB law. *Education Week,* April 13.

———. 2006. State chiefs offer views on NCLB renewal. *Education Week,* October 26.

———. 2007a. Bush plan would heighten NCLB focus on high school. *Education Week,* February 2.

———. 2007b. Senate panel begins examination of NCLB. *Education Week,* February 13.

———. 2008a. Debate emerges over proposed rules on SES, choice. *Education Week,* May 7.

———. 2008b. Steep climb to NCLB goal for 23 states. *Education Week,* June 2.

———. 2009. Schools struggling to meet key goal on accountability. *Education Week,* January 7.

Hoff, David J., and Kathleen Kennedy Manzo. 2007. Bush claims about NCLB questioned. *Education Week,* March 9.

Hoff, David J., and Lynn Olson. 2007. As NCLB turns 5, Washington outlines ways to change it. *Education Week,* January 9.

Jacobson, Gary C. 2008. *A divider, not a uniter: George W. Bush and the American people.* New York: Pearson Longman.

Jeffords, James M. 2001. *My declaration of independence.* New York: Simon and Schuster.

Jennings, John F. 1998. *Why national standards and tests? Politics and the quest for better schools.* Thousand Oaks, Calif.: Sage.

Jimerson, Lorna. 2005. Special challenges of the "No Child Left Behind" Act for rural schools and districts. *The Rural Educator* 26 (3):1–4.

Jones, Bryan D. 2001. *Politics and the architecture of choice: Bounded rationality and governance.* Chicago: University of Chicago Press.

Kaagan, Steve, and Michael D. Usdan. 1993. Leadership capacity for state reform: The mismatch between rhetoric and reality. *Education Week,* May 5.

Kaestle, Carl F., and Marshall S. Smith. 1982. The federal role in elementary and secondary education, 1940–1980. Special issue, *Harvard Educational Review* 52:384–412.

Kahlenberg, Richard D., ed. 2008. *Improving on No Child Left Behind: Getting education reform back on track.* New York: Century Foundation Press.

Kane, Thomas J., and Douglas O. Staiger. 2001. Rigid rules will damage school. *New York Times,* August 13.

———. 2002. Volatility in school test scores: Implications for test-based accountability systems. In *Brookings papers on education policy,* ed. D. Ravitch. Washington, D.C.: Brookings Institution.

Kane, Thomas J., Douglas O. Staiger, and Jeffrey Geppert. 2002. Randomly accountable. *Education Next* 2 (1):57–61.

Kanstoroom, Marci, and Eric C. Osberg. 2008. *A byte at the apple: Rethinking education data for the post-NCLB era.* Washington, D.C.: Thomas B. Fordham Institute.

King, Ledyard. 2007. Data suggests states satisfy No Child law by expecting less of students. *USA Today,* June 6.

Kingdon, John W. 1995. *Agendas, alternatives, and public policies.* 2nd ed. New York: HarperCollins.

Klein, Alyson. 2006. Spellings won't seek minimum subgroup size for NCLB. *Education Week,* December 19.

———. 2007. Bush budget would boost NCLB efforts. *Education Week,* February 12.

———. 2009. Duncan aims to make incentives key element of ESEA. *Education Week,* November 30.

Klein, Alyson, and Michele McNeil. 2010. Administration unveils ESEA reauthorization blueprint. *Education Week,* March 16.

Koppich, Julia E. 2005. A tale of two approaches—the AFT, the NEA, and NCLB. *Peabody Journal of Education* 80 (2):137–155.

Kowal, Julie, and Bryan C. Hassel. 2007. Remedies in action: Four "restructured" schools. In *No remedy left behind: Lessons from a half-decade of NCLB,* ed. F. M. Hess and C. E. Finn Jr. Washington, D.C.: American Enterprise Institute.

Lazarín, Melissa. 2006. Improving assessment and accountability for English language learners in the No Child Left Behind Act. Washington, D.C.: National Council of La Raza.

LeTendre, Mary Jean. n.d. Defining adequate yearly progress: Strengthening responsibility for results without toppling state accountability systems. Typescript.

Levine, Arthur. 2006. Educating school teachers. Washington, D.C.: The Education Schools Project.

Lewin, Tamar. 2007. States found to vary widely on education. *New York Times,* June 8.

Light, Paul C. 1997. *The tides of reform: Making government work, 1945–1995.* New Haven, Conn.: Yale University Press.

Lipsky, Michael. 1980. *Street-level bureaucracy: Dilemmas of the individual in public services.* New York: Russell Sage Foundation.

Loveless, Tom. 2000. *Conflicting missions? Teachers unions and educational reform.* Washington, D.C.: Brookings Institution.

Lusi, Susan F. 1997. *The role of state departments of education in complex school reform.* New York: Teachers College Press.

Magnuson, Katherine, and Jane Waldfogel, eds. 2008. *Steady gains and stalled progress: Inequality and the black-white test score gap.* New York: Russell Sage Foundation.

Manna, Paul. 2006a. Control, persuasion and educational accountability: Implementing the No Child Left Behind Act. *Educational Policy* 20 (3):471–494.

———. 2006b. *School's in: Federalism and the national education agenda.* Washington, D.C.: Georgetown University Press.

———. 2006c. Teachers unions and No Child Left Behind. In *Collective bargaining in education: Negotiating change in today's schools,* ed. J. Hannaway and A. J. Rotherham. Cambridge, Mass.: Harvard Education Press.

———. 2007. NCLB in the states: Fragmented governance, uneven implementation. In *No remedy left behind: Lessons from a half-decade of NCLB,* ed. F. M. Hess and C. E. Finn Jr. Washington, D.C.: American Enterprise Institute.

———. 2008. Federal aid to elementary and secondary education: Premises, effects, and major lessons learned. Washington, D.C.: Center on Education Policy.

Manzo, Kathleen Kennedy. 2005. National clout of DIBELS draws scrutiny. *Education Week,* September 28.

Marsh, Julie A., John F. Pane, and Laura S. Hamilton. 2006. Making sense of data-driven decision making in education. Santa Monica, Calif.: RAND.

Mathews, Jay. 2006. Let's teach to the test. *Washington Post,* February 20.

Maxwell, Lesli A. 2006. State steps in under NCLB in Baltimore. *Education Week,* April 5.

———. 2009. Immigration transforms communities. *Education Week,* January 8.

McCarty, Nolan, Keith T. Poole, and Howard Rosenthal. 2006. *Polarized America: The dance of ideology and unequal riches.* Cambridge, Mass.: MIT Press.

McClure, Phyllis, Dianne Piché, and William L. Taylor. 2006. Days of reckoning: Are states and the federal government up to the challenge of ensuring a qualified teacher for every student? Washington, D.C.: Citizens' Commission on Civil Rights.

McGuinn, Patrick J. 2006. *No Child Left Behind and the transformation of federal education policy, 1965–2005.* Lawrence: University of Kansas Press.

McKluskey, Neal P. 2007. *Feds in the classroom: How big government corrupts, cripples, and compromises American education.* Washington, D.C.: Cato Institute.

McNeil, Michele. 2006. Glitches, data errors delay Illinois test-score release. *Education Week,* December 6.

———. 2007. Governors edge toward position on NCLB. *Education Week,* March 7.

———. 2008. Hard times hit schools. *Education Week,* August 27.

———. 2009. Rural areas perceive policy tilt. *Education Week,* September 2.

———. 2010a. Duncan carves deep mark on policy in first year. *Education Week,* January 19.

———. 2010b. Obama to seek $1.35 billion Race to Top expansion. *Education Week,* January 19.

Mead, Sara. 2007. Easy way out: "Restructured" usually means little has changed. *Education Next,* 7 (1): 52–56.

Medler, Alex. 2007. Colorado: The misapplication of federal power. In *No remedy left behind: Lessons from a half-decade of NCLB,* ed. F. M. Hess and C. E. Finn Jr. Washington, D.C.: American Enterprise Institute.

Meier, Deborah, and George Wood, eds. 2004. *Many children left behind: How the No Child Left Behind Act is damaging our children and our schools.* Boston: Beacon Press.

Merrow, John. 2007. A 'surge' strategy for No Child Left Behind? *Education Week,* February 14.

Milbank, Dana. 2002. With fanfare, Bush signs education bill. *Washington Post,* January 9.

Miller, Gary J. 1992. *Managerial dilemmas: The political economy of hierarchy.* New York: Cambridge University Press.

Mintrom, Michael. 1997. Policy entrepreneurs and the diffusion of innovation. *American Journal of Political Science* 41 (3): 738–770.

———. 2000. *Policy entrepreneurs and school choice.* Washington, D.C.: Georgetown University Press.

Moe, Terry M. 1989. The politics of bureaucratic structure. In *Can the government govern?* ed. J. E. Chubb and P. E. Peterson. Washington, D.C.: Brookings Institution.

———. 2006. Political control and the power of the agent. *Journal of Law, Economics, and Organization* 22 (1):1–29.

Monroe, J. Ryan. n.d. Standardized testing in the lives of ELL students: A teacher's firsthand account. www.elladvocates.org/issuebriefs.html.

Moynihan, Donald P. 2008. *The dynamics of performance management: Constructing information and reform.* Washington, D.C.: Georgetown University Press.

National Center for Education Statistics. 2007. Mapping 2005 state proficiency standards onto the NAEP scales. Washington, D.C.: U.S. Department of Education.

National Center for Learning Disabilities. 2007. Rewards and roadblocks: How special education students are faring under No Child Left Behind. New York: Author.

National Commission on Excellence in Education. 1983. A nation at risk: The imperative for educational reform. www.ed.gov/pubs/NatAtRisk/risk.html.

National Conference of State Legislatures. 2001. Letter to congressional conferees regarding the re-authorization of the Elementary and Secondary Education Act. September 26.

———. 2005. Task force on No Child Left Behind final report. Denver, Colo., and Washington, D.C.: National Conference of State Legislatures.

———. 2010. Education at a crossroads: A new path for federal and state education policy. Denver, Colo., and Washington, D.C.: Author.

National Council of La Raza. 2006. Press release: The National Council of La Raza's position on the No Child Left Behind Act and English language learners. December 11. www.nclr.org/.

National Council on Disability. 2008. The No Child Left Behind Act and the Individuals with Disabilities Education Act: A progress report. Washington, D.C.: Author.

National Education Association. 2010. NEA president: Reauthorization 'blueprint' disappointing. March 13. www.nea.org.

National Rural Education Advocacy Coalition. 2009. Legislative agenda. Arlington, Va.: Author.

Neal, Derek, and Diane Whitmore Schanzenbach. 2009. Left behind by design: Proficiency counts and test-based accountability. Paper presented at NCLB: Emerging Findings Research Conference, August 12, at Urban Institute, Washington D.C.

O'Connor, Sandra Day, and Lee H. Hamilton. 2008. A democracy without civics? *Christian Science Monitor,* September 17.

Olson, Lynn. 2002. States gear up for new federal law. *Education Week,* January 16.

———. 2003. States' plans likely to test ESEA pliancy. *Education Week,* February 19.

———. 2006. Citing new tests, many states late with AYP results. *Education Week,* August 31.

Osborne, David, and Ted Gaebler. 1992. *Reinventing government.* Reading, Mass.: Addison-Wesley.

Paige, Rod. 2002. Remarks to meeting of chief state school officers. January 9. www.ed.gov/news/speeces/2002/01/20020109.html.

———. 2004a. Focus on the children. *Washington Post,* February 27, 23.

———. 2004b. Letter to Senator Edward M. Kennedy on No Child Left Behind implementation progress. February 24. www.ed.gov/news/pressreleases/2004/02/02242004.html.

Paley, Amit R. 2007. Ex-aides break with Bush on 'No Child.' *Washington Post,* June 26.

Perkinson, Henry J. 1991. *The imperfect panacea: American faith in education 1865–1990.* 3rd ed. New York: McGraw-Hill.

Petrilli, Michael J. 2005. Improving teacher quality: Better luck next time. *Education Week,* August 31.

Petrocik, John R. 1996. Issue ownership in presidential elections, with a 1980 case study. *Journal of Politics* 40 (3): 825–850.

Popham, W. James. 2003. The 'No Child' noose tightens—but some states are slipping it. *Education Week,* September 24.

Pressman, Jeffrey L., and Aaron Wildavsky. 1984. *Implementation.* 3rd ed. Berkeley, Calif.: University of California Press.

Radin, Beryl A. 2006. *Challenging the performance movement: Accountability, complexity, and democratic values.* Washington, D.C.: Georgetown University Press.

Radin, Beryl A., and Willis D. Hawley. 1988. *The politics of federal reorganization: Creating the U.S. Department of Education.* New York: Pergamon Press.

RAND. 2009. Policy brief: Increasing participation in No Child Left Behind school choice. Santa Monica, Calif.: RAND Education.

Ravitch, Diane. 1995. *National standards in American education: A citizen's guide.* Washington, D.C.: Brookings Institution.

———. 2001. The history lesson in Bush's school plan. *New York Times,* January 27.

———, ed. 2004. *Brookings papers on education policy.* Washington, D.C.: Brookings Institution.

Reder, Nancy D. 2007. Accountability for students with disabilities. Washington, D.C.: Center on Education Policy.

Resnick, Lauren B., Mary Kay Stein, and Sarah Coon. 2008. Standards-based reform: A powerful idea unmoored. In *Improving on No Child Left Behind: Getting education reform back on track,* ed. R. D. Kahlenberg. New York: Century Foundation Press.

Richard, Alan. 2005. Federal efforts lacking, rural advocates say. *Education Week,* February 2.

Robelen, Erik W. 2002. ESEA to boost federal role in education. *Education Week,* January 9.

———. 2003a. Department levies $783,000 Title I penalty on Ga. *Education Week,* May 28.

———. 2003b. State reports on progress vary widely. *Education Week,* September 3.

———. 2005. Wyoming pragmatist set to lead Senate education panel. *Education Week,* January 5.

Rosenberg, Gerald N. 2008. *The hollow hope: Can courts bring about social change?* 2nd ed. Chicago: University of Chicago Press.

Rothstein, Richard, Rebecca Jacobsen, and Tamara Wilder. 2008. *Grading education: Getting accountability right.* Washington, D.C., and New York: Economic Policy Institute and Teachers College Press.

Rudalevige, Andrew. 2003. No Child Left Behind: Forging a congressional compromise. In *No child left behind? The politics and practice of school accountability,* ed. P. E. Peterson and M. R. West. Washington, D.C.: Brookings Institution.

Rural School and Community Trust. 2006. Position paper on the reauthorization of NCLB: The rural perspective. Arlington, Va.: Author.

———. 2007. Title I weighted grants skewed toward largest districts. Arlington, Va.: Author.

Salzer, James. 2003. Feds yank funds over test delay. *Atlanta Journal-Constitution,* May 22.

Samuels, Christina A. 2009. Special ed. advocates making to-do list for Duncan. *Education Week,* February 11.

Sawchuk, Stephen. 2009. Report finds achievement gap continuing to narrow. *Education Week,* October 1.

Schemo, Diana Jean. 2002. States get federal warning on school standards. *New York Times,* October 24.

————. 2004. States' end run dilutes burden for special ed. *New York Times,* June 7.

————. 2007. Failing schools strain to meet U.S. standard. *New York Times,* October 16.

Seitz, Patrick. 2009. Three scholars come up aces study hard. *Investor's Business Daily,* April 27.

Senge, Peter M. 1990. *The fifth discipline: The art and practice of the learning organization.* New York: Currency Doubleday.

Sheingate, Adam D. 2003. Political entrepreneurship, institutional change, and American political development. *Studies in American Political Development* 17 (2):185–203.

Skowronek, Stephen. 1997. *The politics presidents make: Leadership from John Adams to Bill Clinton.* Cambridge, Mass.: Harvard University Press.

Smarick, Andy. 2010. Toothless reform. *Education Next* 10 (2):15–22.

Spellings, Margaret. 2005. Letter to chief state school officers on flexibility and highly qualified teachers. October 21. www.ed.gov/print/policy/elsec/guid/secletter/051021.html.

————. 2007. Letter to chief state school officers on highly qualified teachers. July 23. www.ed.gov/print/policy/elsec/guid/secletter/070723.html.

Stone, Deborah A. 1989. Causal stories and the formation of policy agendas. *Political Science Quarterly* 104 (2):281–300.

Strach, Patricia. 2007. *All in the family: The private roots of American public policy.* Palo Alto, Calif.: Stanford University Press.

Strange, Marty, Jerry Johnson, and Ashton Finical. 2009. Many children left behind: How Title I weighted grant formulas favor the few at the expense of the many in Pennsylvania. Arlington, Va.: Rural School and Community Trust.

Sunderman, Gail L. 2007. Supplemental educational services under NCLB: Charting implementation. Los Angeles: The Civil Rights Project, UCLA.

————, ed. 2008. *Holding NCLB accountable: Achieving accountability, equity, and school reform.* Thousand Oaks, Calif.: Corwin Press.

Sunderman, Gail L., James S. Kim, and Gary Orfield, eds. 2005. *NCLB meets school realities: Lessons from the field.* Thousand Oaks, Calif.: Corwin Press.

Sundquist, James L. 1968. *Politics and policy in the Eisenhower, Kennedy, and Johnson years.* Washington, D.C.: Brookings Institution.

Sweeping program cuts would fund proposed Bush high-school initiative. 2005. *Title I Monitor,* March.

Test scores released in Illinois after lengthy series of delays. 2007. *Education Week,* March 21.

The Education Trust. 2003a. In need of improvement: Ten ways the U.S. Department of Education has failed to live up to its teacher quality commitments. Washington, D.C.: Author.

———. 2003b. Telling the whole truth (or not) about highly qualified teachers. Washington, D.C.: Author.

———. 2004. The ABCs of "AYP": Raising achievement for all students. Washington, D.C.: Author.

———. n.d. ESEA: Myths versus realities. Washington, D.C.: Author.

Thompson, Ginger. 2009. Where education and assimilation collide. *New York Times,* March 15.

Timpane, P. Michael, and Laurie Miller McNeill. 1991. Business impact on education and child development reform. New York and Washington, D.C.: Committee for Economic Development.

Toch, Thomas. 2006. Margins of error: The education testing industry in the No Child Left Behind era. Washington, D.C.: Education Sector.

Tonn, Jessica L. 2007. States seeking greater rural flexibility under NCLB. *Education Week,* April 4.

Turque, Bill. 2009. Staff shakeup is ordered at six schools. *Washington Post,* May 12.

Tyack, David, and Larry Cuban. 1995. *Tinkering toward utopia: A century of public school reform.* Cambridge, Mass.: Harvard University Press.

U.S. Department of Education. 1993a. Reinventing Chapter 1: The current Chapter 1 program and new directions. Final report of the national assessment of the Chapter 1 program. Washington, D.C.: Author.

———. 1993b. Statement of the independent review panel of the national assessment of Chapter 1. Washington, D.C.: Author.

———. 1998. The Eisenhower Professional Development Program: Emerging themes from six districts. Washington, D.C.: Author.

———. 1999a. Designing effective professional development: Lessons from the Eisenhower program. Washington, D.C.: Author.

———. 1999b. Designing effective professional development: Lessons from the Eisenhower program, executive summary. Washington, D.C.: Author.

———. 2001. High standards for all students: A report from the national assessment of Title I on progress and challenges since the 1994 reauthorization. Washington, D.C.: Author.

———. 2003. President Bush, Secretary Paige celebrate approval of every state accountability plan under No Child Left Behind. June 10. www.ed.gov/news/pressreleases/2003/06/06102003.html.

———. 2005. Press release: Secretary Spellings announces more workable, "common sense" approach to implement No Child Left Behind law. April 7. www2.ed.gov/news/pressreleases/2005/04/04072005.html.

————. 2006. Title I accountability and school improvement from 2001 to 2004. Washington, D.C.: Author.

————. 2007a. Evaluation of flexibility under No Child Left Behind. Volume III—the Rural Education Achievement Program (REAP flex). Washington, D.C.: Author.

————. 2007b. State and local implementation of the No Child Left Behind Act, Volume I—Title I school choice, supplemental educational services, and student achievement. Washington, D.C.: Author.

————. 2007c. Status and trends in the education of racial and ethnic minorities. Washington, D.C.: Author.

————. 2007d. Status of education in rural America. Washington, D.C.: Author.

————. 2008a. *Digest of education statistics.* Washington, D.C.: Author.

————. 2008b. State and local implementation of the No Child Left Behind Act, Volume IV—Title I school choice and supplemental educational services: Interim report. Washington, D.C.: Author.

————. 2009a. Achievement gaps: How black and white students in public schools perform on mathematics and reading on the National Assessment of Educational Progress. Washington, D.C.: Author.

————. 2009b. President Obama, U.S. Secretary of Education Duncan announce national competition to advance school reform. July 24. www.ed.gov/print/news/pressreleases/2009/07/07242009.html.

————. 2009c. State and local implementation of the No Child Left Behind Act, Volume VIII—Teacher quality under NCLB: Final report. Washington, D.C.: Author.

————. 2009d. Title I implementation—Update on recent evaluation findings. Washington, D.C.: Author.

————. 2010a. A blueprint for reform: The reauthorization of the Elementary and Secondary Education Act. Washington, D.C.: Author.

————. 2010b. Secretary Duncan's testimony before the Senate Health, Education, Labor, and Pensions Committee and the House Education and Labor Committee on the Obama administration's blueprint for reauthorizing the Elementary and Secondary Education Act (ESEA). March 17. www2.ed.gov/print/news/speeches/2010/03/03172010.html.

Walsh, Mark. 2009. Federal appeals court weighs union's suit over NCLB. *Education Week,* January 7.

Walton, Mary. 1986. *The Deming management method.* New York: Perigee Books.

Wayne, Andrew J., and Peter Youngs. 2003. Teacher characteristics and student achievement gains: A review. *Review of Educational Research* 73 (1):89–122.

Weisman, Jonathan, and Amit R. Paley. 2007. Dozens in GOP turn against Bush's prized 'No Child' act. *Washington Post,* March 15.

Weiss, Janet A. 1998. Policy theories of school choice. *Social Science Quarterly* 79 (3):523–532.

White House Office of the Press Secretary. 2002. President signs landmark education bill. January 8. www.whitehouse.gov/news/releases/2002/01/20020108–1.html.

————. 2003. President highlights progress in education reform. June 10. www
.whitehouse.gov/news/releases/2003/06/print/20030610–4.html.

————. 2009. Remarks by the president at national and state teachers of the year
event. April 28. www.whitehouse.gov/briefing_room/PressReleases/.

Wiener, Ross. 2006. Guess who's still left behind. *Washington Post,* January 2.

Willner, Lynn Shafer, Charlene Rivera, and Barbara D. Acosta. 2008. Descriptive
study of state assessment policies for accommodating English language learners.
Washington, D.C.: George Washington University Center for Equity and Excellence in Education.

Wilson, James Q. 1989. *Bureaucracy: What government agencies do and why they do it.*
New York: Basic Books.

Winerip, Michael. 2003a. A failure of logic and logistics. *New York Times,*
October 1.

————. 2003b. No Child Left Behind law leaves no room for some. *New York
Times,* March 19.

————. 2003c. On front lines, casualties are tied to new U.S. law. *New York Times,*
September 24.

————. 2003d. A star! A failure! Or caught between unmeshed yardsticks? *New York
Times,* September 3.

Wirt, Frederick M., and Michael W. Kirst. 1997. *The political dynamics of American
education.* Berkeley, Calif.: McCutchan Publishing.

Wong, Kenneth K., Francis X. Shen, Dorothea Anagnostopoulos, and Stacey Rut-
ledge. 2007. *The education mayor: Improving America's schools.* Washington, D.C.:
Georgetown University Press.

Wood, George. 2004. A view from the field: NCLB's effects on classrooms and
schools. In *Many children left behind: How the No Child Left Behind Act is damaging our children and our schools,* ed. D. Meier and G. Wood. Boston: Beacon Press.

Zehr, Mary Ann. 2006. No child effect on English-learners mulled. *Education Week,*
March 1.

Index